Capacity Building
for Peacekeeping

**RELATED TITLES FROM POTOMAC BOOKS
AND NATIONAL DEFENSE UNIVERSITY PRESS**

The Armed Forces Officer
by the U.S. Department of Defense

*African Counterterrorism Cooperation:
Assessing Regional and Subregional Initiatives*
edited by Andre Le Sage

Seeing the Elephant: The U.S. Role in Global Security
by Hans Binnendijk and Richard L. Kugler

Capacity Building for Peacekeeping

THE CASE OF HAITI

EDITED BY JOHN T. FISHEL
AND ANDRÉS SÁENZ

Center for Hemispheric Defense Studies

National Defense University Press Potomac Books, Inc.

Washington, DC

Copublished in the United States by National Defense University Press and Potomac Books, Inc. The opinions, conclusions, and recommendations expressed or implied within are those of the authors and do not necessarily reflect the views of the Department of Defense or any other agency of the Federal Government. This publication is cleared for public release; distribution unlimited. Portions of this book may be quoted or reprinted without further permission, with credit to both National Defense University Press and Potomac Books, Inc.

Library of Congress Cataloging-in-Publication Data
Capacity building for peacekeeping : the case of Haiti / edited by John T. Fishel and Andrés Sáenz.—1st ed.
p. cm.
Includes bibliographical references and index.
ISBN 978-1-59797-123-2 (alk. paper)
1. Peacekeeping forces—Haiti. 2. Conflict management—Haiti. 3. Conflict management—Methodology. 4. Haiti—History—1986– I. Fishel, John T. II. Sáenz, Andrés, 1927–
JZ6374.C365 2007
972.9407'3—dc22

                                                        2007025925

Printed in the United States of America on acid-free paper that meets the American National Standards Institute Z39-48 Standard.

Potomac Books, Inc.
22841 Quicksilver Drive
Dulles, Virginia 20166

First Edition

10 9 8 7 6 5 4 3 2 1

Contents

Figures and Tables

FIGURES

TABLES

Foreword

In many respects, this book is the outgrowth of a groundbreaking and highly successful effort by Mr. Ryan Henry, Principal Deputy Undersecretary of Defense for Policy, to expand the outreach and scope of the five Department of Defense (DOD) Regional Centers. Recognizing the remarkable potential for policy-relevant academic research by talented academic faculties with broad contacts, Ryan allowed each center to compete for year-end research funds to be used for a valuable project.

On extremely short notice, I alerted my team at the Center for Hemispheric Defense Studies (CHDS) to prepare some proposals. The most promising was an effort originally titled "Capacity Building for Peacekeeping in Latin America and the Caribbean: The Case of Haiti," which developed into this book. I felt strongly about the value of this project, as it touched on many of the issues that CHDS had addressed in seminars, workshops, and other activities. Moreover, as this book emphasizes, the extensive cooperation among hemispheric partners necessary to achieve the peacekeeping effort in Haiti truly reflects the CHDS motto, "Understanding and mutual trust" (*Mens et fides mutua*).

Given the short time frame in which funds for this project had to be committed, the CHDS faculty and staff, led by Research Director Professor John Fishel and Associate Research Professor Andrés Sáenz, organized the project around a series of commissioned papers by a distinguished group of practitioners and scholars—many of whom are both. This dual set of skills is exemplified by Andrés Sáenz, who has since returned to his home in Colombia as Deputy Director of its national intelligence agency known as the Departamento Administrativo de Seguridad (DAS). Others include the team from the Chilean National Academy of Political and Strategic Studies, Ricardo Benavente, a CHDS graduate, and Enzo di Nocera; Enrique Obando from Peru, a noted scholar of civil-military relations who, at the time of the decision to participate in the Haiti operation, was third in the hierarchy at the

Ministry of Defense; Glen Milne, from Canada, a scholar who has advised Prime Ministers and Ministers of Defence; Guillermo Pacheco from Guatemala, a CHDS graduate, who was once the sole civilian advisor to the Minister of Defense in his country, and is now an Associate Professor at CHDS; and General Jorge Rosales, who is now the Commander in Chief of the Army in Uruguay. The remaining contributors bring similar credentials that are spelled out in their biographies at the end of this volume.

This illustrious team has produced a study that has provided unique insights to its sponsor, to the U.S. Department of Defense, to the governments of participating countries, and to the scholarly community on defense issues in the hemisphere. We were almost immediately able to make all the papers available in the language in which they were written (with abstracts in the other two languages) in the CHDS electronic journal, *The Security and Defense Studies Review*. The publication of this book makes the study available to the English-speaking defense studies community, with the expectation that it will also be published in Spanish and Portuguese.

I am proud of this pioneering effort and am honored to congratulate the eminent team that produced it. We at CHDS are also especially pleased to present the results of this project to a wider audience, within and beyond the defense communities of the Western Hemisphere, where it will add significantly to a more informed and well-grounded debate on many aspects of peacekeeping and stability operations.

RICHARD D. DOWNIE, PH.D.
DIRECTOR, CENTER FOR HEMISPHERIC DEFENSE STUDIES

Acknowledgments

As the editors, Andrés Sáenz and I would like to thank those who made this book possible. First, and foremost, we appreciate the work of all the individuals who participated in the workshop that resulted in this book. This includes not only the participants and the chapter authors but those who worked to set it up. A special thanks goes to those usually unsung heroes who work behind the scenes—in this case, Claudia Provitina, Monica Stapleton, Audete Ramos, and Frank McGurk and his team of translators from the Ventura Group.

Another set of thanks goes to people who helped recruit some of the participants and chapter authors. These include Dr. Juan Belikow, Juan Ramon Quintana, Dr. David Last, and Dr. Thomaz Costa. We want to thank the Director of CHDS, Dr. Richard Downie, who not only recruited a key participant but, more importantly, guided the project from beginning to end.

Thanks also goes to the Senior Editor of *The Security and Defense Studies Review*, Dr. Herb Huser, who shepherded this book through its original publication in that journal to its publication now in book form. We also thank George Maerz, our editor at NDU Press, who has been especially helpful as this project moved toward book publication.

On a personal note, I want to express my sincerest *gracias* to my co-editor, Andrés Sáenz, for his efforts in organizing the workshop and editing all the Spanish language articles. His knowledge and hard work were essential to the success of this project in all its stages.

Finally, we thank Mr. Ryan Henry, then Principal Deputy Undersecretary of Defense for Policy, without whose vision and financial support this book would never have been produced.

Needless to say, this work represents the views of the authors alone and is not the official view of the Center for Hemispheric Defense Studies, the National Defense University, or any government in the hemisphere.

Chapter One
Capacity Building for Peacekeeping: The Case of Haiti

JOHN T. FISHEL

I n 2004, for the second time in a decade, the international community found it necessary to intervene in the Caribbean Republic of Haiti to enforce and keep a peace. For the first time under a United Nations (UN) mandate, Latin American countries stepped up to lead the mission. Political leadership, in the form of the Special Representative of the Secretary-General, was provided by Chile. Brazil agreed to provide the force commander as well as troops. A number of other Latin American states also offered troops.

As a result of this unique circumstance, the Center for Hemispheric Defense Studies (CHDS) at the National Defense University led a research project that looked at capacity building in the hemisphere for the countries that participated in the peacekeeping operation (PKO) in Haiti. The objective of the project was to identify the strategic-level lessons learned in capacity building for peacekeeping operations by the contributing countries. The countries included those that contributed to the Multinational Interim Force–Haiti (MIFH) as well as those contributing to the UN Stabilization Mission in Haiti (MINUSTAH). Those countries, at present, are Argentina, Bolivia, Brazil, Canada, Chile, Guatemala, Paraguay, Peru, the United States, and Uruguay.

METHODOLOGY

The method of the project was to commission research papers elaborated by individual researchers or teams from each of the participating countries. All of the papers address the issues on the basis of nine common research questions, thus making for comparability among the cases. One paper looks back to the 1994 intervention in Haiti (Operation *Uphold Democracy* and the United Nations Mission to Haiti [UNMIH]) to set the stage for the current PKO. These papers were then presented and discussed at a workshop held in Washington, DC, on December 3, 2004. Based on that discussion and further guidance, the authors revised their papers for publication in this book. Although we were not able to include a separate chapter on one of the partici-

1

pating countries, Paraguay, we were able to include the important insights of the Paraguayan research in the final analytical chapter.

The project produced several outputs in addition to this book. First, an executive summary report was prepared for the Office of the Secretary of Defense (OSD) and other U.S. Government stakeholders. Second, the individual research papers appeared (in the language in which they are written—English, Portuguese, and Spanish—with abstracts in the other two languages) in a special issue of the CHDS electronic journal, *Security and Defense Studies Review*.[1] Third, hardcopy books will be published in each of the three languages of the contributing countries, of which this is the first. While the executive summary report was aimed at the U.S. policy community, the other venues address the larger community of influence and interest throughout the hemisphere. The result, we expect, will be something that is useful to policymakers, implementers, and academics throughout the region.

We designed the project to achieve three broad, policy-related outcomes. As a result of this study, we hoped that OSD would be able to increase its ability to motivate and achieve heightened regional participation in peacekeeping and other multilateral missions. Second, we hoped that OSD would be able to identify the kinds of incentives and disincentives that lead regional countries to sustain their participation in these kinds of missions. And third, our goal was that regional countries would be able to identify their own strengths and weaknesses in terms of participation in PKO and similar missions. We also expected that all participant countries would be able to learn from the experiences of one another, thereby increasing their individual and collective capacity for PKO and other integrated operations.

DEFINITIONS AND CONCEPTS

Because this project focused on capacity, it is critical to explain exactly what we mean by the concept. For our purposes, *capacity* is a capability (or capabilities) that is sustained over time; a *capability* is a function of equipment, personnel, support, information, and doctrine, and can be expressed as a formula: $C = f(E,P,S,I,D)$. Clearly, this formulation implies that training is important, as are command, control, communications, computers, intelligence, surveillance, and reconnaissance (C^4ISR). What we have described here is a *military* or, what we might call, an *integrated capability*. In general, we would identify three broad categories of integrated capabilities—those of military, police, and interagency actors. With regard to military capabilities, each service has a set of combat, combat support, and combat service support capabilities defined in the form of the function expressed above. Similarly, the police have a series of capabilities—paramilitary/gendarme, dispersed, and investigative. These integrated policing capabilities address the paramilitary constabulary function, the uniformed beat "cop" or patrol car operating in a dispersed way, and the investigative role of a local, state/provincial, or national detective force. And the interagency actors, if we were to explore them, would have a similar set of integrated capabilities—for example, intelligence, representation, consular, and support (in a foreign ministry).

There is, however, a second type of capability that we have come to believe is crucial. It is a *political* capability that is made up of a national strategy and political will.[2] A national strategy links the integrated capabilities with political capability, while political will determines, and is determined by, a state's willingness to bear the burden necessary to achieve its strategic objective. The result is that political capacity is the key to success or failure. Lack of political will guarantees failure. Sustained political will over time gives the possibility of success. Integrated capabilities linked to political capability by a national strategy likely will strengthen political will. Integrated capabilities that are not well developed will tend to undermine political will. A strategy that fails to make full use of integrated capabilities likewise will tend to undermine political will. Thus, we expect that there is likely to be a strong relationship between political will and integrated capabilities in which increased integrated capabilities will strengthen political will, while a decrease or weakness in integrated capabilities will have the opposite effect.

HYPOTHESES AND RESEARCH QUESTIONS

Initially, we conceived of this study in inductive terms. As a result, we developed a series of nine major research questions, each of which had several supporting questions. These were shared among the researchers and served to make certain that the products had a high degree of comparability.

As we considered the project in greater detail, we revisited the issue of the study objective and the associated research questions. Starting with a clean slate, we looked again at the concept of capacity and its building block concept of capabilities that were discussed in the previous section. Based on this analysis, we developed two major hypotheses, each with two sub-hypotheses, as follows:

- H1: Countries decided to participate in Haiti based on their political capabilities.
- H1a: Participating countries chose their role based first on their political capabilities and then on their integrated capabilities.
- H1b: The same incentives that affected the decision to participate will affect the political capacity to sustain the effort.
- H2: More countries would participate in PKO if their political capacity for the conduct of PKO were strengthened.
- H2a: Perceived lack of integrated capabilities adversely affects political will.

- H2b: Countries would participate at a higher level if their political and (to a lesser extent) integrated capabilities were increased.

When we address hypothesis H1, it becomes obvious that objectives are critically important. As the Cheshire Cat told Alice in the children's novel *Alice in Wonderland*, "All roads lead there if you don't know where you are going." But *there* may not be where you want to be. Indeed, where you want to be at the end of the journey is the objective, and it should be found in a national strategy. Thus, the political objectives of participating in a PKO are the first consideration in testing this hypothesis. A national strategy, however, consists of two additional parts beside the objectives. First, there are the courses of action (COA) that lead to the objectives. The COA answer the *how* question: how do we achieve the objective? Given that we can describe what we must do to achieve the objective, we must address the third part of the strategy resources. This answers the question, "With what?" The assumed answer in H1 is that the resources are adequate to carry out the COA or can be made so. In other words, a third party will supply missing resources. If a third party does not provide missing resources, then we would expect to find the force-providing country waiting on the sidelines.

With regard to the first sub-hypothesis, we expect to find that force-providing countries weighed the interaction between their political capabilities and their integrated capabilities before offering to provide forces. However, we strongly suspect that the driving force behind their decisions was the assessment of their political capabilities. In some cases, we would expect to find linkage between types of capability to have been made explicitly and addressed clearly. In other cases, the linkage is likely to have been only implicit. If this is indeed the nature of the relationship, it suggests that an appropriate direction for U.S. policy of support for capacity building in the region is to assist in improving the analytical skills required to assess the capability requirements for participation in peacekeeping operations.

The second sub-hypothesis states that the incentives that affected the original decision to participate will be at least equally important to the decision to sustain the effort. Some of those incentives are capability (both political and integrated), prestige, perception of obligation, treaty obligation, sense of hemispheric solidarity, and politics (both domestic and international). Clearly, however, experience over time will modify perception and the weight of particular incentives may very well change, resulting in possible changes of policy.

Hypothesis H2 focuses on political capacity as the driving force behind participation in PKO. If political capabilities over time can be strengthened, then we would expect to find more countries willing to commit forces to PKO missions. Nevertheless, the first sub-hypothesis suggests that there is an important relationship between political capability and integrated capabilities. The expected relationship is between the perception of integrated capabilities and political will. Stated in the opposite manner, it suggests that as the perception of a state's integrated capabilities increases, its political will to participate in PKO will also increase.

The second sub-hypothesis focuses on the level of participation. Here the expectation is that as political and integrated capabilities increase, participation in PKO would rise to a higher level. In this case, we would expect to find states with greater political capabilities undertaking more leadership roles. We would also expect those states to have greater integrated capabilities and to assume a wider variety of tasks with larger numbers of deployed personnel.

In brief, our hypotheses suggest that capacity for PKO, and other integrated operations, is a result of the development of a number of discrete but related capabilities and the ability to use and sustain them over time. We expect to find that there is a powerful relationship between the components of the political capability—national strategy and political will—and the several integrated capabilities. We do not, however, expect to find that the relationship is one to one. Instead, as in most sociopolitical relationships, we expect the relationship to be complex between the two hypothesized variables both in that they may well tend to interact in reciprocal ways and in that there are likely to be a number of intervening variables to further add to the complexity. The structure of this research did not allow us to show quantitatively the expected degree of correlation. However, we were able to demonstrate in a rigorous qualitative fashion how these variables relate to each other through the conduct of a series of comparative case studies among the participants in the MIFH and MINUSTAH missions. As mentioned, comparability has been ensured by the use of a common series of research questions (see below).

ORGANIZATION OF THE BOOK

The following chapters address each of the comparative cases beginning, first, with an overview of Haitian history and the antecedents to the current intervention. Next, we look at the states that participated in the Multinational Interim Force: the United States, Canada, and Chile. Chile forms a bridge case between MIFH and the UN mission, MINUSTAH. The next chapters examine the countries with the largest contingents and longest PKO experience, as well as the state providing the force commander—Brazil, Argentina, and Uruguay. Finally, we look at some of the countries that have not played such a large role in peacekeeping operations in the past—Bolivia, Guatemala, and Peru. We conclude with recommendations for countries that wish to conduct peacekeeping and other integrated operations, as well as suggestions for states that seek to support those who would be force providers.

RESEARCH QUESTIONS

Researchers for each of the participating countries were asked to address the following questions:

1. What factors influenced the decision to participate in the Haiti PKO?
   - Capability
   - Prestige
   - Sense (perceived) of obligation
   - Legal (treaty) obligation
   - Hemispheric solidarity
   - U.S. (bilateral) influence
   - Feeling of threat
   - Politics (domestic and international)

2. How was the decision taken? Was it top down, bottom up, or a combination?
   - What institutions were involved/consulted?
   - Foreign Ministry
   - Defense Ministry
   - Interior Ministry
   - Finance Ministry
   - Other ministries
   - International governmental organizations and nongovernmental organizations
   - What criteria were employed in making the decision?
   - What was the concept?

3. How was the mission designed and planned? By whom? To what extent was it shaped by external influences?
   - Which ministries?
   - Which institutions? (Role of the Armed Forces [individually and collectively] and joint staff?)
   - Which ones dominated?
   - What were the external influences, if any?

4. What were/are the political objectives of the mission? Economic objectives (if any)?
   - How do they relate to the criteria used to decide to participate?

5. What were/are the military/security objectives of the mission?
   - Are they congruent with the political objectives? Economic objectives?

6. Have the objectives changed over time? In what way? Why?
    - Political
    - Economic
    - Military (security)

7. What independent variables influence the effectiveness of combined military forces, police forces, and civilian agencies in international missions to support governance, law and order, and institution building of fragile states (PKO)?

8. What performance measures can be used to evaluate the effectiveness of combined forces conducting integrated operations in international PKO either in the Western Hemisphere or conducted by nations of the Western Hemisphere?

9. What are the key recommendations for policymakers to enhance the capabilities for PKO and other integrated operations within a framework of regional security cooperation?

NOTES

[1] Center for Hemispheric Defense Studies, *Security and Defense Studies Review* 5, no. 1 (Spring 2005), available at <http://www.ndu.edu/chds/journal/indexarcspring05.htm>.

[2] See Ray S. Cline, *The Power of Nations in the 1990s* (New York: Rowman and Littlefield, 1994).

Chapter Two

Haiti's Quest for Democracy: Historical Overview

WALTER E. KRETCHIK

On February 29, 2004, Haitian President Jean Bertrand Aristide resigned his office and fled into exile after internal upheaval and external pressure from both France and the United States, both of which had ordered their citizens out.[1] On the same day, after a request for support from the interim Haitian government, United Nations Security Council Resolution (UNSCR) 1529 authorized a 3-month Multinational Interim Force (MIF) to secure and stabilize the country and to "support [newly appointed] Haitian President Boniface Alexandre" in his quest for political harmony.[2] MIF troops from Canada, Chile, France, and the United States arrived to ensure stability until a robust UN peacekeeping force appeared. In April 2004, UNSCR 1542 created the UN Stability Mission in Haiti (MINUSTAH), a force capped at 6,700 troops and 1,600 civilian police. Brazil provided the largest contingent of forces (about 1,200 troops) under Brazilian Lt. Gen. Augusto Heleno Ribeiro Pereira, with mission handover occurring on June 1, 2004.[3]

Aristide's departure signaled the continuation of yet another troubled period in Haiti's history, an account rife with political discord and human rights violations. In considering these political woes and repeated multinational efforts to assist in rectifying them, at least two questions come to mind: How did Haiti's security situation evolve into its present situation? And, arguably more importantly, how effective has multinational force been in assisting the government of Haiti in its quest for democracy? By properly analyzing these queries, the Haiti case may yield valuable lessons that will aid hemispheric nation-states seeking to build capacity for the conduct of current and future multinational peacekeeping missions. That said, no analysis of present conditions in Haiti can be considered adequate without understanding past events. Haiti's current circumstances are rooted in experiences that can be divided into two categories suitable for the purposes here: what transpired before the intervention of multinational forces in 1994, and what has occurred since that point.

8

THE PRE-MULTINATIONAL ERA: 1804–1994

Recent United Nations (UN) and other organizational forays into the Western Hemisphere's most impoverished country follow in the wake of what Donald E. Schulz calls periodic waves of political violence with the Haitian people as its victims.[4] The evidence for such social pandemonium is both profuse and well documented. Scholars such as Robert Debs Heinl, Deidre McFadyen, Pierre Laramee, Mark Fried, Fred Rosen, and Robert Fatton have described Haiti as a place where violence reigns and people are victimized. Once considered by many observers as the pearl of the Caribbean for its natural beauty and French colonial architecture, Haiti now conjures up images of filth, utter despair, and endemic political corruption.[5]

The 2004 example of violent behavior notwithstanding, Haitian political mayhem can be traced at least to a late 18th-century uprising against French colonialism. In 1791, Haiti's revolution commenced when inspired Haitian veterans of the American Revolution gained knowledge of the French Revolution's recognition of the rights of man. Political intrigue with Britain, France, Spain, and the United States soon followed, as well as a bloody revolt to eradicate French colonial power. Ultimately, the so-called first Black Republic in the Western Hemisphere emerged on January 1, 1804.[6]

Fearing that mob rule might affect them in the same way it had their former French masters, the revolution's leaders cast aside the ideals of liberty, equality, and freedom to impose an iron-fisted caste system upon the country. Rooted in Haitian mulatto and slave culture, the rigidly controlled political framework embraced privilege, family allegiance, and racism.[7] Trickery kept the superstitious masses terrified, illiterate, impoverished, and powerless. Meanwhile, political tactics designed to retain power through fear and distrust imposed both dread and a respect for authority upon Haitian society.

Consequently, while Haitians considered themselves a separate people due to language and culture, Haiti's elites consolidated power—the ability to make, execute, and enforce policy—at the top. The masses became quarry for the upper class and soon trusted few individuals outside of family bloodlines. Over time, a predatory society developed, one so lacking in public virtue that John Sweeney described it as "the poorest, least educated, and most socially polarized country in the Western Hemisphere."[8]

Emerging from these restless social conditions was Jean-Jacques Dessalines, an illiterate military commander who named himself governor-general for life. Elites quickly opposed Dessalines for seeking popular support through land reform; he was murdered in 1806. The homicide served to reveal three Haitian societal realities: civic virtue (for political gain or otherwise) leads to intimidation or assassination, violent removal of officials or the opposition is an accepted engine for social change, and populist leaders threaten the privileged classes. Guided by those social rudders, the Haitian people endured 22 heads of state between 1843 and 1915, with 14 removed by force, 2 with fates unknown, and only 1 completing the term of office.[9]

By 1915, Haiti's geographic location along the Windward Passage enmeshed it within a U.S. Government hemispheric quest to expunge European imperialism and thus protect liberty through the creation, shaping, and regulation of stable, free market societies.[10] Haiti, as with many Latin American and Caribbean states of the time, was a target country for such policy due to the high amount of debt owed to foreign banks, primarily German. But one regional entity that often defaulted on repaying foreign loans, the Haitian government, was particularly adept at siphoning money gathered from import taxes to enrich itself.

More importantly, in the late 19th and early 20th century, European powers projected naval power into the Western Hemisphere and occasionally shelled regional states to encourage the payment of foreign debt. After August 1914, the Great War in Europe incited an American government fear of Haitian debt collection by foreign powers. Capital was required to pay for the conflict, and Europeans had already demonstrated a willingness to use coercive force to extract money owed from Western Hemisphere states. If rival fleets clashed in the Caribbean or sought bases there, the region was certain to become destabilized and the Panama Canal threatened. A neutral America would then be dragged into a foreign conflict.

In 1915, the murder and public dismemberment of Haitian President J. Vilbrun Guillaume Sam provided President Woodrow Wilson with a motive to invade the troubled country and prevent international mischief there. Citing the rationale of protecting U.S. citizens and property as legal justification for intervening in sovereign states, a small invasion force led by Rear Admiral William B. Caperton landed in Haiti on July 28, 1915. Although intended to provide temporary security and stability characteristic of the Banana Wars era of U.S. history, initial success evolved into an enduring occupation lasting until 1934. For 19 years, the U.S. Government improved Haiti's politics, economics, culture, and infrastructure, fought off uprisings, and created national police forces to help ensure order.[11] American efforts succeeded in the short term, but the methods used often reflected racial attitudes of the time that alienated the elites. Moreover, the American occupiers shunned training and educating the Haitians to maintain their rejuvenated society, which soon returned to pre-invasion norms after 1934 due to the lack of interest, funds, and job skills.

Between 1940 and the 1960s, a relative political calm ensued in Haiti as bipolar Cold War maneuverings kept the country in the U.S. orbit. Under Haitian strongman and proclaimed anticommunist François "Papa Doc" Duvalier, Haiti followed a policy of *negritude*, which combined mysticism, Haitian *voudoun*, and African-roots revivalism while also promoting terror and brutality to keep social order. Duvalier transformed the U.S.-created Haitian police or *gendarmierie* into a predatory force that only served him and also formed the *tonton macoutes*, a militia named after the Haitian folklore figure "Uncle Knapsack," the malevolent kidnapper of troublesome children.

After Papa Doc Duvalier's death in 1971, Jean Claude "Baby Doc" Duvalier succeeded his father by a resolution that passed 2,391,916 to 0.[12] Yet the younger Duvalier shunned ruling, even to maintain his own position. After $2 million was spent on his wedding to a wealthy mulatto, the impoverished masses were so sickened by the extravagances of wealth that many fled across the Caribbean by boat and thus attracted international attention. Forced to resign in 1986, Duvalier's absence led to an ill-fated junta under Haitian Lt. Gen. Henri Namphy. Ousted in 1988, Namphy was replaced by Prosper Avril, who served for a year before leaving office for an interim presidency.

By early 1990, events suggested that the country's grim past might take a more sanguine twist. Centuries of dictatorship and military rule ended in 1990 when Jean-Bertrand Aristide, a populist and Roman Catholic priest, campaigned as a political reformer with *Lavalas* (*flood* in Haitian Creole) as his platform. After 6 weeks of stumping, Aristide became Haiti's first democratically elected president after garnering 67 percent of the votes.

After assuming office on February 7, 1991, Aristide spoke of an aggressive and unachievable array of social reform programs, to include minimum wage increase, a national literacy campaign, land reform, the abolition of rural section chiefs, tax collection from the rich, ending drug trafficking, and cracking down upon government corruption. Initially, Aristide's publicly mandated government showed signs of competency and general acceptance. His populism, however, signaled his downfall. One month after Aristide took office, Roger Lafontant, the former interior minister and head of the *tonton macoutes*, attempted a coup. The overthrow failed, but Aristide never reconciled his political agenda with Haiti's elites, military leaders, and the masses.

In the wake of Lafontant's power bid, President Aristide verbally attacked the prevailing upper class in his *Pe Lebrun* speech of September 27, 1991. Although claiming non-Marxist leanings, Aristide chastised the predatory upper class as "bourgeoisie thieves." Demanding that the wealthy and powerful cease the fleecing of the people and instead invest money in jobs, Aristide warned, "If you don't do it, I am sorry for you! It's not my fault, you understand?"[13] Such threats rattled Haiti's elites and the military; Aristide soon fled to Venezuela after a coup led by Lt. Gen. Raoul Cedras.

Numerous acts of barbarism marked the Cedras regime to include the arrest, murder, torture, and rape of thousands of Haitian citizens and prominent Aristide supporters. At least 5,000 Haitians were killed, while another 10,000 fled the country. About 300,000 people became internally displaced out of fear for their lives.[14] Pressure by the United Nations, the Organization of American States (OAS), and the United States brought economic sanctions upon the country, a situation that barely affected the Cedras junta while driving the masses into further despair. The sanctions had some positive effect, however, for on July 3, 1993, both Cedras and Aristide separately signed the Governors Island Accord, setting an October 1993 date for the junta to leave Haiti, with amnesty.[15]

On October 11, 1993, the junta orchestrated a potentially violent dockside demonstration that repulsed a UN peacekeeping force aboard the USS *Harlan County* that was sent to set conditions for Aristide's return. Cedras and his thugs embarrassed both the UN and the U.S. Government as the naval vessel departed without discharging the multinational force. Military planning soon commenced, headed by the U.S. Atlantic Command in Norfolk, Virginia. Negotiations and sanctions failed to convince the junta to leave and, on July 31, 1994, UNSCR 940 authorized all means necessary to restore democracy in Haiti under Chapter VII of the UN charter.[16]

The passage of UNSCR 940 allowed the U.S. Government to forcibly invade Haiti in September 1994. On September 18, one day prior to the intervention, U.S. President William Clinton announced that the multinational force (MNF) was deploying "under the terms of UN Security Council Resolution 940," as a heavily-weighted U.S.-led international coalition from 25 nations tasked to create a safe and secure environment and support the return of exiled President Jean-Bertrand Aristide to Haiti.[17] With military forces converging on Haiti by air and sea on the night of September 19, only a last-minute peace delegation approved by President Clinton and led by former President Jimmy Carter averted combat operations. While saving lives, the decision proved unwise. Combat was required to conquer the country and thus force the junta's unconditional surrender or obliteration, a necessary condition for reinstating democracy by force.[18] Without a conquering army on the ground upon Aristide's return, a complete societal overhaul by the occupying nations, something that Haiti clearly required, was now impossible.

THE POST–MULTINATIONAL FORCE ERA

Humanitarian efforts may have spared lives and property damage, but they also left the American-led invasion force in the ignoble position of orchestrating both the removal of the junta and the return of President Aristide while working alongside the unrepentant Haitian military. The international community and the Haitian people were stunned as the UN forces of democracy apparently tolerated a military known for brutality and predatory traits. The situation set the tone for future UN force rotations in Haiti: international agencies sought to build democracy through a variety of cooperative and persuasive measures rather than by outright domination.

Operation Uphold Democracy *(September 1994–March 1995)*

Under the moniker of Operation *Uphold Democracy*, the U.S.-led multinational peacekeeping force underwrote Aristide's ensuing return to office.[19] About 20,000 American Servicemembers and approximately 5,000 non-U.S. forces served in the MNF.[20] While the United States had the capacity to accomplish the invasion without outside help, Caribbean Community and Common Market (CARICOM) forces provided the multinational gilding authorized under UNSCR 940.[21] MNF operations achieved the peaceful restoration of President Aristide to office while propping up a frail government and creating something Haiti never had: a police force that embraced Western democratic views of civic virtue.

Possibly the MNF's greatest contribution was to improve but not totally eradicate a malevolent human rights situation. Violence continued, however, spawned by a variety of cutthroats such as section chiefs, attaches, and alleged members of the Revolutionary Front for the Advancement and Progress of Haiti, although the last assassination attributed to those groups occurred on November 4, 1994, in Mirebalais.[22] Under the watchful eye of foreign military power, Haitians assembled freely and expressed their opinions, with the exception of the Artibonite region where former junta thugs still wreaked havoc. Nonetheless, large numbers of internally displaced persons came out of hiding, and a sense of security returned where the multinational force established a presence. However, one or two criminal murders occurred daily without respite, an indicator that military security occurs only where the forces are physically located.

Under MIH assistance, Aristide's government took steps to disband the military. Yet confusion reigned over the former soldiers, particularly with compensation and reemployment. Promises were made to offer jobs within government ministries and to set up retraining programs. Yet as assurances proved slow to materialize, a deadly incident on December 26, 1994, at the Haitian army headquarters confirmed the anger of former Haitian Army (*Forces Armées d'Haïti*, or FAd'H) members who needed money, not words, for sustenance. Moreover, although paramilitary forces had declined in visibility, section chiefs and other ruffians continued to intimidate and extort.[23]

Although Aristide placed justice system reform high on his list of priorities, finding qualified and incorruptible legal officials proved problematical. The majority of the country remained under the legal interpretation of *commissaires du government*, some of whom were closely involved with the Cedras régime or had records of human rights violations. Haitian legal system authorities were either incapable of or unwilling to prosecute criminals, fearing family retribution or future lack of patronage. In response, frustrated citizens often resorted to vigilante action and revenge, two well-established Haitian cultural values.

Local assemblies were to appoint Haitian judges, but that had not occurred by mission handover. Indeed, many judges were illiterate or not grounded in the law; U.S. Army Colonel Mark Boyatt recalled having to provide copies of the Haitian Constitution to such individuals and then offering classes in citizenship.[24] Suitable jails for detaining prisoners until trial were in short supply, although some were upgraded due to independent Special Forces initiatives, not the MNF. The lack of electricity for the facilities was also a concern, for Haiti lacked a power grid and was dependent upon dozens of diesel-driven power generators. Escapes were commonplace, records nonexistent, and families provided prison food, not the state. Although the Haitian government established the Commission on Justice and Truth to investigate and correct such matters, little was accomplished by the MNF in this area, for nation-building was not a task.[25]

Interlaced with the Haitian justice system was law enforcement, in this case the formation of an Interim Public Security Force (IPSF). This police organization, under the training and supervision of the International Criminal Investigative Training Assistance Program, numbered approximately 3,000 personnel and was comprised of former Haitian military police, FAd'H, Guantánamo detainees, and Haitian expatriates. The force was vetted to ensure they had no human rights violations attributed to them and provided basic police functions until a permanent Haitian national police force came into being. After a dubious background screening, the recruits underwent a 6-day training course to instill a police code of conduct and civil rights concern where none existed for 200 years.

About 800 international police monitors provided the force with 2 hours of on-the-job-training each day with mixed results. While enthusiastic at first, many IPSF members became skittish of going on patrol, especially at night when criminal activity intensified. In some cases, international policemen made arrests (although these actions were forbidden by mandate and Haitian law) when crimes occurred but an IPSF officer failed to act. Moreover, the IPSF lacked essential equipment, such as communications gear and proper vehicles, and their effectiveness was limited. By March 1995, the United Nations had serious doubts that most IPSF members could join the to-be-formed Haitian National Police (HNP) due to its minimum education requirement for police school being the tenth grade and a baccalaureate required for academy entrance.[26]

Foreign intervention alone under the MNF did not end the turbulent undercurrents in Haitian society although, to some pundits, political violence tempered to some degree. While true when comparing the rate of violent incidents taking place before and after intervention, Haiti's imbedded social beliefs, attitudes, and values remained virtually untouched. One informed

Haitian said, "It won't take much for things to go back to what they were." [27] As with an outwardly calm volcano, lava bubbled deeply within.

United Nations Mission in Haiti (March 1995–June 1996)

With a belief that international military power might remedy Haiti's troubled political situation, UNSCR 944 of September 29, 1994, also set the stage for eventual mission handover from the MNF to the UN Mission in Haiti (UNMIH). Over the next few weeks, UN observers and their equipment flowed into the country, and by October 5, the advance team totaled 49 personnel. UNMIH personnel worked with the MNF to keep track of ongoing events and also achieved a mission first. In late February to early March 1995, the UNMIH headquarters staff underwent group training in planning and decisionmaking before mission assumption under the tutelage of a U.S.-led international team. [28] For reasons that remain unknown, no UN mission since then has undergone similar predeployment training.

For all that the MNF accomplished in providing stability, Haiti was still a dysfunctional country in March 1995. Despite MNF command proclamations of a secure environment as UNMIH mission handover approached, Haiti's violent political realities resurfaced. On March 28, 1995, 3 days before UNMIH assumed its mission, Mireille Durocher Bertin and Eugene Baillergeau, Jr., were shot dead in their car along Martin Luther King Boulevard in Port-au-Prince. Bertin was a prominent lawyer and an outspoken Aristide critic. Baillergeau was a client and had the misfortune of accompanying her to a meeting. Members of the MNF and the IPSF responded quickly, albeit too late to save either Bertin or Baillergeau. Doubtful that the investigation could be handled with internal security forces, U.S. Department of State representatives contacted the Federal Bureau of Investigation and asked them to investigate the brutal killings. [29]

After 6 months of MNF intervention to stabilize the country and to support the UN mandates and various agencies involved, the responsibility for assisting the government of Haiti fell to UNMIH on March 31, 1995. Operating under Chapter VI of the UN Charter, the force supported the legitimate constitutional authorities of Haiti in establishing free and fair legislative elections. The 6,000-personnel multinational force was led by U.S. Army Major General Joseph Kinzer.

Upon arrival, Kinzer found that Haiti was more unstable than imagined. Finding Chapter VI unsuitable and requesting what he called "Chapter VI and a half," he proceeded to establish six patrol districts that covered Haiti in its entirety. A Pakistani battalion controlled zone I, while a Nepalese battalion was responsible for zone II. A Dutch company operated within zone III, and CARICOM located itself within zone IV. U.S. forces patrolled zone V (Port-au-Prince), and zone VI fell to the Bangladesh force.

By March 1995, Haiti's government was to have assumed responsibility for its own security with UNMIH support. Crime, however, was even higher than acceptable Haitian norms, and the IPSF was not up to the task. While the people were joyous at having Aristide back as president, a feeling of public insecurity and mistrust permeated society, for the police proved incapable of securing the country from violence.

The lack of an effective police force posed problems for the national elections scheduled for June 1995. In March, 43 Haitians died due to vigilante killings, while three more incidents occurred in the first few weeks of April. The Haitian government's response was to make the public aware of the legal consequences of vengeful murder, although that had limited effect. For some UN observers, UNMIH's operating under Chapter VI instead of Chapter VII led to continued crime because the probability of coercive measures was reduced, although the threat to UNMIH personnel was low. Regardless, as the UN Secretary General reported, "The possibility of incidents during routine operations should not be underestimated."[30]

UNMIH faced two significant issues in its initial stages, the status of the Haitian police and parliamentary and local elections slated for June 2 and 25, respectively. The force was also involved with the Haitian Police Academy, established on February 3, 1995, and its 4-month academic program. In the meantime, the IPSF continued to operate at a low level of motivation; members' future unemployment possibilities and failure to be paid were but several factors. Morale slumped due to the government's failure to consider the IPSF members for alternative employment when their mission ended.[31]

As far as the elections were concerned, the process was complicated by 27,000 candidates for 2,200 office positions and 45 political parties, of which 18 were considered viable. UNMIH personnel attempted to work with Haiti's Provisional Electoral Committee but found most of the members inexperienced in how to plan, prepare, and execute legitimate democratic elections. UN troops found themselves assisting Haitians not only to comprehend the intricacies of democratic elections, but also to locate polling stations, arrange for ballot security and distribution, and provide discreet site security. The UN charter forbade personal protection for candidates, although several people asked for such security.[32]

International support for the Haitian elections fell to the International Civilian Mission in Haiti (MICIVIH), a group chartered to monitor unrestricted ability to express public opinions, resolve differences, and investigate irregularities. When the OAS recruited and deployed international observers for the elections, UNMIH military personnel assisted in this effort, a significant assignment considering that only 15 to 20 percent of Haiti's estimated 2,500,000 voters were literate. Handbills and leaflets were of limited worth, so UNMIH relied more upon radio and television broadcasts when announcing election-related information.[33]

The road to Haitian elections in June 1995 was filled with pitfalls. Haiti's streets were places of murder and attacks during all hours of the day, and UN and OAS observers talked of likely voting irregularities. For both the Haitian government and UNMIH, however, the elections were a necessary step toward legitimizing the progress of democracy, both internationally and nationally, and for gauging the success of multinational forces in such endeavors. For his part, Aristide and his government had to prove that their own and international efforts to democratize Haiti were not in vain.

The weeks prior to the election saw violent attacks on candidates and the loss of 800,000 voter registration cards. Although the government claimed 3 million Haitians were registered to vote, all the parties criticized the process. Growing apathy among the populace indicated a fear that their vote was insignificant or would result in additional violence. Their concern was well founded, for a candidate from the *Union des Patriotes Democrates* was shot and wounded at a political meeting on May 28, 1995. Two days later, Senate candidate Renaud Bernadin, head of *Pati Louvri Barye* and an Aristide advisor, was attacked in Cap-Haitien, apparently in an effort to influence the elections.

In the wake of this violence, 408 Haitian police officers graduated from the academy on June 4. At the highly publicized ceremony, President Aristide announced that the new force was to increase from 3,300 officers to 6,000— almost the size of its predecessor, the 7,000-man FAd'H. Unlike their repugnant predecessor, however, the new force was to embrace democratic but alien societal views of being removed from politics and having a sense of civic virtue. President Aristide, a product of his own societal norms, failed to make the transition when he reminded the "apolitical" graduates, "Alone we are weak, together we are strong, [and] together we are *Lavalas!*"[34]

When elections were held in June, both Haitians and neutral observers contested the results. While some saw Haiti's voting as "generally free and fair with some irregularities," the voter turnout was hardly overwhelming— about 70 percent of the eligible electorate. Several polling stations were burned down, and 2 weeks later, the results were still not officially announced, partially due to accommodating voting places that had remained open for only a short time. UNMIH had provided sufficient logistical assistance to ensure that ballots were delivered, used properly, safeguarded, and counted. A pro-Aristide, multiparty coalition called the *Lavalas* Political Organization won a landslide victory at all levels.

June also brought a UN resolution to extend UNMIH and its monitoring of Haiti's human rights policies until February 1996. Tension was heightened during this time by anticipated violence in reaction to the eightieth anniversary of the U.S. intervention in 1915, but no major incidents occurred. With UNMIH now in continued support of the Haitian government for several additional months, Haiti's political leaders created several new ministries, to include administration and public service, social affairs, environment, and commerce and industry.[35]

During fall 1995, UNMIH forces continued to patrol the Haitian countryside in anticipation of a government announcement for the expected presidential election. The announcement came on October 13, and 2 days later, UN Secretary-General Boutros Boutros-Ghali attended ceremonies commemorating Aristide's return of the previous year. As with the previous elections, much was expected both domestically and internationally regarding Haiti's transition to democracy, and UNMIH again played a role.[36]

An unfortunate incident soon marred Haiti's anticipated elections. On November 9, the killing of President Aristide's cousin, Jen Hubert Feuille, and the wounding of pro-*Lavalas* supporter Gabriele Fortunet nearly derailed the elections scheduled for December 17, 1995. Aristide accused UNMIH of providing insufficient security for the tottering country, thus directing the fury of his own personal grief onto the international agency. In a way, Aristide menaced the democratization process by talking of remaining in office for 3 additional years, since he had been denied a full term because of the coup. Although supported by his followers, Aristide came to understand the ramifications of this course of action and later decided not to attempt to extend his term of office. He then unleashed a flurry of activity in his final weeks in office: firing his police chief, announcing plans to marry, and phasing out the tiny Haitian navy with a coast guard.

When the election came, Rene Préval took 88 percent of the vote. Sworn to a 5-year term on February 7, 1996, Préval became the first person in Haiti's history to transition between two democratically elected presidents. Although Préval agreed to uphold the constitution and enforce its laws, his vision for Haiti's future was not immediately clear. In sweeping statements calling for Haitians to "join intelligences and unite efforts" in order to do away with "the profound inequities of our society," Préval was leading a country wracked by political violence. Knowing that UNMIH was scheduled to depart on February 29, 1996, Préval requested that the force to remain in Haiti for his transition period, resulting in a UN extension of the mission until June 1996.[37] On March 1, 1996, command transferred from Major General Kinzer to Canadian Brigadier General J.R.P. Daigle.

Haiti's transformation to democracy lurched forward under UNMIH supervision. The headquarters provided technical and logistical support to the Haitian authorities responsible for organizing and conducting parliamentary and presidential elections in 1995, but ensuring that the elections were free and fair was never its charter. Although UNMIH provided some assistance in support of the new HNP, transferring democratic values of civil responsibility and apolitical views to a society where such things were unfamiliar concepts went unaccomplished. In truth, UNMIH civilian police were much more adept at organizing Haiti's new criminal investigation unit and helping with formal police training at the Haitian Police Academy under the International Criminal Investigative Assistance Training Program than changing Haitian attitudes toward society and each other.

According to Kinzer, UNMIH's most significant efforts occurred through more than 1,000 small projects, to include bringing electrical power to the people when such contrivances had never functioned properly or at all. As with the American occupation force of 1915–1934, UNMIH personnel worked with Haitians to improve living conditions in areas such as water, sanitation, electricity supply, and roads. Police stations, schools and other public facilities were repaired, and training was provided in disaster management, first aid, and other fields.[38] Unlike the occupation, UNMIH forces also attempted to educate the Haitians to appreciate such things and to maintain them.

There are, of course, problems when foreign powers intervene to advise and assist desperate countries, especially among Haitians who can prove recalcitrant when it comes to accepting outside ideas. Thus, UNMIH officials had to be culturally sensitive when working with Haiti's government and people as it assumed its responsibilities and functions. Patience, not paternalism, was extremely important in maintaining a secure and stable environment, not only when guarding Aristide but also when providing security to humanitarian convoys, airports, seaports, and storage locations and a myriad of other missions. Haiti's people also required nurturing by building lasting relationships that in turn developed into something that Haitians lacked: trust for perceived authority.

Sensitivity was also necessary when cooperating with representatives of the Haitian government, the Friends of the Secretary General for Haiti (Argentina, Canada, Chile, France, the United States, and Venezuela), and MICIVIH, the entity that assisted with Haiti's many democratic transitional issues. UNMIH efforts thus complemented those of numerous countries and agencies. The burden of overall responsibility, however, remained firmly situated upon the back of the Haitian government as UNMIH's mandate finally drew to a close.

United Nations Support Mission in Haiti

With the end of UNMIH, the UN Support Mission in Haiti (UNSMIH) was established under UNSCR 1063 of June 28, 1996, to operate under Chapter VI. Consisting of 1,300 UN personnel (including 300 police trainers) drawn from Canada and Pakistan, 700 troops remained under separate control of the Canadian government. According to UN political affairs officer Karin von Hippel, the operation was more a U.S.-Canadian venture than an international one, despite the absence of American troops and the presence of Pakistani forces.[39]

The UNSMIH mandate continued in the same vein as UNMIH: to assist the government of Haiti in professionalizing its police force and to maintain a secure and stable environment for establishing and training an effective national police.[40] These missions proved difficult to attain due to ongoing turmoil within Haitian society. Haiti's police force was not competent enough to maintain security, a situation that Préval freely acknowledged when stating, "Withdrawal of international support at this juncture could jeopardize the objective of completing the creation of the new civilian police" and furthering democracy in Haiti. Indeed, Préval had requested an extension of the UNMIH mandate, or some sort of multinational presence, for 6 months, noting, "The current context of the social climate in Haiti requires the Government to have at its disposal an adequate public force for the maintenance of order and security. Our newly established national police force is unfortunately not fully in a position to assume that responsibility."

That request, plus UN understanding of the situation, led to the establishment of UNSMIH.[41] It also meant that UNSMIH's civilian police were thinly spread across Haiti, with 5 detachments in Port-au-Prince and 10 in the provinces. Regardless of location, they accompanied the Haitian National Police and informed the public about the benefits of community police work, as well as supervising police training through the *programme de formation*, which focused on conflict resolution, human rights issues, immigration, and narcotics, among other matters.

As with previous Haiti missions, UNSMIH missions were subject to Haitian political chicanery and violence. No sooner had Préval settled into office than former President Aristide verbally attacked his designated replacement as encouraging corruption. Préval, highly dependent on Aristide's nod for popular support, as well as constitutional authority, soon lacked a strong political base to further his own aims. In November 1996, Aristide broke with *Lavalas* and formed the *Lavalas Family*, claiming that the intent was not to undermine the Haitian president but to revitalize the parent organization that had been split into several factions, to include the *Organization Politique Lavalas* and the *Front National pour le Changement et la Democratie*.[42]

July through September saw increased amounts of violence despite UNSMIH's presence and its augmenting of HNP crowd-control units (*compagnies d'intervention et de maintien de l'ordre*, or CIMO) that deployed when trouble arose. Beginning in October, however, politically motivated violence actually decreased but did not end completely, for reasons that still remain unclear. Perhaps the reduction in violence was due to the arrest of

Sergeant Joseph Jean-Baptiste, the leader of the Committee for the Defense of Demobilized Military (*comite revendicatif pour la defense des militaires*), who led former soldiers in militant actions against the government. Nevertheless, UNSMIH's rules of engagement allowed for the use of force in self-defense and in attempts by any individual or group to impede the execution of the mandate. In an attempt to deflect such incidents, 17 Creole-speaking policemen arrived from the United States in mid-October, a requirement for not only interacting more effectively with the populace but also gathering information about criminal activities.

If UNSMIH could claim any early mandate successes, the training of police certainly fell into that category. On October 23, 1996, 60 Haitian university graduates undertook the required entrance examinations for civilian police training. UNSMIH police assisted the Haitian government in selecting applicants, as well as reviewing files to identify up to 30 candidates for a new criminal investigation unit. Infrastructure repair was also accomplished, to include UNSMIH personnel renovating 20 police stations. More significant, however, was that the Haitian police received paychecks and new police cars, a timely boost to morale. HNP competency also improved, and absenteeism dropped but was not totally eradicated in most districts. One blot on such improvements was that some officers abused their powers, with 40 being dismissed for serious infractions of their code.[43]

Despite some success, it was apparent to both the UN Security Council and the government of Haiti that the HNP had not yet attained sufficient proficiency and confidence to undertake their duties without multinational assistance. This was especially true once civil violence again broke out in November 1996, the result of high unemployment, inflation, and the Haitian people's ebbing tolerance for the slow pace of change. Several police officers were killed in the capital, and gang warfare over control of drug trafficking along Haiti's borders and coastline increased. The rise in such incidents, coupled with President Préval's November 13 request for yet another mandate extension, resulted in UNSCR 1086 of December 5, 1996, that set a new mission termination date of May 31, 1997.[44]

The extension brought a change in force structure, with 800 additional personnel financed with voluntary contributions from Canada and the United States to augment the authorized 800 troops on the ground. During the extension period, UNSMIH troops continued their patrols, renovated additional police facilities, assisted with community policing, and prepared study guides and information sheets for Haitian police and detectives. Unfortunately, many of the Haitian officers refused to avail themselves of these tools, again reflecting a cultural proclivity to treat foreign assistance with suspicion.

Shunning the advice and experience of professional law enforcement officers was an unfortunate course of action for many policemen, given that the inhabitants of Haiti's cities were only partially obeying the rule of law. Indeed, frustrated Haitian security forces were known to engage in "thuggery and disintegrated into warring factions," apparently to impose their own brand of righteousness at a quicker pace than the one at which the fledgling justice system operated. Such actions were more characteristic of a frontier zone than a nation-state and caused the Haitian government to declare on December 10, 1996, that the HNP was the only sanctioned law enforcement entity and parallel organizations were not to be tolerated.[45]

Such announcements did little to change matters. By March 1997, gangs, an illegitimate but de facto source of power at the local level of society, caused the deaths of 10 people in Cite Soleil. The HNP's ability to arrest gang leader suspects calmed matters for the moment but did little to staunch the flow of drug trafficking and contraband smuggling across Haiti's porous borders and coastline. When the police attempted to crack down, local thugs organized protests that resulted in the burning of a police station and the blocking of roads. Such actions served to demonstrate the strength of self-appointed local potentates through their ability to shun law enforcement and to embarrass the government in its failings to meet the security needs of the people.

By mid-July 1997, with the UNSMIH mission ending in 2 weeks, the Haitian people's ability to transition to democracy was in doubt due to a demonstrated lack of voter confidence and continuing incidents of political violence. Haiti's government was smarting after the April 6 senatorial election, where turnout was only 10 percent of registered voters, and also the forced resignation of Prime Minister Rosny Smarth on June 9.[46] For many Haitians, irregularities in the electoral process and perceived lethargic government reform created public doubt as to the efficacy of it all.

Clearly, the UN forces had little effect upon Haiti's political transformation, but it was not their mission to do so. Focused upon security and legal matters in the realm of law enforcement and assistance, UNSMIH members continued to provide instruction (albeit reluctantly accepted or even ignored) to Haitian police in the areas of conflict resolution, marksmanship, human rights issues, basic driving skills, and immigration and narcotics investigations. UNSMIH's training of CIMOs and their movement by helicopters proved essential for crowd control and delivering voting materials to remote areas for the election process. Regardless of such progress, the Haitian police remained a partially trained force incapable of dealing with the magnitude of the security situation.

In July 1997, the Haitian government's fragility was apparent to many pundits. While the Haitian people in general viewed the reinforcing of democratic institutions as fundamental to a better life, the economic growth and employment opportunities necessary for creating public confidence in a democratically based society had not achieved realization. Progress was slow, and both the UN Secretary-General and Haiti's political leaders believed that long-term international support was necessary to thwart a potentially deteriorating security situation.

United Nations Transition Mission in Haiti

On July 30, 1997, the day before the expiration of UNSMIH's mandate, UNSCR 1123 established yet another multinational force, the UN Transition Mission in Haiti (UNTMIH). As the third UN effort in Haiti to date and acting under Chapter VI, the force consisted of 50 military personnel and 250 policemen from Argentina, Benin, Canada, France, India, Mali, Niger, Senegal, Togo, Tunisia, and the United States. Headed by Canadian Brigadier General Robin Gagnon, UNTMIH's police advisors were tasked to train Haitian policemen in crowd control, rapid reaction force procedures, and national palace security. UNTMIH members also followed past practice and worked with the UN Development Program to assist with improving law enforcement expertise while furthering the development of the Haitian judicial system. The mandate was to remain in effect until November 30.[47]

As part of its mission, UNTMIH security forces were also to protect any personnel who assisted the Haitian police. This mandate nuance demonstrates the realities of the situation; not only Haitian police but also those who stood by them were subject to attack. This was no insignificant matter, for previous UNSMIH diagnostic studies had revealed numerous problems in the area of Haitian police leadership. Among the nine police districts, only three had shown progressive improvement in police behavior toward the populace; the remaining six continued to violate human rights and demonstrate abuses of authority.[48] When UNTMIH forces were deployed to these districts, their ability to influence and reform local police authority remained questionable.

Some analysts may point to the lack of resources and facilities as diluting the effectiveness of the HNP, but the issue is much more complex. Traditional Haitian cultural tendencies to form vigilante groups that seek retribution, as well as the formation of private security firms to earn much-needed revenue, served to undermine government authority. Moreover, the government failed to break toleration of such practices due not only to a weak police force, but also to the lack of public education in such matters. Eliminating the public's desire for revenge requires both education and observable positive results, something that the United Nations and the Haitian government had yet to achieve.

Haitian security woes were in part due to a government that had not functioned for at least 4 months. A major rift existed between the two principal factions of *Lavalas* that amplified Haiti's long-established social divisions. Polarization forces not only kept Haitians living on the island from benefiting from the wealthier diaspora who had fled to safer environs, but also further divided the privileged and the impoverished, educated and illiterate, and mulatto and black.[49] Such political and social disarray created an atmosphere of international and public doubt over Haiti's ability to make democracy work and further complicated the UN mission.

For 4 months, UNTMIH forces achieved marginal mission results. The Haitian government remained paralyzed due to internal divisions while human rights violations continued; many abuse cases were attributed to the police. In response, the government removed many untrustworthy police commissioners from office, although the replacements in some cases were no better. Poor discipline concerns, absenteeism, uniform violations, and lack of motivation continued despite ongoing UN supervision and training.

By 1997, it was apparent to many observers that police problems originated from the character of the individual policemen. UNTMIH troops were forced to work with what the Haitian academies produced, and despite a system of examinations and preliminary requirements to cull out only the best-qualified individuals, what passed as the fittest recruits were substandard. Civil responsibility had never been a national virtue and thus was difficult at best to institute.[50] Moreover, immature policemen, some issued a weapon for the first time, turned to the hasty use of firearms, resulting in eight people shot dead by the HNP between September and October 1997. While some of the killings were in self-defense, others were determined to be unnecessary. During the same period, one detainee died in jail, allegedly from being beaten by the police.[51] Such scandals did little to win public trust and eventually contributed to the failure of an HNP experiment to train northern Haitian communities in mediating their differences peacefully.

United Nations Civilian Police Mission in Haiti

UNTMIH's mandate furthered Haitian police professionalism but was not absolute; all UN military personnel left Haiti in November 1997 upon expiration of the mission's mandate. To honor President Préval's request for continued international support, the UN Security Council passed UNSCR 1141 on November 28, 1997, and created the UN Civilian Police Mission in Haiti (MIPONUH), a force to serve for 1 year beginning on December 30, 1997. The mandate was later extended by UNSCR 1277 (on November 30, 1999) until March 15, 2000, to ensure a phased transition to another organization, the International Civilian Support Mission in Haiti (MICAH). MIPONUH was authorized 300 civilian police personnel from Argentina, Benin, Canada, France, India, Mali, Niger, Senegal, Togo, Tunisia, and the United States, and was tasked to further assist the Haitian government in its continuing efforts to professionalize the national police.[52] As of February 12, 1998, 285 police officers and a special 90-man police unit were in country, headed by Colonel Claude Grude of France.

Soon after MIPONUH's arrival, President Préval praised the HNP in a February 1998 speech. While violence, banditry, and drug trafficking continued to mar the official record, the national police had become less dependent upon their foreign mentors for assistance. This was due in part to eliminating unsuitable officers and placing more competent ones in positions of authority while simultaneously improving police coverage throughout the country. Yet police-driven human rights abuses still occurred, and policemen continued to arrest Haitians on grounds of subversion against the state, an indicator that free speech was not yet a universally accepted democratic value.

Part of the problem was that the HNP was city-based for resource purposes, which in turn led to outbreaks of lawlessness and vigilantism in the countryside where the police had little to no presence. In an effort to extend police coverage to outlying areas, President Préval suggested that a rural police force be created. The proposal elicited numerous complaints from government officials concerned that the rural police would be less qualified than the national police, paid less, and be subjected to local political pressures that were more intense than those within the more developed cities. The proposal stalled due to political and financial constraints, yet such discourse demonstrated that the government recognized a security problem and sought a solution to it.

In spite of Haiti's political gridlock, the national police showed major improvement by fall 1998. Efforts continued to clear away corrupt leaders such as the director of the *Police Judiciaire*, who resigned and was later prosecuted under government defamation charges. When compared with previous years, fewer violent incidents between Haitians and their police forces occurred. Still, detainee abuses continued, as well as police beatings of protestors in Cabaret, Cite Soleil, Ile de la Tortue, and Ganthier, which led to angry crowds besieging police stations. International policemen found themselves mediating strained civil relations between an enraged citizenry seeking retribution and local law enforcement.

By late November 1998, the United Nations found the stalemated political conditions in Haiti such a risk for peace and development that MIPONUH's charter was extended for an additional year.[53] The extension paid dividends by early 1999, for the HNP displayed remarkable professionalism in the face of numerous demonstrations while enduring a continued political crisis and several incidents where heavily armed criminals broke the law. One indicator of the growing competency of the police was a decrease in shooting incidents: 59 in 1996, 31 in 1998, and 3 in early 1999.[54] However, many incidents occurred where the local police officials showed reluctance to punish officers who took part in citizen beatings or other forms of illicit behavior. Haitian culture again played a role, for many local policemen refused to take action against one of their own out of fear of reprisal by the particular officer's family.[55] In a society where familial ties are stronger than national agendas, apprehension over revenge can be a power unto itself.

Despite MIPONUH and HNP efforts, political violence continued in Haiti's streets. On January 11, 1999, President Préval broadcast a speech to the nation that declared the end of terms for deputies, one-third of the senators, and all local authorities. Citing Haitian law, Préval was unable to dissolve parliament or extend its mandate, calling upon all Haitians to find a solution to the problem. Taking emergency measures, the council of ministers froze bank accounts and cancelled diplomatic passports in what many political parties interpreted as a coup. In the wake of such measures, Préval's sister and a personal secretary were seriously wounded in an assassination attempt in which their automobile driver was killed. In spite of such security setbacks, MIPONUH policemen continued weekly training on police administration, arrest procedures, community relations, crowd control, and report writing, among other subjects.[56]

Despite continuous training efforts, MIPONUH members and Haitian police were unable to prevent the politically motivated violence endemic to Haitian society. On April 20, 1999, a member of the *Lavalas Family*–associated group *Jeunesse Pouvoir Populaire* was killed, allegedly by Haitian policemen. Two days later, several deputies of the *Organisation du Peuple en Lutte* (Organization of People in Struggle) sought refuge in the Chilean embassy after threats were made against their lives and property. They subsequently left the country, but these incidents continued a pattern of violence against political figures that local law enforcement alone was powerless to prevent. The atmosphere was inauspicious as Colonel George Gabbardo of France assumed command of the force.

By November 30, 1999, the security situation in Haiti became more unstable, with frequent incidents of violence, robbery, and civil unrest. Yet the UN Security Council believed that sufficient progress had been made to extend MIPONUH until March 15, 2000, under UNSCR 1277 with the intent of transitioning to yet another headquarters, the MICAH. Under UNSCR Resolution A/54/193, a phased transition from MIPONUH to MICAH was envisioned, with in-place officers gradually relinquishing responsibility for assisting the HNP to the new international support mission.

Haitian realities soon marred this planned changeover. With national elections scheduled for November 2000, the winter of 1999–2000 saw continued outbreaks of violence. In December 1999, politically motivated arson was blamed for the burning of several homes in Jeremie. A 14-year-old boy was killed on January 11, 2000, when a mob in Fort Liberte attempted to free and then lynch a police-held prisoner.[57] Yet despite these outbreaks of violence, plans to remove MIPONUH's law enforcement became finalized, and force withdrawal occurred on March 15.

International Civilian Support Mission in Haiti

MICAH's 1-year mandate consisted of building upon the mixed results of previous UN force missions and MICIVIH in the further promotion of human rights in Haiti. Specifically, the support mission was to "reinforce [the] institutional effectiveness of Haitian police and judiciary, and to coordinate and facilitate international dialogue with Haiti's political and social leaders." With assistance as the primary mission, MICAH consisted of 80 nonuniformed UN technical advisers advising the Haitian government in the areas of policing, justice, and human rights. Participating countries included Argentina, Benin, Canada, France, India, Mali, Niger, Senegal, Togo, Tunisia, and the United States.

Under MICAH's mission term, the security situation in Haiti eroded significantly. Much of the turmoil was due to a year dominated by numerous elections, to include local and parliamentary polls on May 21, additional voting through August, and presidential and partial senatorial contests planned for November and December 2000. Complicating matters was a parliament not functioning since being dissolved in January 1999. By 2000, political stagnation had generated tremendous international pressure upon the Haitian government and the termination of multilateral funding totaling US$500 million.

Despite the international community's efforts to improve police work, Haiti's propensity for political violence continued throughout 2000. Human Rights Watch recorded at least 70 cases of murder, intimidation, beatings, and assorted thuggery between January and June. Respected journalist Jean Dominique was one such victim, shot to death along with security guard Jean-Claude Louissant on April 3. Criminals stole and burned election ballots after the May 21 elections in several districts, forcing election workers to tally votes in police stations to avoid intimidation. When open ballot boxes and their spilled contents littered Haiti's streets the following day, the government undertook no serious investigation, and cries of fraud were soon raised among the international and domestic communities.[58]

Public outcry against the police also increased. Many members of Haiti's law enforcement community continued to side with the party in power and either participated in the beatings of opposition members or failed to intervene when witnessing such episodes. Of note was that inappropriate Haitian police behavior continued despite 673 police officers having been dismissed for wrongdoing between 1995 and 1999. Even the threat of job dismissal had little influence over police conduct in a society where fear of retribution and family intrigue are imbedded into the cultural fabric.

In November 2000, with multinational presence having succeeded in some areas and failed in others, UN Secretary-General Kofi Annan recommended against renewing MICAH's mandate. Annan remarked, "Haiti's political and electoral crisis has deepened, polarizing its political class and civil society," conditions unsuitable for the international organization to function successfully. In an exclamation point to Annan's statement, 7 bombs exploded in Port-au-Prince on November 22, killing a young boy and injuring 14 people. MICAH's mandate ended on February 6, 2001, coinciding with the end of the Préval administration and Aristide's subsequent return to office the next day.[59]

Multinational Interim Force

On February 7, 2001, Aristide returned to the presidency with promises of national reforms, an independent judicial court, and new schools, roads, and electrical systems.[60] Yet the Haitian security situation continued to worsen even with the numerous multinational military and civilian missions that had attempted to alter police practices since 1994. Between 2002 and early 2004, Haiti's security situation reflected that of a frontier, not a nation-state, with numerous cases of murder, intimidation, bombings, and the fleeing of refugees. While many of the incidents were related to criminal activity, political violence also was prevalent. The police were either unwilling or unable to handle such situations; for example, on November 14, 2003, a number of law enforcement officials were swept away by a crowd of rock-throwing protestors at an anti-Aristide demonstration.

In February 2004, in the face of increased shootings and beatings by the police and thugs attributed to Aristide and others, the United States and France exerted pressure upon the United Nations to act. With Aristide reluctantly fleeing the country and under UNSCR 1529, the UN authorized the deployment of a Chapter VII Multinational Interim Force for up to 3 months to contribute to security and stability in support of interim Haitian President Alexandre's request for international assistance. On June 1, 2004, the force transitioned to MINUSTAH, as authorized by UNSCR 1542.

CONCLUSION

In exploring 200 years of Haitian history, this study sought to shed additional light upon the role of multinational force in assisting the Haitian government and its transition to democracy. To answer the question of how Haiti's security situation evolved into its present situation, Haiti's current political and social instability goes back at least 200 years. While Haitians espouse republican government, actual practice deviates from that claim. This circumstance does not bode well for building democracy in Haiti, where the lack of a concept of powersharing for the betterment of society is a major obstacle to institutionalizing democracy.

Haitian culture is thus a major hindrance to democratic reform, particularly in implementing law enforcement to create a secure and stable environment.

In Haitian society, two levels of public violence affect stability and security: routine criminal activity and politically motivated action. Although routine criminal activity slowed to nuisance levels between 1994 and 2004, culturally embedded societal practices surfaced within Haitian police behavior. Law enforcement's decisionmaking was weighed against the possibility of revenge or vigilantism by the arrestee's family. Moreover, eradicating political violence in Haiti is impossible without altering cultural values. As long as Haitians believe that intimidating or killing political figures is an effective way to force governmental and social change, it will continue.

How effective has multinational force been in assisting the government of Haiti in its quest for democracy? True effectiveness in that troubled country would mean that no further multinational intervention is required. Since the Haitian government has yet to implement and sustain democracy under the rule of law, multinational force did little to bring permanent change to Haitian society from 1995 to 2004. As this study suggests, multinational forces only assisted in the transformation process with the United Nations and other international groups working with the Haitian government across a broad band of issues at many levels.

International forces have made little headway in stopping political violence, for that has not been the focus, as the United Nations has pointed out. For example, a Secretary-General report notes in the case of MIPONUH that the force trained the police in border police operations, crowd control, and first aid, as well as community policing, maintaining law and order, fighting capital crimes and drug trafficking, and reinforcing police administration and logistics.[61] Yet the missions did not seek to directly educate the Haitian people that political violence is not a legitimate means for change. The question remains: Should the United Nations or other foreign agencies proceed in this direction? Given the Haitian people's tendency to shun foreign advice, this approach does not seem likely to succeed.

Education, however, has at times proven to be an effective tool in furthering democracy by force. Unfortunately, the two most significant cases of this are post–World War II Germany and Japan, countries that were conquered and then occupied by outside forces that still linger there today. According to some experts, building democratic institutions in those occupied countries also depended upon high literacy rates, industrialization, and unconditional surrender, in addition to a respect for mass education. Haiti lacks all of these components. Thus, an unconquered Haiti is more of a peacekeeping experiment where the government allows a foreign presence to assist in establishing democracy by invitation, not by force.

Multinational force effectiveness has been limited by two additional factors: Haiti's propensity for lawlessness and the ad hoc nature of the multinational forces. Where a very volatile situation periodically displays stability, progress is still far below what is expected of Western-oriented governments. Corruption can only be blamed for part of this problem, for time and resources are also factors. It is helpful to remember that the United States formed professional law enforcement agencies in the 19th century, but it took decades to professionalize the thugs that constituted many police forces. U.S. law enforcement agencies still suffer from corruption, but politically motivated killings by such officials are atypical. Haiti cannot make the same claims. As far as the multinational forces are concerned, they were mostly unplanned and the continuous rotations impeded mission performance. UNMIH, with its dedicated headquarters training prior to mission assumption, was the exception, and lead nations undertaking future missions should consider similar practices.

While stability and security missions dominate the role of multinational forces in Haiti, the various rotations address only the symptoms of social disorder and not the causes. Between 1995 and 2004, Haitian stability and security proved to be temporary in nature, given that yet another UN force is in that country at the time of this study. Law enforcement is necessary, but so is cultural overhaul through education, a necessity for building legitimate institutions that care for the needs of the people. To have social order, people must believe in their system of government and society, and for Haitians that means confidence from results, not promises. Until human rights are guaranteed and enforced by an incorruptible government dedicated to making life better for all, Haiti's stability and security will remain problematic no matter how many rotations of UN or other forces occur.

NOTES

[1] Paisley Dodds and Ian James, "Aristide Flees into Exile; U.S. Dispatches Marines," Associated Press, March 1, 2004.

[2] United Nations Security Council Resolution 8015, available at <http://www.un.org/News/Press/docs/2004/sc8015.doc.htm>.

[3] United Nations Security Council Resolution 1542, April 30, 2004, available at <http://www.globalsolutions.org/programs/peace_security/peace_ops/conflicts/Haiti_Articles?SCRes_1542.pdf>. Other force contributors included Argentina, Chile, Sri Lanka, and Uruguay.

[4] Donald E. Schulz, "Whither Haiti?" *Parameters* XXVII, no. 4 (Winter 1997/1998), 73–91.

[5] Robert Debs Heinl, *Written in Blood: The Story of the Haitian People, 1492–1995* (New York: University Press of America, 1996); Deidre McFadyen, Pierre Laramee, Mark Fried, and Fred Rosen, *Haiti: Dangerous Crossroads* (Cambridge, MA: South End Press, 1995); Robert Fatton, *Haiti's Predatory Republic: The Unending Transition to Democracy* (Boulder, CO: Lynne Rienner Publishers, 2002).

6   James G. Leyburn, *The Haitian People* (New Haven, CT: Yale University Press, 1966), 22–23. The point of Haiti being a republic is debatable, for autocracy, not republicanism, has driven Haitian politics for two centuries.

7   Haitian racism is based upon skin tone; the lighter the skin, the better. See Karen Richman, "The Protestant Ethic and the Dis-Spirit of Vodou," in *Immigrant Faiths: Transforming Religious Life in America*, ed. Karen Leonard (Lanham, MD: AltaMira Press, 2004).

8   John Sweeney, "Stuck in Haiti," *Foreign Policy* no. 102 (Spring 1996), 1142–1151.

9   Leyburn, 16–17, and Robert Heinl and Nancy Heinl, *Written in Blood: The Story of the Haitian People, 1492–1995*, rev. ed. Michael Heinl (New York: University Press of America, 2005), 33.

10   In 1823, the Monroe Doctrine, an outcome of Thomas Jefferson's views of the so-called American System, had proclaimed that the Western Hemisphere was no longer open to European colonization as a reaction to a British treaty suggestion that also involved Russia. An unenforceable proclamation given the weakness of the American military and economy relative to the powers it had just threatened, it regardless indicated a growing U.S. Government intolerance for European empires and their economic hegemonic polices. The Monroe Doctrine later served as a driver for U.S. Government foreign policies in penetrating regional countries to expand free trade and to further U.S. business interests.

11   See, for example, Lester D. Langley, *The Banana Wars: United States Intervention in the Caribbean, 1898–1934* (Belmont, CA: Wadsworth Publishing Company, 1988).

12   Elizabeth Abbott, *Haiti: An Insiders' History of the Rise and Fall of the Duvaliers* (New York: Simon and Schuster, 1988), 159.

13   Jean Bertrand Aristide, speech, September 27, 1991, translated by the *Haitian Observateur*, available at <http://www.hartford-hwp.com/archives/43a/009.html>.

14   Karin von Hippel, *Democracy by Force: U.S. Military Intervention in the Post–Cold War World* (Cambridge: Cambridge University Press, 2000), 98.

15   Governors Island Accord, available at <http://www.globalsecurity.org/military/library/report/1998/kretchik-appendixd.htm>.

16   United Nations Security Council Resolution 940, July 31, 1994.

17   William J. Clinton, speech on Haiti, September 18, 1994, available from <http://www.findarticles.com/p/articles/mi_m2889/is_n38_v30/16354742>.

18   von Hippel, 185–189.

19   UNMIH was originally established by Security Council Resolution 873, September 23, 1993, to help implement certain provisions of the Governors Island Agreement signed by the Haitian parties on July 3, 1993. Its

mandate was to assist in modernizing the armed forces of Haiti [to instill civic values] and establishing a new police force. However, due to non-cooperation of the Haitian military authorities, UNMIH could not be fully deployed at that time and carry out that mandate. After the U.S. invasion, UNMIH assisted the Haitian Constitutional Government and multinational force. UNMIH's mandate was revised under UN Security Council Resolutions 940 and 975 to assist the government of Haiti in sustaining a secure and stable environment and protecting international personnel and key installations, as well as professionalization of the Haitian armed forces and the creation of a separate police force.

[20] United Nations Security Council Report S/1994/1143, "Report of the Secretary-General on the Question Concerning Haiti," September 28, 1994.

[21] Interviews with Lieutenant Colonel Phil Idiart, USA, and Lieutenant Colonel Chris Olson, USA, December 1995, United States Atlantic Command, Norfolk, Virginia. Both officers were involved in creating Contingency Plan *Jade Green*, the plan for invading Haiti.

[22] United Nations Security Council Report S/1995/46, "Report of the Secretary-General on the Question Concerning Haiti," January 17, 1995.

[23] Ibid.

[24] Interview with Colonel Mark Boyatt, February 28, 1997, Fort Leavenworth, Kansas.

[25] United Nations Security Council Report S/1995/46; von Hippel, 103–104.

[26] United Nations Security Council Report S/1995/46.

[27] Interview with Anthony Ladouceur, March 1996, Fort Leavenworth, Kansas. Schultz described Haitian culture as dysfunctional and the development of a "syndrome of destructive/self-destructive political behavior marked by authoritarianism, paternalism, personalism, patronage, nepotism, demagogy, corruption, cynicism, opportunism, racism, incompetence, parasitism, rigidity, intolerance, rivalry, distrust, insecurity, vengeance, intrigue, superstition, volatility, violence, paranoia, xenophobia, exploitation, class hatred, institutional illegitimacy, and mass apathy, aversion and submission." See Schultz, "Whither Haiti?" 3. Interviews with various U.S. military members revealed that they reflected little upon the time they spent in Haiti and their views regarding effectiveness contained only personal experiences. Thus, opinions varied from Soldier to Soldier.

[28] Walter E. Kretchik, "Multinational Staff Effectiveness in UN Peace Operations: The Case of the U.S. Army and UNMIH, 1994–1995," *Armed Forces and Society* 29, no. 3 (Spring 2003), 393–413.

[29] See *A National Security Strategy of Engagement and Enlargement* (Washington, DC: The White House, 1994), 19. As reported in that document, Haiti plagued American foreign policy because "in the Western Hemisphere, only Cuba and Haiti are not democratic states." For an assessment of

half-way measures and Haitian cultural intrigue, see Schultz, "Whither Haiti?" 2–3. For Clinton's rationale for invasion, see Schultz, "Wither Haiti?" 20, and Bob Shacochis, *The Immaculate Invasion* (New York: Viking Press, 1999), 51–53. For a detailed report on the Bertin-Baillergeau murders, see the testimony of William E. Perry, March 30, 1995, available at <http://www.us.net/cip/perry.txt>.

[30] United Nations Security Council Report S/1995/305, "Report of the Secretary-General on the United Nations Mission in Haiti," April 13, 1995.

[31] Ibid.

[32] Kinzer interview.

[33] Ibid.

[34] "U.S. pushes for 7,000 Haitian cops," *Weekly News Update on the Americas*, issue 227, May 21, 1995; Warren Christopher, remarks at Haiti Police Academy graduation ceremony, Port-au-Prince, Haiti, June 4, 1995.

[35] John R. Ballard, *Upholding Democracy: The United States Military Campaign in Haiti, 1994–1997* (Westport, CT: Praeger, 1998), 173–174.

[36] Ibid., 175.

[37] United Nations Security Council Resolution 1048 (February 29, 1996) extended and modified the United Nations Mission in Haiti mandate until June 30, 1996; available at <http://www1.umn.edu/humanrts/resolutions/SC96/1048SC96.html>.

[38] Kinzer interview.

[39] von Hippel, 105.

[40] United Nations Security Council, Press Release SC/6237, June 28, 1996.

[41] Ibid.

[42] Rebecca Bannister, "Former President Jean Bertrand Aristide Forms New Political Group," *Latin American Affairs* 6, no. 42, November 8, 1996.

[43] United Nations Security Council Report S/1996/813/Add. 1, "Report of the Secretary-General on the United Nations Support Mission in Haiti," November 12, 1996.

[44] United Nations Security Council Resolution 1086, December 5, 1996.

[45] United Nations Security Council Report S/1997/244, "Report of the Secretary-General on the United Nations Support Mission in Haiti," March 24, 1997.

[46] United Nations Security Council Report S/1997/564, "Report of the Secretary-General on the United Nations Support Mission in Haiti," July 19, 1997.

[47] United Nations Security Council Resolution 1123, July 30, 1997.

[48] United Nations Security Council Report S/1997/832, "Report of the Secretary-General of the United Nations Transition Mission in Haiti," October 31, 1997.

[49] Michele Wucker, *Why the Cocks Fight: Dominicans, Haitians, and the Struggle*

for Hispaniola (New York: Hill and Wang, 1999), 238–239.

50 Interview with Anthony LaFontaine by author, November 1997, Port-au-Prince, Haiti. Mr. LaFontaine was instrumental in recruiting Haitian police academy cadets.

51 United Nations General Assembly A/52/687, "The Situation of Democracy and Human Rights in Haiti," November 18, 1997.

52 United Nations Security Council, Resolution 1141, November 28, 1997.

53 United Nations Security Council, Resolution 1212, November 25, 1998.

54 United Nations General Assembly Report A/53/950, "The Situation of Democracy and Human Rights in Haiti," May 10, 1999.

55 LaFontaine interview.

56 United Nations Security Council Report S/1999/181, "Report of the Secretary-General on the United Nations Civilian Police Mission in Haiti," February 19, 1999.

57 United Nations Security Council Report S/2000/150, "Report of the Secretary-General on the United Nations Civilian Police Mission in Haiti," February 25, 2000.

58 Human Rights Watch, "World Report 2001," available at <http://www.hrw.org/wr2k1/americas/haiti.html>.

59 British Broadcast Corporation, "UN Mission in Haiti 'To End'," available at <http://www.globalpolicy.org/security/issues/general/2000/haiti.htm>.

60 "Aristide Picks Premier for an 'Open Door Government'," *Haïti Progrès*, February 14–20, 2001.

61 United Nations Security Council Report/2000/150, "Report of the Secretary-General on the United Nations Civilian Police Mission in Haiti," February 25, 2000.

Chapter Three
The United States Role

JOSEPH NAPOLI

Haiti is clearly unable to sort itself out, and the effect of leaving it alone would be continued worsening chaos. Our globalized world cannot afford such a political vacuum, whether in the mountains of Afghanistan or on the very doorstep of the sole remaining superpower.
—KOFI A. ANNAN, SECRETARY-GENERAL OF THE UNITED NATIONS

Only 10 years after the United States last intervened in Haiti to reinstall President Jean Bertrand Aristide, on February 29, 2004, U.S. military forces once again entered Haiti to stabilize the country after President Aristide was forced to flee in the face of violence and demonstrations against him. Unlike the 20,000 troops, significant resources, and ambitious objectives of Operation *Uphold Democracy* in 1994, the second intervention (Operation *Secure Tomorrow*) was executed with a much smaller force and more limited U.S. Government goals, objectives, and expectations. Reflecting significant changes in the international security environment since 1994, Washington did not devote large quantities of troops and resources to a crisis deemed unrelated to the war on terror. Instead, the United States led an intervention for a very brief period while it enlisted the support of, and relied upon, the countries in this hemisphere to invest in and determine Haiti's long-term future. While the United States commanded and dominated the United Nations (UN) mission after the 1994 intervention, only four U.S. servicemen remained with UN forces after the 2004 intervention.

Although it was U.S.-led, Operation *Secure Tomorrow* emerged as a coalition effort with contributions made rapidly by France, Canada, and Chile. Equally significant was the quick decision by Brazil to lead the follow-on UN stabilization mission under Chapter VII of the UN Charter and the successful transfer of responsibility of the Multinational Interim Force (MIF) to the UN force. The UN force, in fact, was dominated in leadership and contributions by nations from the Western Hemisphere other than the United States. The response by countries in this hemisphere relieved the United States of the need to tie up precious forces and resources as the country's focus remained on the wars in Iraq and Afghanistan. This was a positive indication that other countries in the region were willing to make strong commitments to resolve crises in the hemisphere. Hence, lost in the difficult and very complex efforts to stabilize Haiti is the subtle sign that the region has made significant progress in collectively dealing with complicated future threats and crises, not necessarily led and dominated by the United States.

This chapter will analyze the events leading to the U.S. decision to intervene and the rationale to limit U.S. objectives and participation. It will then examine the planning, organization, objectives, and effectiveness of the MIF and the smooth transfer of responsibility to the UN stabilization force. The paper will conclude with recommendations on how the United States might build upon and strengthen the demonstrated capacity for future collective security operations for Latin America and the Caribbean.

THE ROAD TO ANOTHER INTERVENTION

Haiti is inextricably linked to the United States by proximity, history, and demographics. Political, economic, and social disorder has prompted U.S. military intervention 3 times within the last 100 years. In 1915, the United States intervened to quell political and economic turmoil and governed Haiti for 19 years until 1934. In 1994, the United States restored Haiti's democratically elected government following a military takeover 3 years prior. Forces remained for 6 years until the disestablishment of the U.S. Support Group Haiti in 2000. Unlike 1994, when the Clinton administration deliberately planned on intervening in Haiti to restore President Aristide, the Bush administration was compelled to action by a rapid escalation of violence and unrest. Up to that point, the Bush administration largely consigned resolving Haiti's problems to working within the Organization of American States (OAS) framework.

The decision and magnitude of the February 2004 intervention in Haiti were heavily influenced by the U.S. focus on the war on terror and its commitments throughout the world in that effort, most significantly in Iraq and Afghanistan. The recognition that to move Haiti forward, a considerable, persistent, long-term involvement would be needed was something the U.S. Government was not willing to undertake while its focus was elsewhere.[1] Additionally, the gradual yet ultimate failure of the substantial U.S. and United Nations intervention in 1994 to improve conditions and reverse Haiti's history of political violence, human rights violations, endemic poverty, and human misery weighed heavily on the minds of decisionmakers. Consequently, the decision was made to intervene with a small force to achieve narrow and limited objectives to stabilize the country, while pushing the UN and countries within the hemisphere to deal with Haiti's long-term future.

The U.S. Government faced three possible options as the political crisis and violence in Haiti escalated and intervention became inevitable in early 2004. The essence of deciding on an option was timing intervention to support Aristide or allowing events to force Aristide to depart. According to Assistant Secretary of State for Western Hemisphere Affairs, Roger Noriega: "We had to make a decision whether we were going to put American lives at risk, knowing what we know about President Aristide, and expect that he would be able to make the most of that opportunity to govern effectively and honestly, nonviolently."[2] Thus, the options included supporting and perpetuating Aristide in office; forcibly removing Aristide; or waiting for an opportunity for Aristide to either leave or be forced out of office with the hope that another era of ending Haiti's troubled history could take place. The first option—to intervene early to stabilize the country and protect President Aristide—was pushed by many members in Congress, the Caribbean Community (CARICOM), and Aristide himself. However, after 4 years of political impasse in Haiti as democratic and human rights conditions worsened, coupled with increasing use of mob violence, politicization of the Haitian National Police (HNP), and a poor record on stemming drug trafficking, the administration no longer viewed progress as possible under Aristide. Consequently, the decision was made "not to put American lives at risk for the sole purpose of buying Aristide more time to perpetuate such policies."[3]

Tired of Aristide and with no enthusiasm for intervening to protect him, decisionmakers had a second option: to forcibly remove Aristide. This, however, would have met with wide-scale national and international condemnation and exacerbated election-year politics already focusing on the decision to intervene in Iraq. Additionally, this option precluded a limited U.S. intervention. It would have given the United States the responsibility and inherent commitment of resolving the crisis between Aristide's supporters and opponents, and would have forced the United States into a major nation-building role. Complicating matters under this option would be the likelihood of limited if any hemispheric support. A U.S. intervention to remove Aristide would rule out legitimacy in the eyes of Latin America and Caribbean countries and consequently the support of the OAS and the hemisphere's militaries and resources for longer term stabilization in Haiti—a critical condition for any U.S. involvement in Haiti.

The option taken instead was to use forceful and hard-line diplomacy and statements by key officials in the administration to press Aristide to resign to avoid further violence and bloodshed. Simultaneously, the United States prepared a small force to stabilize the country while enlisting the support of nations within the hemisphere to take responsibility for Haiti's future in the long run. Evidence of the evolution of the policy became clearer as events unfolded and the administration's rhetoric gradually changed.

PRECURSORS

For the remainder of the decade following the 1994 intervention, Haiti received an extraordinary degree of U.S. policy attention and resources in an attempt to strengthen democratic institutions, alleviate poverty, and stem illegal migration and drug trafficking. The peaceful transfer of the presidency following elections in 1995 provided hope for Haiti's future. However, a combination of the international community's failure to follow through on its long-term commitment for Haiti's future and the inability of Aristide and other Haitian political leaders to reconcile differences and take the necessary steps to build democratic institutions, improve economic conditions, and enforce the rule of law loomed on the dark horizon. Following the flawed parliamentary elections and meaningless presidential election in 2000 bringing Aristide back to power, the political system in Haiti essentially collapsed, a political impasse ensued, and international assistance concomitantly receded. The hope that Haiti would emerge as a modern democratic society, respectful of human rights and the rule of law, and raise itself from being the poorest country in the hemisphere (and one of the poorest in the world), faded as the country was marked by ever-increasing demagoguery, lawlessness, impunity, and rampant drug trafficking. For Haiti watchers, it became a matter of "when" and not "if" intervention would again be necessary.

Diplomatic efforts to resolve the political impasse and avoid another repeat of history proved futile. After condemning the 2000 elections, the OAS was ineffective in negotiating a political solution between President Aristide and his opponents. CARICOM's plan of action had also failed. The UN pulled its mission out in 2001, lamenting that it had no governmental institutions with which to work.

U.S. RELATIONS WITH HAITI

Following the 2000 elections in Haiti, the Clinton administration stopped providing assistance directly to the Haitian government until the problems of the elections were addressed. Nevertheless, the U.S. Government remained Haiti's largest bilateral aid donor, focusing on humanitarian and economic assistance through nongovernmental organizations (NGOs) and working toward a political solution with the OAS and CARICOM.[4] Meanwhile, Haiti emerged as a major transshipment point for cocaine being transported from South America to the United States with either direct involvement or complicity by Haitian government officials.[5] The U.S. Government consequently decertified Haiti in 2001 for its lack of effort in countering drug trafficking. Relations with Haiti were further reduced, and assistance became more targeted and restrictive. U.S. military and security assistance programs and engagement activities were curtailed and assistance was limited to the Haitian

Coast Guard since it was the only security institution that remained professional, had not been politicized, and stayed relatively free of corruption.

The Bush administration's Haiti policy focused on four areas. The first was implementing the 2002 Organization of American States Resolution 822 that called for a resolution of the political impasse, eventually leading to free and fair elections. Second was providing targeted humanitarian aid and assistance to meet the Haitian people's needs. Third was reducing the flow of illegal narcotics through Haiti to the United States. The fourth was reducing illegal migration and, more importantly, avoiding a mass migration to the United States triggered by political events or ambiguous U.S. policy regarding migration.[6] With the administration's focus on the war on terror, resources for events in the hemisphere waned. Thus, although Haiti was increasingly isolated from the world community and spiraling toward becoming a failed state, the administration placed responsibility for solving Haiti's troubles on the OAS.

ESCALATION OF VIOLENCE

The opposition movement's ability to unify many of its elements and demand the resignation of President Aristide in late 2003 proved to be the trigger to the crisis.[7] However, the state of affairs compelling intervention proceeded quickly in early 2004 as the government rapidly collapsed and the country was terrorized by a few hundred armed thugs and gangs.[8] In a 3-week period, the opposition groups rode a wave of public discontent and were able to easily defeat the ineffective Haitian National Police, capture key towns and villages around the capital of Port-au-Prince, and force President Aristide to flee as they threatened to enter the capital.

The opposition gangs consisted primarily of former military members and other thugs led by former police chief Guy Phillipe and Louis Chamblain, both notorious for attempted coups, death squads, violence, and murder. In Haiti's environment of lawlessness, impunity, and drug trafficking, they had easy access to arms and had no real political agenda, except to force out Aristide. On the other side, Aristide created, armed, and directed the *chimeres*—gangs loyal to him—to intimidate and protect him from the opposition. The politicization, rampant corruption, and lack of resources of the Haitian National Police made it an ineffective and undisciplined force incapable of preventing violence and restoring order.

In early February 2004, events accelerated rapidly and violently. Anti-Aristide protests increased throughout the country, and armed opposition gangs began taking control of cities in the north, most notably, Gonaives, Haiti's fourth largest city, on February 5. Twelve Haitian National Police were killed on February 12 in an attempt to retake the city. On February 17, the police chief in the town of Hinche was murdered, and the rest of his force fled. Violence had reached such a level that on February 18, the U.S. Embassy evacuated nonessential personnel and their families.

On February 23, Cap-Haitien, Haiti's second largest city, fell to opposition groups. A multinational team from the United States, France, OAS, and CARICOM traveled to Haiti with a power-sharing plan to resolve the crisis and end the violence.[9] Fully aware that his hold on power was diminishing rapidly, Aristide agreed to the proposal and called for an international force to intervene and restore order. However, emboldened by their success, the opposition refused. At the U.S. Embassy's request, a fleet antiterrorism security team of approximately 50 personnel deployed to augment protection of the Embassy and other key U.S. facilities. Statements by U.S. officials began blaming Aristide for the current crisis and called on him to do what was best for the country, implying that he needed to step down. This was a significant change in tone from previous announcements, which placed blame on both sides and called for an end to the violence.

As the opposition began to move toward the capital of Port-au-Prince, pro-Aristide gangs set up blockades throughout the city while looting and violence became rampant. Nearly a hundred Haitians had been brutally killed since the violence began. By February 27, 2004, Aristide's hold on power was teetering, and rumors were rampant that he would resign. However, Aristide continued to posture, hoping that an international force would arrive. As Port-au-Prince braced for a bloodbath and with a humanitarian crisis on the verge of unfolding, demands for intervention increased within the United States and internationally. Members of the U.S. Congress criticized the administration's inaction and called for unilateral or multilateral intervention, as did editorials in major newspapers.[10] The United States and France became increasingly active in trying to resolve the crisis.

The UN Security Council met on February 26 and endorsed the CARICOM/OAS power-sharing plan to resolve the crisis while committing to studying an international force to support a political settlement.[11] The French government publicly called for President Aristide to leave and along with CARICOM called for a peacekeeping force to be inserted to stabilize the violence.[12] Not wanting to intervene to perpetuate Aristide and perhaps seeing an opportunity for his leaving office, the administration instead ramped up its rhetoric to pressure Aristide to resign, stating on February 28 that "his failure to adhere to democratic principles has contributed to the deep polarization and violent unrest that we are witnessing in Haiti today."[13]

At the same time, crisis planning by the United States began in earnest. United States Southern Command (USSOUTHCOM) worked on plans in case of a mass migration from the violence and began assessing options and possible forces if an intervention was ordered.[14] Informal calls to potential troop contributors in the hemisphere were initiated, to facilitate the rapid response of countries if needed. Within Latin America, Chile provided an almost immediate commitment. Other countries cited the lack of resources and political constraints for immediate response but gave positive indications for future commitments. Due mostly to rough ocean conditions, few Haitians fled the country by boat. Nevertheless, determined to avoid a mass migration crisis, those who did chance the seas were picked up the U.S. Coast Guard and quickly repatriated to Haiti. The direct repatriation efforts were well planned and coordinated to maximize the deterrent effect on Haitians contemplating migration.

With Guy Phillipe threatening Port-au-Prince, and amid escalating violence and rampant looting, President Aristide determined early on the morning of February 29 that he could no longer hold on to power and requested U.S. assistance to depart the country. In his resignation letter, President Aristide indicated he was departing to prevent massive bloodshed and casualties.[15] Later accusations by Aristide that he was kidnapped by U.S. forces were unfounded. Through constitutional succession, the president of the supreme court, Boniface Alexander, assumed the presidency and immediately requested a UN force to stabilize the country.

During the evening of February 29, the UN Security Council passed Resolution 1529, authorizing the MIF to stabilize the country for 90 days and prepare conditions for a follow-on UN Stabilization Force. The United States, France, Chile, and Canada made commitments for troops. Later that evening, the first elements of the U.S. Air Contingency Marine Air Ground Task Force began arriving in Port-au-Prince. French forces, the Chilean contingent, and Canadian soldiers began arriving on March 1 and 2. By March 9, Combined Joint Task Force Haiti (CJTF–Haiti), consisting of the U.S., French, Canadian, and Chilean forces, stood up under the command of U.S. Marine Brigadier General Ronald Coleman with a French colonel as the deputy commander. The force would eventually reach a total of about 3,700 personnel, with 2,000 from the United States, 900 from France, 330 from Chile, and 530 from Canada. The MIF transferred responsibility to the follow-on UN force led by Brazil on June 25. The UN security force currently has 20 contributing nations with 12 from this hemisphere.[16] Only four U.S. Servicemembers remain as part of the current UN force.

U.S. OBJECTIVES

Assistant Secretary of State for Western Hemisphere Affairs, Roger Noriega, outlined the U.S. Government's objectives for the intervention, which included stabilizing the security situation, providing emergency humanitarian assistance, promoting the formation of an independent government, restoring the rule of law, and encouraging steps to improve Haiti's dire economic conditions.[17] However, the administration made it clear early on that the size of the U.S. force, along with these goals and objectives, would be limited.[18] The administration viewed Haiti as a hemispheric and not strictly a U.S. problem. Therefore, the position was that other countries in the hemisphere should assist with Haiti, as the United States focused on worldwide events and commitments.[19] Secretary of Defense Donald Rumsfeld made this apparent on March 1, 2004, the day after the United States deployed forces, when he stated "we are already working to establish a UN force that will take over for the interim force. . . . Indeed, the leadership of the interim force might very well pass even before the UN force arrives."[20] Mr. Rumsfeld emphasized that the Department of Defense (DOD) had been working to improve the capabilities of the region's militaries to conduct peacekeeping and stability operations and thought it therefore appropriate to pass the mission off to other hemispheric countries.[21] Clearly limiting the MIF's mission and perhaps to lower the international community's expectations, Mr. Rumsfeld publicly envisioned a U.S. force size of 2,000 personnel.[22]

General James T. Hill, USSOUTHCOM Commander (whose command the MIF came under), indicated that the military objectives were to secure critical sites in Port-au-Prince to contribute to a more stable environment; assist in delivering humanitarian assistance; protect U.S. citizens; and facilitate the repatriation of Haitian migrants interdicted at sea.[23] The size of forces provided, along with the expected duration of only 90 days, forced the MIF to restrict its initial planning to securing Port-au-Prince and key northern cities. Forces were not available to place throughout the country; therefore, planners had to determine which cities, towns, and infrastructure were most critical to temporarily stabilize Haiti until the larger UN force would arrive. Planning for the operation was therefore constrained by limited objectives, limited forces, and a clear signal that U.S. participation would be brief and passed on to other countries as soon as possible.

DESIGN AND PLANNING OF THE MULTINATIONAL INTERIM FORCE

The design and planning of the Multinational Interim Force was done primarily at U.S. Southern Command with guidance from DOD and the Joint Staff on the limited mission, scope, and size of the force. The early involvement of coalition partners, U.S. interagency actors, and UN planners was key to smoothly and effectively deploying the MIF, stabilizing key portions of the country, and transitioning to the UN in accordance with United Nations Security Council Resolution (UNSCR) 1542 that authorized the follow-on UN Stabilization Mission in Haiti force (*Mission des Nations Unies pour la stabilisation en Haïti,* or MINUSTAH).

Critical to organizing the multinational force mission, objectives, organization, and employment of its forces was the immediate establishment of a MIF–Haiti Coordination Center at USSOUTHCOM Headquarters, where members of the U.S. interagency community, coalition partners, and representatives to the follow-on UN Stabilization Force would meet and plan on a daily basis.[24] With the rapid escalation of the crisis and swift deployment of forces, this forum proved essential to identifying requirements, resolving and coordinating country-specific issues, coordinating humanitarian aid, receiving arriving forces, and facilitating communications between USSOUTHCOM, CJTF–Haiti, the Department of Defense, the Department of State, coalition countries, and the United Nations. Additionally, this group worked closely in identifying and coordinating potential contributors and capabilities to the follow-on UN force.

A Joint Interagency Planning Group (JIAPG) was convened, consisting of senior representatives from USSOUTHCOM, the Department of Defense, the Department of Homeland Security, the Department of State, the U.S. Coast Guard, the U.S. Agency for International Development, the United Nations, and coalition nations. The JIAPG met March 3–5 to plan and coordinate the initial efforts and again on April 29–May 1 to plan and coordinate the transition to the UN. Additionally, USSOUTHCOM members participated in the Policy Coordination Committee meetings on Haiti chaired by the National Security Council and the Department of State and had frequent interaction with the UN Secretary-General's assessment team, which prepared the report to the Security Council to authorize the size and scope of the follow-on force. The successful integration of the interagency and coalition expertise expedited precise action and guidance for the deployed forces.

The employment of an experienced advance party from the U.S. Southern Command Standing Joint Force Headquarters (SJFHQ) contributed to the early synergy of deployed forces at the optimal locations and led to the rapid activation of CJTF–Haiti.[25] Secretary of Defense Rumsfeld had previously directed the regional combatant commanders to establish SJFHQs within their commands to increase the ability to respond rapidly to global crises and to serve as the core of a joint task force until it was fully staffed.

The MIF was organized under a U.S. commander with a French deputy commander. Subordinate commands included a French infantry battalion with a support battalion and special operations forces; a Chilean infantry battalion; U.S. and Canadian Forces under one command consisting of Marine Air Ground Contingency Task Force 8 and a Canadian infantry company; a U.S. aviation force; a Canadian aviation force; and a maritime component under the command of the U.S. Coast Guard, a first for such operations (see figure 3–1).

To avoid an expanded mission, initial directions given to USSOUTHCOM were to have U.S. forces remain in Port-au-Prince with the hope that their presence would sufficiently stabilize the country until the UN stabilization force arrived. Unlike the 20,000 soldiers used in 1994, MIF planners grappled with being able to stabilize the country with a small force.

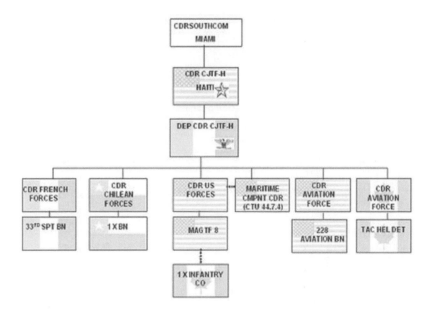

FIGURE 3–1. COMBINED JOINT TASK FORCE (CJTF)–HAITI TASK ORGANIZATION

Consequently, rather than wait for the full MIF force to arrive, elements immediately began patrolling and securing key sites in Port-au-Prince once they landed. MIF forces aggressively defused any violence and immediately established control in volatile areas. The commander of U.S. forces met with Guy Philippe and bluntly warned him against interfering with the MIF and inciting future violence. MIF forces had sporadic incidents with both *chimeres* and rebel groups. By the end of the week, Port-au-Prince was relatively calm and had generally returned to precrisis activity, with isolated looting and gunfire versus the widespread anarchy of the previous week, allowing President Alexander to begin assembling an interim government.[26]

However, it was evident that stabilizing only Port-au-Prince would not be sufficient. Reporting and assessments from other parts of the country indicated that many cities, notably Cap-Haitien and Gonaives, continued being run by gangs, with ongoing instability and violence. The French forces agreed to deploy to the northern part of the country. On March 15, the French began moving troops to Cap-Haitien, Gonaives, St. Marc, Ft. Liberte, and Port de Paix. Without sufficient forces to move to the south, U.S. Special Operations Forces and Canadian troops were used as a show of force and to establish a presence by conducting frequent assessment missions to cities and population centers, while elements of the Chilean force moved to Hinche to the east of Port-au-Prince. The remainder of U.S., Chilean, and Canadian forces deployed throughout Port-au-Prince (see figure 3–2).

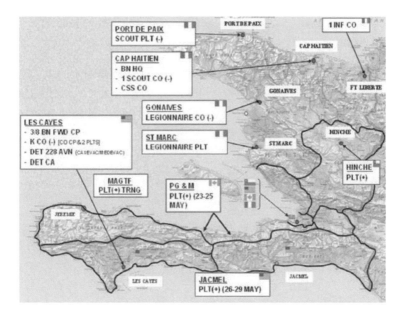

FIGURE 3–2. MULTINATIONAL INTERIM FORCE, MAY 2004

Although disarmament was not specified in UNSCR 1529, or in planning guidance for the MIF, it was recognized that disarming the factions was necessary to establishing a secure environment. Consequently, MIF forces began disarming illegally armed Haitians and conducting operations with the HNP against known and suspected caches. Clearly, however, the MIF did not have the forces or resources to conduct wide-scale disarmament throughout the country.

TRANSITION TO THE UNITED NATIONS

The critical element for the MIF to transfer responsibility to the follow-on UN Force was the designation of a force leader and a UNSCR authorizing its deployment. The Brazilian foreign minister confirmed his country's willingness to lead the follow-on effort on March 23. Anticipating this commitment, the Brazilians began coordination with USSOUTHCOM and CJTF-Haiti. On March 19, a Brazilian reconnaissance element arrived in Haiti to gather information. On April 12, a Brazilian liaison team was stationed at USSOUTHCOM, and another contingent deployed to Haiti in advance of the anticipated UNSCR authorizing the follow-on force deployment. An Argentine liaison detachment also was stationed at USSOUTHCOM to begin coordination as it awaited a formal commitment of forces to the follow-on force from the Argentine government. On April 30, UNSCR 1542 was adopted, establishing MINUSTAH under Chapter VII of the UN Charter. The resolution included a military component of up to 6,700 military troops and established a transfer of authority date from the MIF to MINUSTAH of June 1. A conference was held in Haiti on May 3–7 to plan the details on the deployment of UN forces and redeployment of U.S. and French forces. Brazilian, Argentine, and Chilean representatives also attended the meeting. Although the transfer of authority occurred on June 1 to MINUSTAH, the transfer of responsibility did not occur until June 25 due to a delay in the arrival of Brazilian forces. Countries committing forces to MINUSTAH were unable to provide them on time, and troop levels actually dropped from 3,700 MIF troops to 2,000 MINUSTAH troops for a short period.[27] It took the United Nations until December to build troop strength to its authorized level of 6,700 and until early 2005 for the mission to become effective.

EFFECTIVENESS OF THE FORCES

Using the stated U.S. objectives and the UN Security Council Resolution authorizing its deployment as measures, the effectiveness of the MIF was clearly positive. During the 90 days following its deployment, the MIF curtailed the rampant violence and stabilized large portions of the country. The constitutional succession of government was allowed to work, and an interim prime minister was selected to begin the difficult task of bringing the factions together and assembling a government. The ports and airports were opened, and humanitarian aid flowed again. Mass migration did not take place and even narcotics trafficking was reduced. A smooth transition to the UN Stabilization Force was conducted within the designated timeframe.

However, outside of areas where MIF forces were present, the situation was more problematic. Many towns and villages had no governmental institutions functioning and the HNP disintegrated, leaving control to armed gangs. The UN assessment team reported Haiti had "calmed down with the MIF but restricted resources, geographic areas, [and] limited disarmament activities constrained the ability to establish a secure and stable environment outside of its presence."[28] Unquestionably, with a larger force and greater commitments from other nations, the MIF could have been much more effective throughout the country.

On another level, the confidence and understanding that developed between the United States and Latin American nations on conducting crisis response, operating together, and organizing forces and operations, were incalculable successes, and perhaps the untold positive story of the 2004 intervention. Although the region's militaries often come together for exercises, they rarely come together to resolve crises. Political, historic, and cultural differences have generally precluded intervention in another country in the hemisphere, particularly when the United States was involved. However, the rapid response by Chile, the willingness of Brazil to lead the UN effort, and the contribution of troops to MINUSTAH should be viewed as a positive indication of the capability and interest of hemispheric countries to cooperate and operate in defusing crises, separating factions, and addressing threats. Also, the fact that MINUSTAH is under Chapter VII of the UN Charter cannot go unnoticed. Early indications from most countries that they would only participate under Chapter VI (traditional peacekeeping) and would not participate under Chapter VII (peace enforcement) proved wrong. However, it cannot be overlooked that most countries were unable (due to a lack of capability or resources) or unwilling (due to political reasons) to be a part of the MIF during the immediate response to the Haitian crisis.

Additionally, it took much too long for many forces to deploy in support of MINUSTAH, allowing security conditions to worsen and violence to spike. The structural conditions that led to the violence compelling the intervention persist, and the future of Haiti remains bleak. This, however, requires more than a military solution. The MIF avoided further violence, bloodshed, and a humanitarian crisis. It remains to be seen whether the 10-year international commitment necessary to move Haiti forward according to UN Secretary-General Kofi Annan will be realized, or if the "cycle of poverty, violence, and instability starts again."[29]

The same observation made by the Commander of Operation *Uphold Democracy* holds true after Operation *Secure Tomorrow* 10 years later:

> The lesson of Haiti . . . is that while military forces have excelled in achieving military tasks such as establishing order, separating combatants, or safeguarding relief supplies, they are less effective in solving non-military problems rooted in persistent cultural, economic and political strife. In cases like Haiti, military forces can help create a secure environment in which to pursue lasting political and economic solutions—but they cannot achieve political outcomes by themselves. The burden still remains on statesmen and the international community to pursue integrated approaches that enjoy a broad range of policy tools and processes to ensure long-term success.[30]

RECOMMENDATIONS

Whether one agrees or not, the United States for the foreseeable future will be focused on the war on terror. Concomitantly, U.S. attention and resources for the Western Hemisphere will be limited. As the 2004 intervention in Haiti indicates, the United States is not willing to commit precious troops and resources unless its interests are directly threatened. Yet the hemisphere faces significant problems from transnational threats, fledgling democracies, potentially catastrophic natural disasters, and endemic social, economic, and political problems in many countries. The potential and need for the region's countries to be prepared to respond to crises and improve their capacity for peacekeeping are therefore necessary. Haiti has proven that the hemisphere is willing to do so.

A first step is to improve the capability to respond more quickly to crises. This should be done through the OAS by establishing standby forces that countries commit to be used in crisis. The OAS has a standing group of experienced and talented senior military officers from throughout the hemisphere located at the Inter-American Defense Board (IADB). This group can and must be energized. It wastes very talented officers doing mundane and anachronistic work, instead of focusing on threats to the region and making sound recommendations and judgments on how collectively to address them. The IADB should continuously study and identify requirements and capabilities needed to respond to various potential crisis and contingencies. The IADB through the OAS would then coordinate these requirements and capabilities by identifying forces on a standby basis through agreements with the various countries. It would next develop mechanisms for coordinating, training, and certifying these forces to ensure they are ready when called upon by the OAS. Finally, the IADB could coordinate with USSOUTHCOM to exercise these forces during the frequent multinational peacekeeping exercises the command sponsors. Since the mobility to crisis spots is a critical liability of virtually all countries, the U.S. contribution to standby arrangements could concentrate on lift, thereby reducing U.S. troop commitments.

At the same time, the OAS must restructure itself to be able to respond to crises by developing protocols and mechanisms to respond with more than delegations and unenforceable resolutions and declarations. It must become a more relevant organization and eliminate self-constraints that preclude it from dealing with crises in the region. This should include a decisionmaking body that would be responsible for authorizing the deployment of the standby forces for crisis, contingencies, or natural disasters. The funding could be worked through the UN for peacekeeping operations or through contributions by members of the OAS for other types of operations.

Latin America has world class peacekeeping training centers; for example, the Argentine Center for Joint Training and Peace Operations (CAECOPAZ, *Centro Argentino de Entrenamiento Conjunto Para Operaciones de Paz*) and Chile's Joint Training Center for Peace Operations (CECOPAC, *Centro de Entrenamiento Conjunto de Operaciones de Paz*) train superior peacekeepers. Additionally, the region has a long and distinguished history of participating in peacekeeping operations throughout the world, leaving a legacy of experience and knowledge in conducting such operations. Nevertheless, despite the commitments of many countries to participate in Haiti, only one participated in the MIF, and many others forces arrived late for the UN force due to a lack of resources and preparation. Designating standby forces would not necessarily alleviate the resource constraints in some countries. The United

States should therefore refocus and refine its efforts in assisting countries to improve their peacekeeping and crisis response capacity. It does provide substantial peacekeeping financing to the region through Enhanced International Peacekeeping Capabilities funding. While instrumental, this funding is by law limited to providing training and infrastructure for peacekeeping training centers. The use of this funding should be expanded to purchasing equipment for designated peacekeeping units and even for peacekeeping operations. In addition to training standby forces during its peacekeeping exercises, USSOUTHCOM could exercise realistic scenarios in coordination with the IADB, which would be focusing on such events full time.

CONCLUSION

The 2004 intervention in Haiti was a step forward for nations in the hemisphere to cooperate with forces and resources to resolve a regional crisis. The U.S. focus on the war on terror, coupled with the ultimate failure of the 1994 intervention, influenced the decision to lead an intervention with limited forces and objectives. While the MIF achieved its limited objectives, much more could have been done with additional forces. Additionally, although the countries in the hemisphere have demonstrated a strong commitment by leading and participating in the UN stabilization force, the slow arrival of many of the troops significantly hindered its effectiveness and even allowed conditions to worsen. The hemisphere must therefore capitalize on this demonstrated progress in cooperative security and develop and institutionalize mechanisms to facilitate much quicker decisionmaking and deployment capability of select forces from the region. This does not require a new structure or institution. Instead, the Organization of American States can develop the protocols and use the moribund Inter-American Defense Board to identify, coordinate, and certify standby forces for immediate response to crisis. The U.S. pledge to such forces would be mobility and security assistance, thereby limiting troop commitments. The United States should refocus its efforts to improving peacekeeping capacity in the region by expanding the use of Enhanced International Peacekeeping Capabilities funding to equip peacekeeping units and fund operations and coordinate peacekeeping exercises with an energized and more active Inter-American Defense Board.

NOTES

[1] Kofi A. Annan, "In Haiti for the Long Haul," *The Wall Street Journal,* March 16, 2004, A20. This article sums up the view of a long-term requirement to resolve Haiti's historical problems.

[2] Roger F. Noriega, U.S, Department of State, interview by Chris Bury, *Nightline,* Washington, DC, March 1, 2004; available at <http://www.state.gov/p/wha/rls/rm/30143.htm>.

3   Sue M. Cobb, *What Happened in Haiti*, March 5, 2004, 3; available at <http:/
    /trinidad.usembassy.gov/trinidad/What_Happened_in_Haiti.html>.

4   Marc Grossman, "U.S. Policy toward Haiti," testimony to the Senate For-
    eign Relations Committee, Washington, DC, July 15, 2003, 1.

5   Maureen Taft-Morales, *Haiti: Developments and U.S. Policy since 1991 and
    Current Congressional Concerns* (Washington, DC: Library of Congress,
    Congressional Research Service, December 1, 2004), 17.

6   Grossman, 2.

7   Kofi A. Annan, *Report of Secretary General on Haiti* (New York: United
    Nations, April 2004), 3.

8   Roger F. Noriega, "The Situation in Haiti," testimony to the Committee
    on International Relations, Washington, DC, March 3, 2004, 33; avail-
    able at <http://commdocs.house.gov/committees/intlref/hfa92343.000
    /hfa02343_0. HTM>.

9   U.S. Southern Command, "Joint After Action Report Operation *Secure
    Tomorrow*" (Miami: Multinational Interim Force Coordination Center,
    United States Southern Command, 2004), 6.

10 Robert Graham, "Crisis in Haiti," remarks in the U.S. Senate, February
    24, 2004; available at <http://thomas.loc.gov/cgi-bin/query/F?r108:1/
    temp /r108hzUvya:e0>.

11 United Nations Security Council, "Statement by the President of the Se-
    curity Council," February 26, 2004, available from <http:/
    daccessdds.un.org/doc/indoc/gen/no4/252/10/pdf/ no425210.pd>.

12 Joint After Action Report, 6.

13 Taft-Morales, 7.

14 Joint After Action Report, 7.

15 Cobb, 2.

16 United Nations Department of Peacekeeping Operations, *Facts and Fig-
    ures: Contributors* (New York: United Nations, February 2005); available
    at <http://www.un.org/Depts/dpkp/contributions>.

17 Noriega, 17.

18 Donald Rumsfeld, "DOD News Briefing Transcript" (Washington, DC:
    United States Defense Department, March 1, 2004); available at <http:/
    /www.pentagon. mil/transcripts/2004/tr20040310-secdeff0501.html>.

19 Ibid., 2.

20 Ibid., 1.

21 Ibid., 2.

22 Ibid., 3.

23 James T. Hill, "Press Availability on Haiti News Transcript" (Washington,
    DC: United States Defense Department, March 10, 2004); available from
    http://www.pentagon.mil/transcripts/2004/tr20040310-0526.html>.

24 Joint After Action Report, 7.

25 Ibid., 8.

26 Hill, 5.

27 Joint After Action Report, 35.

28 Annan, 7.

29 Ibid., 2.

30 Henry H. Shelton, "Contingency Operations in an Uncertain World: The Case of Haiti," *Strategic Review* (Fall 1998), 40.

Chapter Four

Canada: Objectives, Decision-making, and Lessons Learned

GLEN MILNE

This chapter provides the Canadian portion of a study on peacekeeping operations (PKO) in Haiti commissioned by the Center for Hemispheric Defense Studies (CHDS) of the National Defense University, Washington, DC. The objectives of the study were to determine the factors that motivated countries to decide to participate and sustain their commitments, the strategic-level lessons learned, and recommendations for the design of similar missions in the future. Eight research questions supplied by CHDS provided the framework for the study. At the time of preparation of this chapter, the Canadian PKO and other support for Haiti were changing in tune with events in Haiti and politics in Canada.

RESEARCH SOURCES AND METHODOLOGY

The author shared the research questions with, and interviewed, a broad range of stakeholders in the Canadian Haiti PKO. These included 12 officials from the range of federal departments involved in mission design and decisionmaking for the Canadian Haiti PKO mission; 2 recently retired officials who previously were responsible for the Haiti file in the Canadian International Development Aid Agency (CIDA) and the Organization of American States (OAS); 4 participants from nongovernmental organizations working on projects in Haiti; 2 academic experts on violence and its effects, crime, and crime prevention; a corporal in the Canadian Forces who recently returned from 2 years of service in Haiti; and a Haitian who currently lives in Montreal with his young family.

All interviews were conducted on a confidential basis with the understanding that there would be no attribution of sources. Some of those interviewed supplied publications and unclassified internal assessment reports dealing with the Haiti PKO. A search of the press produced about 30 articles from Canadian newspapers such as *Globe and Mail*, *National Post*, *Le Devoir*, *Ottawa Citizen*, and *The Hamilton Spectator*. Also, a Web search produced about 100 useful press releases, articles, and summaries of assessments and opinions.

CANADA'S RELATIONSHIP TO HAITI

Haiti is the underdeveloped country closest to Canada in terms of geographic distance, aid programs, shared language (French), and political visibility. Montreal's Haitian population is estimated at between 70,000 and 120,000 and is the third largest Haitian community outside the Caribbean (after New York and Boston). Haitians living in Canada are an important source of money to their families in Haiti and to the Haitian economy. Some Canadian churches and voluntary groups have been contributing to Haiti for over 50 years. The government of Canada has been assisting Haiti since approximately 1994. Canada is one of Haiti's key bilateral development partners (albeit referred to as a "difficult partner"). For example, in 2002–2003, Canadian official development assistance to Haiti totalled $23.85 million. The scope of Canada's aid program in Haiti includes:

- social development and basic human needs
- food aid, health, and education
- governance, democracy, and human rights
- peacekeeping, public security, justice, prisons, elections, human rights
- economic and private sector development
- institution building.

Since the political crisis triggered by the disputed legislative and local elections of May 2000, the government of Canada's position has been to work toward a political agreement in Haiti that would be the result of broad-based consensus among the government, political parties, and civil society. Canada takes part in the work of the OAS and the Caribbean Community (CARICOM) in supporting development of democratic processes and institutions by Haitians.

KEY EVENTS

The following chronology of events provides an overview of the recent Canadian role in Haiti. In March 2003, the Canadian Forces used four C–130 Hercules aircraft to evacuate 350 Canadians and others to the Dominican Republic to escape gangs battling each other for power in Port-au-Prince. In December 2003, the Canadian embassy issued a statement condemning acts of violence and urging the government of Haiti to ensure respect for human rights. Canada issued two other statements to the United Nations (UN) Commission on Human Rights and the General Assembly condemning the abuse of human rights in Haiti. Minister Denis Coderre spoke in similar terms at the ministerial conference of *La Francophonie* in Paris. At the Special Summit of the Americas, Canada proposed that the Inter-American Commission on Human Rights consider the possibility of establishing a permanent observer mission in Haiti.

In February 2004, armed conflict broke out in Gonaives and spread throughout Haiti. President Jean-Bertrand Aristide left the country on February 29, and a UN resolution later that day led to the creation of the United Nations Multinational Interim Force–Haiti (MIFH). The MIFH had a 90-day mandate to contribute to a secure and stable environment in Haiti, to facilitate the delivery of relief aid to those in need, and to help the Haitian police and coast guard maintain law and order and protect human rights. In early March 2004, Canada deployed Task Force Haiti (TFH), consisting of 500 personnel and 6 CH–146 Griffon helicopters, as part of the MIFH. In June 2004, at the request of the United Nations, the TFH mandate was extended to permit it to transfer to the larger follow-on United Nations Stabilization Mission in Haiti (*Mission des Nations Unies pour la stabilisation en Haïti*, or MINUSTAH). On July 6, 2004, Prime Minister Paul Martin announced a change in the nature of Canada's commitment to Haiti from a *military* to balanced *military and police* emphasis by sending 100 police officers to Haiti for 2 years to help with security and training of Haitian police. The prime minister's announcement cited a "hemispheric and moral responsibility" and noted: "The police will be responding to an immediate need in Haiti as the country strives to restore law and order following the recent political crisis. Re-establishment of the rule of law is essential for all other economic, social and political efforts to succeed. This contribution is appropriate given Canada's well known and respected international policing expertise, and our past and on-going engagement in the region." Sixteen million dollars in funding for this police deployment came from CIDA through a special program, the Canadian Police Arrangement, made up of Foreign Affairs Canada, Public Safety and Emergency Preparedness, and the Royal Canadian Mounted Police (RCMP).

In addition to the funding for this deployment, since February 2004, Canada, through CIDA, contributed a total of $15 million: $5 million in support of UN programming including humanitarian, transition, and reconstruction efforts; $5 million to strengthen the special mission of the OAS in Haiti; almost $2 million to Canadian, Haitian, and international organizations working in Haiti to support reconstruction, rehabilitation, and humanitarian aid activities, primarily in the areas of health, education, human rights and efforts to stop violence against women; $1.95 million in humanitarian assistance and food aid to the World Food Program, the Pan American Health Organization, and the International Committee of the Red Cross; and $1 million to the International Organisation of *La Francophonie* to help restore and maintain Haiti's democratic institutions. A further $1 million was provided in humanitarian assistance to flood victims in Haiti and the Dominican

Republic. On July 18, 2004, Canada announced a contribution of more than $180 million over 2 years to Haiti's reconstruction and development efforts, including $147 million in support for the transitional government's interim cooperation framework. Following the devastation caused by Tropical Storm Jeanne in September 2004, Canada contributed $6.5 million through CIDA to support relief in Haiti, out of $11.1 million for the whole Caribbean region. In March 2004, the premier of the province of Quebec, Jean Charest, announced that Quebec was contributing $1 million to Haiti for food, education, and health. In November, he announced an additional $200,000 in emergency aid to flood-stricken Haiti and assured Quebecers that help would reach those suffering.

On November 14, 2004, Prime Minister Martin visited Haiti to discuss the country's social and economic reconstruction and stabilization efforts with the interim president, prime minister, members of the cabinet, leaders of political parties, and representatives of civil society. During these meetings, Prime Minister Martin reasserted the need for all parties to participate in the implementation of the democratic process leading to elections in 2005. On November 26, 2004, Prime Minister Martin announced the appointment of a special adviser for Haiti, Denis Coderre, member of parliament for Bourassa, in the province of Quebec, where the majority of Haitian immigrants to Canada reside. He reports to the minister of foreign affairs on issues surrounding the crisis in Haiti, represents Canada at international meetings on the topic of Haiti, and works with civil society to help find solutions for Haiti.

The Canadian approach to Haiti can be summed up by the following statement from the prime minister in July 2004:

> The Government of Canada continues to examine all available ways to meet Haiti's needs and to ensure that Canada effectively helps the people of Haiti to find a solution to the political and humanitarian crisis and the violence that rock Haiti. As long as the political situation in Haiti continues, Canada remains prepared to play an active role, and to support the UN, the OAS and other international bodies in implementing support measures.

FACTORS INFLUENCING CANADA'S DECISION TO PARTICIPATE IN HAITI PKO

Canada's defense policies were last clearly articulated in the 1994 Defence White Paper. It refocused Canadian defense policy in light of the end of the Cold War. The key tenets of the policy are as follows:

- while the possibility of a global conflict is extremely remote, the world continues to be highly unstable and unpredictable
- the Canadian Forces' mandate is to defend Canada; to defend North

America in partnership with the United States; and to contribute to global stability

- Canada will maintain multipurpose, combat-capable maritime, land, and air forces able to defend Canada and Canadian interests while providing the government with the flexibility to contribute to international peace and security initiatives.

In the past four decades, the government of Canada has preferred that international peace and security be pursued through multilateral cooperation, rather than unilateral action. When Prime Minister Martin took office in November 2003, his priorities included a more outward-looking global agenda and organizational structure in and around his cabinet, particularly with regard to strengthening Canada-U.S. relations, domestic and continental security from international terrorists, and participation in international affairs via multilateral policies and mechanisms. For instance, in January 2005, he advanced and sought support for the formation of a G–20 group of nations that would provide a middle way between the U.S. model of "unilateral with support from allies" and the UN model of "comprehensive multilateral process and debate for every decision" that limits and delays their effectiveness and timeliness. Although Canada has been involved in peace operations with non–UN organizations such as the North Atlantic Treaty Organization (NATO), it has generally tried to promote the use of the United Nations as the only international organization with the charter authority to promote peace and security throughout the world.

All the Canadian political parties that have formed the federal government in the past 35 years have embraced high immigration levels and multiculturalism as defining characteristics of Canada, as well as a potential source of new voters. Between 70,000 and 120,000 Haitians live in Montreal in the province of Quebec where French is the official and most spoken language. As voters, they have considerable strategic political importance within Canada. The distribution of population in Canada makes it necessary for a political party to win at least half the seats in the province of Quebec in order to form a majority government at the federal level. Haitian votes are important in three or four key ridings [electoral districts] in both federal and provincial elections, and in past and potential future referendums on the question of whether or not the province of Quebec stays within Canada or becomes an independent nation-state. Keeping Quebec in the Canadian confederation is a paramount interest of major federal political parties other than the *Bloc Quebecoise*—a Quebec-based party that is devoted to taking Quebec out of Canada. In the last (1995) referendum held in Quebec, the "stay in Canada" side won by a margin of only 1 percent. The former minister of foreign affairs and current special adviser for Haiti, Denis Coderre, is the member of parliament for the community in Quebec with a significant Haitian population.

Canadian interests in the global organization *La Francophonie*, of which Haiti is a member, are directed to reflecting abroad the fact that a significant part of Canada speaks French as its native tongue, and ensuring that French culture and institutions in Canada are connected to that world.

The Caribbean region, including Haiti and Cuba, is important to Canada in economic terms. Many Canadian companies have been involved in banking, tourism, and extraction of natural resources in the region for over 50 years. Immigrants and seasonal workers from all over the region provide key parts of the Canadian labor force. Stability and development in the Caribbean region are also important to Canada in order to avoid large numbers of refugees being added to Canada's relatively open and overloaded refugee system, the spread of disease, and the growth of traffic in illegal drugs with its associated criminal gangs and activities.

DESIGN OF CANADA'S PKO CONTRIBUTION

Peacekeeping has become a primary role for Canada in the international arena. Since 1947, Canada has participated in more than 36 peacekeeping operations, starting when Prime Minister Lester Pearson created the modern concept of multinational peacekeeping forces during the 1956 Suez crisis. Canada is currently the 31st largest contributor of military troops and observers to the United Nations out of 90 contributing countries. Canadian military and police personnel are in demand for peacekeeping and stabilization projects in part because they have established a good international reputation and have considerable experience in terms of values, attitude, skills and ability to work with indigenous institutions and international partners. This legacy causes Canada to consider participating in almost every PKO.

Haiti is generally regarded in Canada as being in need of almost everything. The Canadian government is committed to do whatever it can for Haiti. That means that the criteria for the design of the mission are primarily related to feasibility of what Canada can supply that Haiti is in a position to use. The key concept of the current Canadian PKO program is to provide contributions to establishing order (stop looting and violence against persons), followed by interim police services in conjunction with Haitian police, and, where feasible, to help build police capacity. The government's other policy initiatives (for example, substantial new funding for the national health care system) and parallel commitment to cutting taxes and paying down the national debt make it very difficult to find new funds. The mission was shaped by determining the niche or highest value role that Canada could feasibly play in the total partnership of nations involved in peacekeeping operations as organized by the United Nations.

After money, the most important resource limitation was the current deployment of the Canadian Forces. They are stretched thinly all over the world in peacekeeping projects. Many units have had their tour of duty extended several times and are functionally overdue for a tour of home duty. The resources devoted to the police function are being drawn from existing RCMP, provincial, and municipal forces, with the result that police service levels in Canada are noticeably lowered.

FEDERAL PLANNING AND DECISIONMAKING

Canada is an unusual confederation with "two plus one" levels of sovereign government: federal; provincial and territorial; and an emerging system of aboriginal governments. The federal and provincial governments have separate constitutional responsibilities and powers, as well as some that are shared. The federal government has responsibility for foreign affairs, including international relations, aid, and defense. Immigration is a shared responsibility. The decisionmaking structures and processes in the federal government center around two components.

FIGURE 4–1. THE CANADIAN GOVERNMENTAL PROCESS

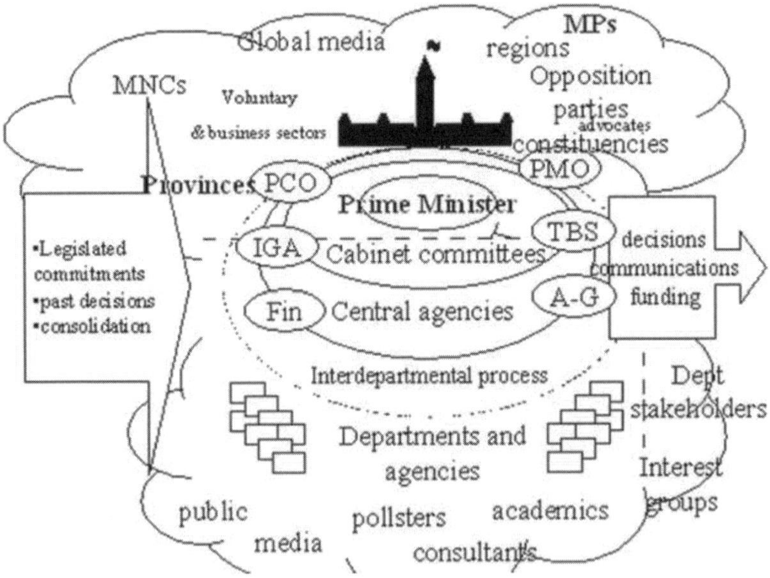

Source: Glen Milne, *Making Policy: A Guide to the Federal Government's Policy Process*, 2004.

The *Prime Minister* has the authority to make or delegate all major decisions and does this with the advice and consideration of senior officials (see figure 4–1).

The interactive network (not chain) of events and organization for the continuing analysis, development of options, funding implications, and decisions like those involved in the Haiti PKO is illustrated in figure 4–2. The current minority government situation at the federal level in Canada means that much more consultation is being done with other parties and parliamentary committees as part of the priority setting and decisionmaking process.

Foreign Affairs Canada (FAC) is the department responsible for the development, execution, and administration of foreign affairs policy, including diplomatic missions and their activities abroad. Previously it was part of the Department of Foreign Affairs and International Trade. In cases such as Haiti, FAC operates in day-to-day collaboration with the Department of National Defence (DND), the foreign aid agency, Canada International Development Agency, the Solicitor General (responsible for the Royal Canadian Mounted Police, the national police force), Public Safety and Emergency

FIGURE 4–2. INTERACTIVE NETWORK FOR DECISIONS LIKE THOSE INVOLVED IN THE HAITI PKO

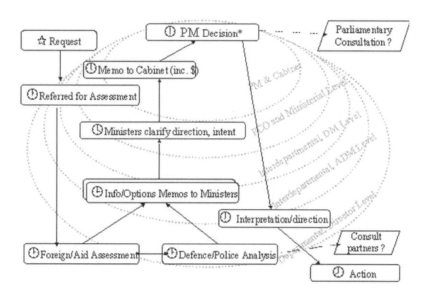

Source: David Last and Glen Milne, *National Security Decision-Making*, 2004.

Preparedness Canada, Canada Security and Intelligence Service, and other agencies as the situation requires. FAC operates a 24/7 watch on global events.

An operations center in Ottawa continuously gathers information and news contacts from Canadian diplomatic posts around the world, DND and other departments, police, intelligence agencies, national and international press media, and so forth. This center provided an early warning of the potential departure of President Aristide and crisis months in advance. The flows of information gathering, analysis, development of briefings and options for ministers, decisionmaking, and coordination in a case like the Haiti PKO are illustrated in figure 4–3.

When an international situation develops that officials identify as involving important Canadian interests, FAC organizes and leads an interdepartmental task force to monitor events, anticipate potential crises, and develop contingency options and plans for action. The mandate of the task force is to provide a forum where analysis and options for action at the strategic level can be developed, coordinated, and directed. The task force is the organization wherein an overall strategic plan is defined for the government as to how Canada will deal with a crisis, what resources the government will use, and so on. In this case, the tools were humanitarian assistance, police assistance, and military power. This approach and these tools were also used in Kosovo, East Timor, and now Darfur.

FIGURE 4–3. THE CANADIAN FOREIGN AFFAIRS DECISIONMAKING PROCESS

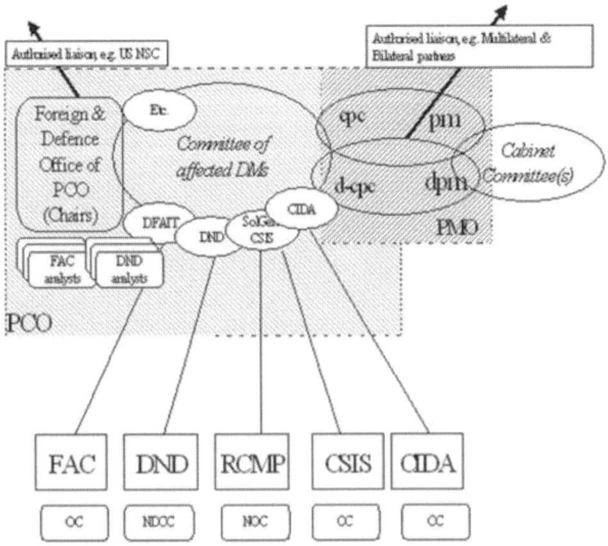

Source: David Last and Glen Milne, *National Security Decision-Making*, 2004.

The task force can be called to meet daily when a crisis is happening. At the first task force meeting on a new topic, FAC provides an update on the situation and guidance on how Canada will respond, in general terms, in accordance with foreign policy imperatives. After discussion, members of the task force disperse to do their own analysis and strategic thinking, then meet again the following day with information on what their departments can provide for the crisis, and begin to formulate the situation assessment, options, resource limits, costs, and recommendations to the FAC minister, the cabinet, and the prime minister. At this stage, approval of the operation is conditional on the government decision and the conduct of an interdepartmental strategic reconnaissance.

HOW THE DECISION WAS TAKEN TO JOIN THE HAITI PKO

Officials in the FAC, along with their partners in DND, CIDA, and the RCMP, were watching events in Haiti carefully in the latter part of 2003 for the reasons noted above. They prepared and continuously updated situation reports for consideration of their ministers and the prime minister. When Haiti fell into crisis early in 2004, the mission design and decision to participate in the PKO came primarily from the top, namely, the prime minister, with assistance from bottom-up scanning, analysis, options and recommendations from committees of officials, and cabinet ministers. These considerations and decisions were undertaken in continuous consultation with the United Nations Department of Peace Keeping Operations (UNDPKO) in New York. UNDPKO was the primary designer of the multipartite mission through an iterative process of asking potential participant countries what resources they might provide and fitting their potential resources into an evolving, overall mission concept and deliverable package. When the UN Security Council passed its resolution regarding Haiti on February 29, 2004, an options paper was prepared within a few hours in Canada by a special interagency task force of middle-level officials from the above group of agencies and sent up to the prime minister via a paper signed by all of the ministers involved. The prime minister's decision on Canada's contribution a few days later was slightly different than the options presented, because it reflected some inputs from his senior advisors, a committee of deputy-ministers (heads of departments), discussion of the options by a cabinet committee, and consideration of costs by the department of finance.

OBJECTIVES OF THE MISSION

The implicit *political*—as opposed to explicit *policy*—objectives of the mission included serving the interests of Haitian-Canadians, and thereby indirectly increasing the probability of Quebec voting to stay in Canada in any future referendum, and increasing voter preference for the governing party among

Haitian-Canadians. Policy objectives included improving Canada-U.S. relations by taking some of the load where the United States might not be able to contribute as much as it wished due to extensive commitments elsewhere.

The implicit economic objectives of the mission included:

- positioning Canada as a *partner* of developing countries and regions. That position may be of strategic economic value to Canada, the Western Hemisphere, and the world as these countries become fully developed over the long term.
- gaining increased respect by doing everything feasible to help Haiti that, in turn, could help Canada's economic relationships with the United States, OAS and UN members, and other hemispheric partners.
- avoiding high costs that could flow from Haiti to Canada and the region via mass migrations, refugees, drugs, crime, and social instability.

The military and security objectives of the mission, as well as MINUSTAH, were ultimately aimed at providing a platform of security and civil order for developmental objectives rather than military objectives such as the elimination of a military or terrorist threat from another country. One might position the gangs fighting for power as terrorists, but in the current context of Haiti, many of those gangs are competing for territory, control, and resources in the current power/governance marketplace of Haiti along with a politicized police force, political parties, clans, and other groups. Accordingly, Canada's military objectives are congruent with its political and economic objectives regarding Haiti.

SITUATION AND MISSION CREEP

The objectives of the Canadian mission in Haiti have been continuously adjusted in light of the frequent setbacks in meeting earlier objectives. In many cases, Canadian officials see the setbacks as due to politicization of the police, diversion of resources, and other interference by the government of Haiti. The thinking about realistic timeframes for substantial progress toward a self-sustaining economy and democracy in Haiti, among those interviewed or read for this study, has shifted from years to decades. A recent strategic assessment by CIDA in an unclassified but unpublished document includes a change in nomenclature for Haiti from "partner" to "difficult partner" in order to reflect the increasing degree of difficulty seen in achieving development progress in some areas. Other assessments by the OAS and CIDA indicate the time has come to step back and learn from the few successes and many failures.

LESSONS LEARNED IN HAITI

The assessments by Canadian government agencies read during the study indicated the need for a more comprehensive mapping of the institutional and regional fabric of Haiti and an equally comprehensive and unified (not just coordinated) vision and strategy among the Haitian people and government, intervening nations, their programs and nongovernmental agencies, to move that entire fabric along a development pathway. They also indicated that the UNDPKO has little capacity to develop on-the-ground intelligence that could make its planning for PKO more effective, and is hampered in its ability to design missions by having to ask member states for what they can provide, rather than arrange the deployment of the right kind of personnel, equipment, logistic supplies, strategies, and tactics by member states.

Several sources pointed to the success South Africa achieved through bringing together key representatives from all competing power groups in the country to develop three scenarios for their potential future. One of those scenarios, which showed a potential win/win pathway to a stable social situation, included making Nelson Mandela the president. The other scenarios showed lose/lose pathways to anarchy and chaos similar to that of Haiti today and had the effect of drawing consensus on a development roadmap from a similar wide (and wild) range of stakeholders. Planning for the feasible emergence of Haiti from its current state of anarchy and economic and ecological devastation might benefit from such comprehensive visioning and participation. Almost all sources thought an empirical model of the emergence of governance from anarchy proffered by the author could help identify and analyze the current state of governance in Haiti. A concept model for such a governance ladder, with a notional example of a country at each level, is shown in table 4–1.

Other independent variables that determine the success of the PKO mission were raised by the research sources, including:

- ability to speak French and Creole
- at least a minimal transportation and telecommunications infrastructure throughout Haiti
- long-term horizons (5-year funding and 10-year planning)
- adequate funding for the scale of resources required.

PERFORMANCE MEASUREMENT OF THE EFFECTIVENESS OF MULTIPARTITE PKO

In the course of this study, recommendations were sought and received on how to measure the outcomes of the PKO mission. Recommendations have been summarized as follows:

TABLE 4–1. GOVERNANCE LADDER

Level	Description	Example
7	Governance includes collaborative vision, transparency, universal education, development and sharing	Scandinavian countries
6	Democratic determination of authority and rule of law	Canada
5	Rule of law made public and enforced	Singapore
4	Order imposed by, or accorded to, one power group, leader, or outside intervener	Saudi Arabia
3	Formal and informal agreements among power groups on territory, trade, rules of engagement, and dominance or hierarchy of power	Iran
2	Emergence of orderly power groups, economic marketplaces, and informal institutions, with some implicit rules of engagement among power groups	Somalia, 11th-century England
1	Disorganized battles for power, without humanitarian rules of engagement, by leaders and members of power groups such as gangs, clans, militia, police, and armed forces	Haiti

- track local and regional rates of economic activity, employment, and crime through preconflict, PKO, and post–PKO periods
- conduct interviews and workshops with representatives of all PKO forces on lessons learned, sharing best practices, and ideas for future operations
- conduct interviews and workshops with local leaders, aid organizations, and citizens on lessons learned, sharing best practices, and ideas for future operations. Develop these with insights gained from the South African post-Apartheid process.

RECOMMENDATIONS FOR FUTURE PKO WITHIN A FRAMEWORK OF REGIONAL COOPERATION

The design of the collective PKO mission should include identifying, assessing, mapping, and developing strategies for engagement of the complete range of social and economic institutions in the country being considered for PKO. These include government institutions, political parties, the military, elements of the justice system, religious groups, clans, gangs, commercial enterprises, opinion leaders, investors, institutions, and all other significant informal and formal organizations and the mechanisms/marketplaces through which they interact.

Analysis of the situation and design of the PKO should be based on an in-depth understanding of the generic and specific regional hierarchy of order, law, and governance, and feasible goals and strategies for moving the local institutional network up the hierarchy.

Mission goals and scope should be system-wide rather than focused on one institution. For instance, building police capabilities and ethics should be done in conjunction with courts, correctional institutions, and support systems for ex-prisoners and youth-at-risk.

The mission should be prepared to work independently of the central government, if there is one, in the event that it is so dysfunctional as to be of no use, or a threat to its citizens.

A future peacekeeping operation should address the issue of postmission systemic sustainability from the beginning of the mission. This includes:

- planned staging from initial replacement or infill of local military, militia, police, and civil governance institutions to postmission mentoring and other follow-up support
- developing a strategy for protection, first aid, and development support for key community and national institutions, governance, infrastructure, and natural resources
- providing expert advice and services to help local populations deal with trauma and improve conditions that are root causes of violence
- maintaining and developing alternatives to loss of identity, jobs, and hope in the local population, particularly with regard to individual and gang violence and lethal weapons among young males
- developing hand-off strategies among mission military and police forces, local military and police forces, courts, correctional services, and other key institutions
- leaving in place a feasible and functional set of institutions equipped with locally sustainable technologies and practices, rather than dependence on those of the PKO forces
- providing adequate funding and making the commitment to provide enough personnel (including rotation) and logistic support to effectively build institutions, change values, establish trust relationships, and establish a sustainable society and economy over a term of 5 or more years
- convincing the Canadian government and citizens of the value received for their money, given that, in Canada's case, a prime issue is cost and capacity
- collaborating on building analytic tools and system-dynamics models that can help each contributing state identify its special role in PKO, and the cost-effectiveness of missions' indirect contributions to their domestic society and economy.

Chapter Five

Chile:
Responding to a Regional Crisis

ENZO DI NOCERA GARCÍA AND RICARDO BENAVENTE CRESTA

C hile decided to send to Haiti one of the largest contingents the country has ever used in a United Nations (UN) peacekeeping mission. This initial participation, along with the other countries (United States, France, and Canada) that constituted the Multinational Interim Force–Haiti (MIFH), opened up the possibility for other soldiers from Brazil, Argentina, and other Latin American countries to be included later in the stabilization phase (the UN Stabilization Mission in Haiti, or MINUSTAH). This was an unusual situation in that regional forces were participating in peacekeeping operations on the same continent.

When Chilean president Ricardo Lagos ordered the mobilization of troops to be deployed in Haiti in the MIFH within the short period of 48 hours, he stated that the decision was in keeping with the doctrine his government has been promoting. He noted that the participation of Chilean troops in peacekeeping missions was authorized because there was a crisis situation in Haiti and it was imperative "to assist in the recovery of peace, the reestablishment of institutional channels, and the general order of a friendly country."[1]

Chilean foreign affairs minister Maria Soledad Alvear, who at the time was in Buenos Aires participating in a meeting of Southern Common Market foreign ministers, commented on Chile's national Radio Cooperativa network, "Since Chile has been a member of the group of Haiti's friends for several years, and is also one of the 17 countries that have a diplomatic mission in Haiti, we feel the obligation and the duty as part of the international community to collaborate in this process." She added, "The Government is absolutely convinced that our presence in Haiti is completely necessary and timely and is one more commitment by Chile to peace, democracy, and human rights." Lastly, she said that Chile "is consistent" and that it only acted after a UN resolution had been approved.

Juan Emilio Cheyre, commander in chief of the Chilean army, pointed out the responsibility his institution was taking on in Haiti, emphasizing that "it is a decision of the government that reflects our foreign policy and our defense policy." Cheyre was careful to stress that the Chilean troops were going there to collaborate for peace, not to participate in supporting one gang or another.

ABOUT THIS CHAPTER

With this background in mind, this research project is aimed at analyzing the participation that Chile has had historically in peacekeeping operations (PKO); analyzing and commenting on existing national policy on the subject; describing how the country has been increasing its capability to participate in this type of operation; and in particular making a detailed analysis of the role Chile has played and is playing in regional security matters with its participation in the peacekeeping operations the United Nations have authorized for Haiti.

The Haitian matter is not completed, but is a process that is still in full development, and therefore very little has been written on this peacekeeping operation. Thus, the research group prepared this work using the following principal reference sources: available written accounts and public statements from authorities; press articles; interviews of authorities in the national and foreign media; structured interviews of Chilean military authorities who have participated in managing and planning this peacekeeping operation; and legal references and other similar available background.

For reasons of time and space, one major section of this chapter is a direct response to the research questionnaire of nine questions that the study director formulated for each of the participating country authors. In the final section of this chapter, some conclusions that resulted from the study are briefly presented.

CHILE AND PEACEKEEPING OPERATIONS: A BRIEF HISTORY

One of the specific objectives of our foreign policy is to increase Chile's
participation in the Peacekeeping Operations sponsored by the United Nations.
—María Soledad Alvear, 2002

Since the 1990s, peacekeeping operations have been increasingly present in the perceptions of authorities and governments. Further, due to the globalization of communications, peacekeeping has also become widely known to the public throughout the world.

When these types of operations began in the late 1940s, they were symbolized by the traditional United Nations "blue helmets." These soldiers were not equipped to confront or contain a conflict, but were mere elements of peace and goodwill placed sporadically and strategically at points of conflict to separate the warring forces that were threatening even the civilian population.

The increasingly spectacular nature and tragic consequences of these confrontations in various parts of the world have made peacekeeping operations a permanent and recurring reality for many nations and their inhabitants. This was due in part to the high casualty rate among the uninvolved innocent population brought on by internal or external conflicts, as well as to the phenomenon of globalization that appeared in the world at the end of the last century. In effect, because of the new interrelationships and multiplying effects that globalization created among all states, any armed conflict that arises in any part of the world causes deep-seated and immediate political and economic repercussions in countries and regions very distant from the site of the events.

One example that dramatically demonstrates the economic effects produced by an international conflict is the case of the first Gulf War in the early 1990s, which had strong and immediate repercussions on the world economy due to the changes it brought about in the oil market and the normal supply of this vital element for all countries, producers and nonproducers alike.

On the effects this type of conflict can produce in the Chilean economy, it is worthy of note that the country's development policy is primarily based on a strategy of opening up to foreign markets. The products that Chile imports and exports are mainly shipped by sea, which makes the country very vulnerable in this aspect and with respect to situations that can restrict its trade with the rest of the world. The commander in chief of the Chilean navy, Admiral Miguel Vergara, clearly related this maritime dependency to international security in an interview with the *El Mercurio de Santiago* newspaper on January 13, 2002, when he said, "For Chile it is important to promote peace, security, and order in the international community, at least in the areas through which our maritime trade transits."

In an interview on July 11, 2004, Chilean undersecretary of war Gabriel Gaspar confirmed the navy leader's statements, saying, "There is nothing more damaging to trade than conflicts that paralyze exports, and from an economic standpoint half of Chile's GDP [gross domestic product] has to do with foreign trade." He later stressed the will of the national government to participate in the resolution of international conflicts, especially those occurring in the region.

The free trade agreements and treaties that Chile has signed with other countries and various political entities such as the European Union and the Asia-Pacific Economic Cooperation group create ties that are not only economic in nature, but also entail significant connotations concerning security.

An example of this is found in the recent words of national defense minister Michelle Bachelet, commenting that the country's future participation in Operation *Althea* (the mission that will replace NATO in Bosnia) is one more link in the series of Chile's contributions to the security of the Balkans— where in addition to participating in the Stabilization Force, it has deployed police forces in Bosnia and Kosovo. Minister Bachelet related this participation to the Partnership Agreement between the European Union and Chile.[2]

From a humanitarian standpoint, and as a result of the high death tolls caused by armed conflicts among the civilian population of the affected countries, peacekeeping operations had to be changed, escalating from the initial image of blue-helmeted soldiers in stress-relieving work, to other scenarios in which regular soldiers act as part of international forces outfitted with modern combat equipment in order to protect the civilian population and to keep, or enforce, peace.

Chile has not been a stranger to this evolution. Early on, the country began its participation in this type of operation in 1949, with the UN Military Observation Group in India and Pakistan. There, and in eight later operations, it played the traditional role of the blue helmets.

Later, starting in the 1990s, the country participated in a second phase, which could be considered intermediate and more specialized. The characteristics of this new phase lie in the nature of the means used and the missions performed; it begins with sending air force helicopters and personnel to Iraq, then participating with marine infantrymen in Cambodia, and later deploying police forces in Bosnia-Herzegovina. This phase comes to a close with sending Chilean army helicopters and resources to East Timor.

Regarding Chilean public opinion, the deployment of military forces and helicopters, first in Iraq and then in East Timor, produced a major change in the sensitivity of the common Chilean citizen. Since these participations, the populace has followed peacekeeping operations with interest and regularity in the national and foreign media. This situation enabled the population to realize that United Nations peacekeeping operations were now closer to their daily lives; they accepted them as a natural element of the country's business and favorably received the country's necessary participation in this type of humanitarian operations

The third phase, the one now facing Chile, is characterized by the use of its military forces in joint or combined units. Two examples of this are a new participation in Bosnia-Herzegovina, but this time using Army resources in integrated form with a combat unit from Great Britain; and in Cyprus, where Chilean Army and Navy forces are participating in combined form with a task force from Argentina.[3]

A question publicly asked by the authority in charge of Chile's foreign policy also contributed to greater citizen awareness of the peacekeeping operations of the time: Why is our country taking an increasingly active part in these operations, although they seem far from our own daily lives and problems? That authority also answered the question publicly with the following thoughts, which have come to summarize the bases of the country's policy on the subject:

> We must remember that the peaceful resolution of conflicts is a fundamental and permanent principle of Chile's foreign policy. The projection of the intrinsic moral value of this principle, as well as the fact that safeguarding national security—among other factors—depends on international and regional stability, has determined that the priorities of the country's external action include promoting and maintaining world peace.[4]

Chile's PKO Policy

Chile's national policy on participating in PKO is based on the fact that world peace is a permanent objective of its foreign policy. The country's participation with troops in missions authorized by a mandate of the UN Security Council is therefore a real, concrete, and sovereign way of reaffirming that commitment to the international community.

This policy establishes a range of political-strategic requirements for participating in PKO. Among these is the fact that the participation of Chilean forces must be in the national interest, so the costs and benefits involved must be weighed on a case-by-case basis, analyzing each time the type of operation to be conducted, the region where the resources are to be deployed, the size of the forces that must be committed, and the expected duration. Other important aspects to be considered are the fact that the operations must contribute to the improvement of the institutions involved and that all the participating personnel, civilian or military, must preferably be volunteers due to the personal risks involved.

According to the same policy, the decision to participate in PKO must be taken by the president of the republic with the joint advice of the ministers of foreign relations and defense, the latter ministry being vested with the responsibility of coordinating the activities. Lastly, and since the decision involves the movement of military forces outside the country, according to article 60 of the Chilean constitution, the matter must be regulated by law.[5]

Law No. 19,067 (1991), resulting from the constitutional provision, states: "The deployment of national troops outside the territory of the Republic must be authorized by executive order signed by the President of the Republic subject to Senate consent and report, or at the proposal of the applicable institution of National Defense issued by the National Defense Ministry and with the signature of the Foreign Affairs Minister." The said decree must state the purpose, schedule, and terms for the deployment of the troops.

In this manner, the sovereign decision made by the president to participate in PKO with Chilean military forces is ratified by another branch of the state and formalized in a rule that commits to and involves in the procedure the two ministers of state participating in this type of operation.

With respect to the hierarchy of the national PKO policy, it is for all intents a policy of the state of Chile and in it, peacekeeping operations are understood to be "any international deployment of civilian or military or public safety resources that under the command and control of the United Nations and with the consent of the parties in conflict, has the purpose of directly contributing to consolidation and the cessation of hostilities."

The first document that was prepared on the subject, in 1996, called "National Policy for the Participation of the Chilean State in Peacekeeping Operations," contained the primary considerations that regulated such activities and referred to the operations the country would conduct under Chapter VI of the United Nations Charter, namely, operations that are more closely related to the peaceful settlement of disputes. This policy was made official by supreme decree 94 dated November 6, 1996, which in turn has its legal basis in articles 24 and 32–8 of the constitution of the republic.[6]

The aforesaid supreme decree also defines the relationships that exist between the country's internal and external security: "In an integral and modern sense, the security of Chile depends on a set of internal and external factors, and among them are international stability and security." Later, the same document states that "due to the globalization of relations, conflicts have a broader and more intense international repercussion, and international stability and security pacts therefore take on greater importance."[7]

The National Defense Book of Chile 1997, which is contemporary with the original policy, said that "Chile will not authorize the use of Chilean forces for seeking and/or capturing offenders, belligerents, or war criminals, missions for the control of public order after the cessation of hostilities, or missions of oversight of the respect for human rights conducted in peacekeeping operations."[8]

In 1999, the original policy on Chile's participation in PKO changed when a memorandum of understanding was signed with the Secretary-General of the UN, which stated that Chile will contribute to the UN Reserve Forces System. In order to formalize this agreement, a new supreme decree was promulgated in the same year that modified the national policy, D.S. (G) No. 68 from the under secretariat of war, which broadened Chile's participation in PKO, authorizing participation in peacekeeping missions with mandates based on chapter VII of the charter, relating to cases of threats to peace or peace-breaking or acts of aggression. This new policy maintained the limitation of not using Chilean forces for seeking and/or capturing offenders, belligerents, or war criminals.

Other elements strengthened Chile's national interest in participating with increasing forces in PKO and becoming more deeply committed in the area of international security. These included the following: the country's participation as a founding member of the Human Security Network since 1999;[9] its role as host country for the Fourth Meeting of Foreign Affairs Ministers of the Human Security Network in July 2002; the meetings of Defense and Foreign Affairs Ministers of the Americas held in several countries during the period; and, especially, its new participation as a nonpermanent member of the United Nations Security Council starting in January 2003.

All these activities and commitments taken on in humanitarian matters resulted in a positive perception on the part of the citizenry and greater receptiveness of Chile's cooperation with other international actors in instituting initiatives that improve regional security. Among these instances, peacekeeping operations still have a major role, and in turn have made it possible to see clear examples of the country's acceptance as a serious and active interlocutor on these matters and others relating to international security.

Motivated by these achievements, the national policy aimed at incorporating the broadest possible spectrum of actors in order to take the greatest possible advantage of the factors that would contribute to increasing Chile's prestige and participation in the agencies charged with overseeing world security. As part of this scheme, it was also felt that it was pertinent to promote the role of women in this area. To that end, and in cosponsorship with Denmark and the European Union, a biregional conference on women's role in peacekeeping operations was held in Santiago in 2002. The initiative, which included the participation of international experts, also responded to Resolution 1,325 of the United Nations Security Council of October 31, 2000, which emphasized the need for the full inclusion of women in all the processes relating to decisions and actions in conflict prevention, peacekeeping operations, and postconflict reconstruction.

When it was deemed appropriate to broaden the country's participation, incorporating other peacekeeping operations ordered by the United Nations Security Council, supreme decree 68 was issued, which ratified the contents of the greater part of the policy that was in force and only amended article 4, now including peace enforcement operations as discussed in Chapter VII of the United Nations Charter. To that end, the pertinent part of the decree said: "This declaration of National Policy includes peace enforcement operations, such as the total or partial interruption of economic relations and railway, maritime, air, postal, telegraph, and radio electric communications, the rupture of diplomatic relations, demonstrations, blockades, and other operations conducted by Air, Naval, or Land Forces as referred to in the United Nations Charter."[10]

When Chile incorporated this new task of peace enforcement, the country was automatically committed to expanding its agenda of participation in the UN-sponsored settlement of international conflicts, joining the concert of nations that carry out the following tasks:

- overseeing cease-fires and collaborating in the separation of forces
- overseeing dividing lines or exclusion zones
- escorting, guiding, and distributing humanitarian aid
- overseeing the demobilization of combatants and the delivery and/or destruction of weaponry
- collaborating in mine removal programs
- contributing to the success of war refugee return and relocation programs
- contributing to the reconstruction of areas affected by conflicts or natural disasters
- observing electoral activities.

Other Actions to Increase Chile's Participation in PKO

As a way of endorsing the will to become increasingly involved in this area and to strengthen the national capabilities it would be necessary to use in the future, Chile's national authorities took the following measures:

- increased their presence in the international agencies that plan and coordinate peacekeeping operations
- created means for the training and education of the civilian and military personnel who would make up the national forces
- maintained standby forces to act when requested by the United Nations
- showed national and international public opinion the country's willingness to participate in this type of operation.

Increased Presence in International Agencies. This task was accomplished by assigning a group of specialized and highly qualified officers to various UN agencies on a rotating basis to serve as military liaisons and advisors. The assigned positions were as follows:

- an army colonel designated as advisor to Heraldo Munoz, ambassador of Chile and a non-permanent member of the United Nations Security Council
- an army colonel as defense attaché to the Chilean mission in the UN, a rotating position with the navy and air force

- an army colonel as permanent delegate to the training department of the UN department of peacekeeping operations.

The work of these officers, which is only minimum representation, provided a liaison and increased contact with the agencies charged with the negotiations and coordination work handled by the United Nations in the area of peacekeeping operations. In addition, it enabled the Chilean authorities to become more familiar with various subjects and procedures relating to such operations and to receive timely and early detailed information on the resources and requests for forces the UN might address to Chile.

Another milestone in the country's commitment to PKO, particularly in Haiti, has been the UN acknowledgment of Chile in appointing Chilean ambassador to Argentina Gabriel Valdes, a former representative of Chile on the Security Council, as special representative of the agency in Haiti.

Ambassador Valdes began work in this highly placed position in Haiti in August 2004, and soon after familiarizing himself with his duties stated in a meeting with the defense minister and the defense chief of staff: "I could not refuse the appointment of the Secretary General; the commitment of President Lagos and the Chilean Armed Forces had to be followed by my personal commitment." He later added that in view of the complex conditions existing in Haiti, this is not a conventional mission, and in that sense he underlined the historical dimension that participation in that country's reconstruction and stabilization represents for regional countries.[11]

Training and Education for Civilians and Military Personnel in Peacekeeping Operations. Participants in UN peacekeeping operations must have specialized training, which was provided by Chilean forces in training centers abroad. For that reason, along with adopting the decision to increase Chilean participation in peacekeeping operations and to expand it to the actions provided in Chapter VII of the UN Charter, the national authorities resolved to commit significant human, material, and economic resources to create a center of this type in Chile. At such a center, personnel from the armed forces, public safety and security agencies, and civilians would receive specialized PKO training. This resulted in the creation of the Joint Peacekeeping Operations Center of Chile (*Centro Conjunto para Operaciones de Paz de Chile*, or CECOPAC) in 2002.[12]

The center was created as a joint agency dependent on the national defense ministry, with a modern headquarters located in the army military camp in Santiago, equipped with all the necessary resources and outside liaisons to achieve its functions. It is the first of its kind to be built specifically for purposes of deployment training and education for civilian, police, and military personnel.[13] Two years after its creation, CECOPAC already has the following regular courses:

- military observers' course
- peacekeeping operations course
- United Nations police monitoring course
- media correspondents' course in peacekeeping missions
- course on international humanitarian law in armed conflicts and PKO
- course in peacekeeping service given by the Pearson Center of Canada
- predeployment courses for national contingents.

The various CECOPAC courses are regularly attended by all the civilian, police, and military personnel the state is training to participate in peacekeeping operations and by others from the private sector and from other countries who are interested in taking special courses on the subject.

Readiness of Standby Forces. The joint training center was also an important step for the readiness of Chilean forces associated with the commitment of Standby Forces, since to date the CECOPAC has prepared and trained numerous personnel in various specialties to respond to the requests of the United Nations with minimum prior notice.

This operational capability was clearly reflected when the United Nations asked Chile to participate in the Stabilization Force in Haiti in March 2004. At the time, presidential instructions ordered that Chilean forces join the Multinational Interim Force along with the United States, France, and Canada as soon as possible. The national forces, a battalion of approximately 350 army infantry and special forces troops plus their respective support groups, which at the time were the most numerous to participate on Chile's behalf in peacekeeping missions, were ready to be deployed within the first 72 hours after the UN request. These forces were part of those that Chile had committed on a standby basis.

Actions Emphasizing the National Will to Participate in UN PKO. The national authorities have given repeated public signals to emphasize the country's manifest interest in participating in UN peacekeeping operations through official visits by the highest national authorities to the forces that Chile has deployed in various parts of the world. For example, in 2001, President Ricardo Lagos visited the Chilean army forces stationed in East Timor, and during 2004 he visited the troops and police personnel in Bosnia-Herzegovina and Haiti. In 2003, national defense minister Michelle Bachelet visited the combined Argentine and Chilean forces deployed in Cyprus. She repeated that visit in 2004 and extended it to the forces Chile has in Bosnia-Herzegovina, and particularly those deployed to Haiti since the beginning of the year.

Another outstanding visit was the one made to Haiti in 2005 by Santiago mayor and presidential candidate and opposition leader Joaquin Lavin. While this visit did not have the importance and official nature of those discussed above, it was a clear demonstration that all the national political groups support the peacekeeping operations in which Chile is participating and consider them very important.

Brazilian president Luiz Inacio Lula da Silva met privately with the Chilean president on August 23, 2004. At a joint press conference, the two emphasized the presence of the region in Haiti and highlighted the work that both Chile and Brazil are doing to stabilize the convulsing Caribbean island. In the same press conference, the Brazilian president summarized the role being played by the two countries in Haiti: "With the same force with which President Lagos, speaking in the name of the people of Chile, said no to sending troops to Iraq in the Security Council, he said yes, when the cause was peace, to sending troops to Haiti, troops that are working with our own, under the civilian coordination of a Chilean and the military coordination of a Brazilian."[14]

RESPONSES TO RESEARCH QUESTIONNAIRE

It is now appropriate to respond to the guideline questions given to the study participants by the PKO project director. Taking account of the specificity of the questionnaire and the possibility of rating the responses, the following section deals directly with each of the questions in the order in which they were presented.

Factors that Influenced Chile's Participation in the Peacekeeping Activities in Haiti

- the fact that Chile was a signer of the United Nations Charter from the beginning
- the existence of a specific national policy for the participation of the Chilean state in peacekeeping operations, made official by supreme decree on October 14, 1999
- the direct request made by UN Secretary-General Kofi Annan to Chilean president Ricardo Lagos to commit to participating in the MIFH
- the existence of an international legal basis with the promulgation of United Nations Security Council Resolution No. 1529 of February 29,

2004, requesting such participation and stating that it should be implemented under the command and control of the United Nations

- the "Memorandum of Understanding between the Government of the Republic of Chile and the United Nations" on the contributions to the United Nations Reserve Forces Agreements System, signed by the two parties in New York on November 11, 1999
- the fact that after Resolution No. 1529, the United Nations asked in Resolution No. 1542 of April 30, 2004, that a UN Stabilization Mission be established in Haiti (MINUSTAH) for a renewable period of 6 months starting June 1, 2004
- the fact that Chile is participating as a nonpermanent member of the Security Council and a Chilean is currently designated in charge of the case of Haiti. This gives the country greater responsibility with respect to world and regional security, tasks that are in keeping with the principles of its foreign policy and absolutely consistent with its intentions of achieving greater international participation and inclusion
- the statement made in Chile's 1997 and 2002 Books of National Defense that one of the guiding principles of its foreign and defense policies is its willingness and commitment to participate in United Nations Chapter VI and VII peacekeeping operations
- the fact that Haiti is a part of Latin America and Chile is interested in cooperating in the search for solutions to the conflicts threatening the region. In addition, the participation of national forces with countries of the region strengthens the goals of bilateral and multilateral trust to which the government is committed.

Lastly, this decision also considered the following political and strategic factors:

- demonstrating Chile's response capability by accepting the challenge of the MIFH to prepare significant resources and deploy them over a long distance in only 72 hours to participate along with the United States, France, and Canada
- showing Chile's capability of acting in certain urgent conditions in the MINUSTAH, since this second request from the United Nations established short readiness deadlines and the use of larger forces, all within a tight decide-and-respond schedule
- making use of these challenges to confirm permanent aspects of Chile's foreign policy and to provide further proof of the country's commitment to peace and international security, and specifically regional security

- emphasizing the national will to contribute to the collective responsibility, particularly during Chile's term as a nonpermanent member of the Security Council, in spite of the fact that the initial 6-month period of operations would coincide with the last half-year of Chile's participation in the Council
- justifying the logic that two Latin American states that are members of the Security Council (Brazil and Chile) should be present in Haiti, the most fragile country in the region, contributing to a multidimensional peacekeeping operation. At the same time, the two countries' participation is a unique opportunity for two traditionally friendly and nearly neighboring countries to work closely together.
- announcing the national will to cooperate in the full establishment of institutionalism and the consolidation of democracy in Haiti, thereby helping to demonstrate that this status can only be achieved with medium- or long-term plans and with UN oversight
- providing an example of Chile's commitment to international solidarity and the fact that Chile wants to fairly share its social responsibilities with other states
- delivering the message that Chile's participation in the MINUSTAH along with Brazil and Argentina is a strong signal of cooperation and leadership in the region
- confirming the efficiency and rapid readiness and deployment of the forces to be used in the mission, and evaluating the quality of the training provided by the CECOPAC. On the same subject, the Chilean authorities realized that if the training had been successful, it would be viewed positively by national and international public opinion, thereby creating favorable internal and external expectations of these processes in the event of Chile's future participation in similar operations.

Finally, Chile's participation showed national public opinion that the significant economic investment required to prepare the forces requested by the United Nations could be partially recovered through reimbursements. The fact that the operations periods are established as 6-months-renewable provides for flexibility in decisionmaking. This enables the country to decide in advance on the forces that must be used in the next period, on whether the forces are to be increased or decreased, and even, if necessary, on discontinuing the mission.

How the Decision Was Made
At the first request from the United Nations and due to the need for a rapid response, President Ricardo Lagos immediately accepted the mission from

the Security Council. Just after receiving the request, on March 1, 2004, and after brief consultations with the foreign affairs minister, the national defense minister, and the commander-in-chief of the army, but without first consulting the senate, Lagos said that Chile would participate in the Multinational Force.

This gave rise to some apprehensions on the part of some representatives of the legislative branch, who were disturbed by the fact that the president had not asked for the prior opinion of the congress. In spite of this brief controversy, on March 2, the senate approved sending the contingent by a large majority. So, within 48 hours, Chile was in a position to send a first contingent of 336 soldiers from the Chilean army to Haiti to join the Multinational Interim Force.

The urgency of accepting and preparing the MIFH was driven by the need to accomplish critical special tasks, such as reversing the situation of crisis Haiti was experiencing, permitting the country's rapid return to peace, normalizing minimum basic services, and creating more suitable conditions for the country's stabilization. This would give the United Nations time to prepare the broader mission that would be deployed 3 months later, in which Chile could also play a leading role.

On March 11, in accordance with Article 4 of Law No. 19,067 regulating the deployment of troops outside the country, the president of the republic asked the president of the senate to extend the contingent's stay until the end of May and to authorize the deployment of more troops. This procedure made it possible to increase Chile's presence in Haiti from 336 to 584 troops in MINUSTAH, with the incorporation of more personnel from the army and, at that time, the navy, the air force, and the *Carabineros* (national police) and investigative police forces of Chile.

The process used in Chile to respond to a request of this type is as follows. When the United Nations makes a request to all countries for peacekeeping operations, the Chilean defense ministry and foreign affairs ministry are informed of the request through their respective channels. Then, an analysis group composed of an interdisciplinary team of military and civilian personnel from various organizations reviews the UN requests and analyzes all the positive and negative factors impacting them. Among others, the group is composed of representatives from the defense, foreign affairs, and treasury ministries, as well as representatives of the army, navy, air force, *Carabineros*, investigative police, and voter registration. This phase ends with a joint recommendation on the appropriateness and feasibility of participating in the operation, with what resources and in what conditions. With this proposal, the foreign affairs ministry and the defense ministry make a final joint proposal to the president of the republic, who decides on the matter. If the decision is affirmative, the president submits the troop deployment request to the senate. At the same time, he reports the result to the ministries involved and, through the defense minister, orders the institutions to ready the resources to be used. As soon as a favorable decision on participation is made by the president and the senate, it is officially reported to the United Nations through the Chilean ambassador, with details on the quantity and type of forces the country will contribute.

Mission Design and Planning, Participants in the Design, and Consideration of External Influences

The first mission (MIFH) has already been explained in detail. The following concerns the second phase, consisting of joining MINUSTAH with resources from Chile's army, navy, air force, *Carabineros*, and investigative police starting on June 1, 2004, for an initial renewable period of 6 months.

At this point, and with more time for decisionmaking, the national defense ministry's advisory committee was charged with reviewing, analyzing, and proposing the legal grounds relating to the task assigned by the United Nations. For its part, the National Defense Staff (*Estado Mayor de la Defensa Nacional*, or EMDN) analyzed the costs the mission would entail, the technical aspects of the operation, and the arrangements for selecting and preparing the force to be deployed.

As an initial document to guide the task, a ministry preparation directive set out the first guidelines for the participating institutions (army, navy, air force, *Carabineros*, and investigations). Then, after the presidential decree making the operation official was promulgated, an implementation directive was issued.

For the detailed work on performing the mission, a joint staff (*Estado Mayor Conjuncto*, or EMC) for Haiti was formed. The national defense chief of staff was designated as the top national authority for the entire operation, and the assistant defense chief of staff became direct head of this joint staff. The EMC was composed of officers from the EMDN and the institutions that would participate with forces to strengthen critical areas. The general organization was in keeping with NATO rules, which are those recognized by the UN.

The joint staff for the MINUSTAH is still functioning under the defense staff, with all the original permanent members and those especially assigned by other institutions. It should be noted that this is the largest Joint Staff that has operated in the country in peacetime.

The national military authority and the EMC, as well as advising the defense minister, oversee and control the tasks performed by the national contingent in Haiti and are also responsible for supporting it until the end of the mission.

As for any external influences that could impact the phases of preparing and deploying forces and operations on the ground, they are considered nonexistent. This is because the decision to participate in this UN peacekeeping operation was a sovereign act by the country and because all the phases of preparation and deployment of forces were carried out in accordance with national standards and procedures. Perhaps the only external factor in the whole process would be that NATO interoperability rules were used for the configuration of the forces, liaison systems, communications, and all means of coordination with other non-Chilean forces.

The national command system is organized as follows: All the participants in the operation are under the authority of the national defense minister, headquartered in Santiago. The national defense chief of staff, by delegation of the minister, has acted as national military authority from the beginning of the operation, and the units deployed in Haiti are under his authority. The command relationship in this case is the one referred to as *full command*, by delegation of the political level.

Political and Economic Objectives

Political. The use of the military to maintain peace and world security has taken on new terms and meaning in the international post–Cold War scenario; as a result, the relative importance given this instrument in Chile's defense and foreign policies developed in a positive sense.

In addition, and due to the political and strategic effects that participating in UN peacekeeping operations has for any country, these operations have been the subject of special concern for the government of Chile. The political decision to participate in a timely manner with special forces in Haiti reflects this development.

Chile's defense policy, as that of any other country, is aimed preferably at achieving a degree of deterrence that ensures territorial protection. However, it also centers its actions on keeping the peace, and that will always be dependent on the degree of international stability, especially regional stability, where peacekeeping operations have an irreplaceable role. Added to this is another basic element of the policy, which is the concept of cooperation, understood as a complementary way of using the country's military to promote Chile's insertion in a globalized world in which it also plays a preponderant role in peacekeeping operations.[15]

In this way, the participation of Chilean forces in MINUSTAH is consistent with the country's defense and foreign policies. In this case, the political objectives of solidarity and commitment to a UN resolution are predominant.

Economic. Chile has no direct economic objectives in the case of Haiti. However, it is interesting to note that the country has maintained increasing openness to the international economy and intensified its participation in economic globalization as a permanent strategy for development. Accordingly, the effects of any international crisis, and, to a greater extent, regional crises, can directly affect its national development, which creates increasingly strict commitments for it to the security of other countries, particularly those of the region.[16]

Among the indirect economic objectives arising from the operations in Haiti are the following:

The National Market. Chile's participation in the MINUSTAH has meant the investment of significant funds in the process of preparing its forces, a situation that has been favorable to the Chilean companies that have participated in the process. This situation makes internal demand more dynamic, and thereby makes it grow, factors that are also essential to reducing the unemployment rate.

International Context of the Operations. Beyond any monetary rewards from the United Nations through reimbursements to participating countries, these countries are able to participate in the search for solutions to the problems of the country that is the subject of the peacekeeping operation. These solutions could involve providing supplies and other elements to relieve the problems of local shortages, transferring technology and sending in specialized people, or other types of contributions that effectively support the reconstruction of Haiti. This situation in turn could result in business opportunities for producers from countries such as Chile.

It is obvious that the normalization of Haiti will be an ambitious job, and that the participation of Chilean businesses will require them not only to discover opportunities for action but also to have an information and incentive process for possible economic agents interested in participating.

Military and Security Objectives
The military and security objectives for the operation were shaped based on the UN mandate. In keeping with that mandate, the primary objective was to create a secure and stable environment. Broadly, the basic idea of both operations was to establish an environment in which the transitional government of Haiti could develop a new political and constitutional process. Among other desirable goals, this included disarming and pacifying the population, overseeing the restructuring and reform of Haiti's national police in accordance with the standards of a democratic police force, and preparing the environment for future elections.

For the forces themselves, the security measures were aimed at achieving the principle of zero casualties among civilian and military personnel. To achieve this goal, the mission's security objectives were grouped into *operational risks* and *health risks.*

The basic assumption was that any military operation involves certain risks and that the operation in Haiti in particular would not be easy, considering the nature of the assigned task, the scope of the human and material resources used, and the Chilean personnel's lack of knowledge of the scenario, the terrain, and the customs and idiosyncrasies of the local population. In the first of the operations, it was possible to minimize these risks by careful planning and by the forces' prior training, which included a brief period of local orientation and exchange of experiences with the forces from other countries that were present. The task was easier for the MINUSTAH since there was sufficient time for more detailed planning and some Chilean officers traveled to Haiti before the operational deployment. Having the experience of the Chilean personnel who had participated in the previous phase was of great value during this phase.

With respect to any special precautionary measures taken in both operations, one of the most effective was not to permit isolated personnel movements in any area of Haiti. For example, whenever a vehicle had to leave the barracks facilities, it had to be accompanied by another vehicle and an escort. The use of helmets and bullet-proof vests was also mandatory in all movements.

In addition to taking extreme security measures, instructions to personnel in connection with carrying and using weapons were always aimed at avoiding any action or show of force that could frighten the civilian population and create an undesirable image for the UN forces in general and the Chilean troops in particular. The general rule was to always use a friendly and deferential approach toward the native population.

With respect to any operational risks that were associated with the MIFH and MINUSTAH, the balance sheet to date has been very positive, since there have been no casualties or accidents of any kind, nor has it been necessary to modify the security objectives set out by the military forces.

Since the environmental health conditions in Haiti were considered deficient, with a high risk of contagious diseases and digestive infections, special preventive measures were taken before deployment, such as vaccinating all participants against the most common illnesses in the area (hepatitis A and B, smallpox, yellow fever, typhoid, dengue, malaria, and toxoid).

In addition, protective health measures were taken against insects, mosquitoes, and other parasites that could threaten the health of the deployed personnel, and special instructions were issued on personal hygiene, environmental hygiene, and other precautions necessary to avoid contagion and infection. For example, due to the high rates of acquired immune deficiency syndrome (AIDS) in the Haitian population, personnel were ordered to avoid any intimate personal contact with the civilian population. In addition, they were prohibited from buying or consuming food from local city markets and for any reason drinking the water or eating elsewhere than in the service areas indicated by the respective command.

Variables Impacting Effectiveness of the Combined Military Forces

After interviewing various military and civilian authorities who participated in the planning and later field work of the MIFH and MINUSTAH, the following conclusions were reached on the independent variables that had or could have a significant effect on the activities carried out by the combined military forces in Haiti.

Terrain and Communications. The area of the operations is insular; it is a small geographic area, and medium-high mountain chains isolate sectors in the north of the island. Land travel is difficult; the road system is poorly laid out and in very poor condition. There are severe difficulties for radio communications, and the local telephone system is nonexistent or permanently out of service.

Experiences with Peacekeeping Missions in Haiti. The combined forces in Haiti are faced with a population that has seen three previous missions. However, to date there have not been any major political, economic, or social results that are really sustainable over time. This could lead the population not to maintain a degree of permanent or at least extended acceptance of this new experience, particularly as it is a Chapter VII operation but has features more closely associated with problems of security and of a police nature.

The mission has very special characteristics. For the first time, a majority regional force has been formed, which is better received by the local population. However, this acceptance could cool if the Haitians see that no major permanent goals are achieved to solve political, social, and economic problems that are endemic in their country. If this situation of rejection occurs, security will be increasingly complex, especially if armed groups are not disarmed and political clashes between warring groups prevented.

It is also felt that if these negative effects arise with respect to the presence of UN troops, it would seriously affect the operations of the combined forces, although they are making efforts to be a beneficial articulator for national reconstruction and development. The major challenge for the Secretary-General's representative in Haiti is to avoid this negative scenario. It is useful to note that he is the political authority charged with coherently integrating the efforts being made to achieve peace and to normalize and develop the country.

Nature of the Mandate. In the case of Haiti, the UN mandate includes applying some measures contained in the resolution sections of Chapters VI and VII, in circumstances in which some participating countries have internal legislation that does not include the action of their forces in accordance with Chapter VII. This situation could lead to the military forces of those countries in general being restricted in their freedom of action, which would make their coordinated and efficient work difficult—as a combined whole—in the field.

Participants' Varying Degree of Experience. The forces now operating in Haiti have different levels of experience and knowledge of peacekeeping operations and the procedures to be used. Although these differences tend to decrease over time and with practice, some inequalities are more noticeable when less experienced countries take over, which does not make it easy, at least initially, to form uniform and standard forces. Other effects of this situation are the difficulties created in better coordinating efforts for the pacification, reconstruction, and development of Haiti according to UN standards and parameters.

In Haiti, as in most peacekeeping operations, the military forces have had to face confrontational situations with the civilian population, which have had to be resolved peacefully and in a manner very different from those associated with a conventional armed conflict. Because of this situation, proper troop education, full indoctrination, and comprehensive training according to UN standards are becoming increasingly important.

Conclusions on Independent Variables. In spite of the variables discussed above that characterize the operations being conducted in Haiti, it was possible to conclude that the achievements to date in that country have been successful since it has been possible to apply accepted measures and procedures that have customarily ensured the effective use of combined forces.

Most of the successes achieved are the result of some specific measures taken, such as a single top command on the basis of an integrated staff that has representatives of all the forces to coordinate harmoniously and to actuate personnel and resources; the use of procedures that have been standardized by the United Nations and are common to all the participating forces; and lastly, the training of forces in training centers that prepared them based on a common doctrine, using up-to-date UN procedures.

As a result, the international community, the United Nations,[17] and the government of Chile have made a positive evaluation of the achievement of the objectives set forth in UN Security Council Resolution No. 1529, which created this Multinational Interim Force.

POSSIBLE RATINGS TO EVALUATE EFFECTIVENESS OF COMBINED FORCES IN PEACEKEEPING OPERATIONS

The actions of the military forces participating in any UN peacekeeping operation are regulated by a mandate from that international organization that clearly defines the task to be performed. Accordingly, the simplest way of measuring the effectiveness of the participating combined forces could be to verify the degree of overall achievement of these tasks. If they are all fully achieved, the efficiency of the forces, in principle at least, could have been total.

However, the above rating formula is complicated when the security factor is added, which is logically the essential requirement to be met. In any peacekeeping operation, casualties in the forces or among the local population take away from the effectiveness of the overall process, even if all the assigned tasks are performed.

Considering the security and risk factors, we find some of the principal differences between peacekeeping operations and the operations of a conventional war. In the latter, in qualified cases, the forces involved can accept some calculated risks and, in extreme situations, even some degree of insecurity that could result in casualties among themselves, which in peacekeeping operations is not acceptable. In addition, in any peacekeeping operation the safety of the forces themselves must be compatible with that of the individuals receiving humanitarian aid, all without losing sight of the achievement of the many tasks assigned in the respective mandate.

If we take as an example the simple activity of distributing humanitarian aid by the forces, we could conclude—erroneously—that it should not present any risk for the troops delivering the aid or for the individuals receiving it. However, the experiences registered in Haiti and in other operations indicate that in many such cases, confrontations, fights, and major disturbances can occur among the people receiving the aid, even including aggression against those attempting to perform this humanitarian act. Only if the distribution ends up as an orderly and peaceful act in which there is no damage among the forces or the population receiving aid can this task be considered successfully carried out.

Accordingly, and based on just this example, the best way of measuring the performance of the forces could be by quantifying the elements distributed and the real benefit to the population, versus any damage, injuries, or casualties among the forces or the recipients of the aid. Similarly, the other tasks assigned to the participating forces could be analyzed, whether they are aimed at contributing to the processes of the country's political, social, or economic reconstruction, the disarmament, demobilization, and reinsertion of the groups in conflict, or others.

For all of the above reasons, some management indexes could be designed to rate the degree of effectiveness achieved by the forces in performing their tasks. These indexes could measure achievements through percentages. What percentage of the local armed population turned over its weapons? What percentage of the population received food, medicine, or other aid? What percentage of the children regularly attends school? Each of these indexes would be weighed with the degree of physical security achieved during the action.

RECOMMENDATIONS TO IMPROVE OPERATIONAL AND SECURITY FACTORS IN THIS TYPE OF OPERATION

Experiences in all types of armed conflicts indicate that from a tactical standpoint, the leader of an operation must have reconnaissance units that help determine and evaluate in advance all the needs for forces and the risks associated with a mission or task. Furthermore, the experience now existing with peacekeeping operations throughout the world teaches something very similar. No mission of this type should be initiated without first having all the necessary preliminary information, which should be the product of reconnaissance and complete analysis aimed at determining the situation, the conditions, and the specific scenario in which the peacekeeping actions will be conducted.

With respect to political decisionmakers and the differences involved in each case, experience in the tactical field can also be applied. Since they must evaluate the situation in detail before deciding on possible participation in a peacekeeping operation, they could use the following agencies and people to supply them with the preliminary information they require: their diplomatic representatives to the United Nations; those of the country that would be the subject of the mission; those in other countries that would also participate in the mission; and those in countries that have previously participated in similar missions.

In addition to the above, it is deemed appropriate in this scheme for each of the aforesaid diplomatic representations to have, or to temporarily assign, the military advisors necessary to make a preliminary estimate of the types of forces it is advisable to use, their size, and the resources that should be contributed by each armed institution individually. In this manner, the initial political analysis would have specialized military advice.

It would also be advisable for political decisionmakers to have a sort of permanent national early warning system to identify in advance the crises in which the country could be involved or participate. This system should have thorough knowledge of the state's capabilities, policies, forces, and resources that could most appropriately respond in order for them to act proactively.

Some tools should be used for the review and analysis of each situation that help define the future scenario in which action would be taken, such as forecasting, and there should be multidisciplinary analysis teams composed of civilian and military personnel. In the same vein, it is also advisable to develop the capabilities for preparing national manuals to be used in peace-keeping operations. These documents could include the national policies and doctrines that are most consistent with those of the United Nations, since such documents are indispensable for achieving instruction and training objectives in keeping with international standards and being able to operate in joint and combined peacekeeping operations according to the concept of interoperability.

For each peacekeeping operation, it is advisable to state in a very transparent fashion the assignment of economic resources it will require. It is also important for these funds not to come exclusively from the budget of the defense sector, since this is a commitment of the state in which not only its military forces are involved.

It is also advisable in all cases to have strong media support that truthfully and accurately reports on what is happening, so that citizens can be informed how important it is for their country to participate in and contribute to this type of operation.

Lastly, it is deemed to be a fundamental responsibility of the political leader to promote the necessary public commitment in the country's society for the country's participation in peacekeeping operations. It is emphasized that this is a political responsibility, because the task exceeds the authority of defense since it is a national commitment that requires decisions at the highest level, major organization, and strong media support.

CONCLUSIONS

The peacekeeping operations in Haiti are the largest combined effort that Chile has carried out with joint military and civilian forces with other countries of the region. In the particular case of Chile, never before has the country committed this amount of human and material resources in a single peace-keeping operation.

United Nations Resolution 1529 of February 29, 2004, creating the MIFH, ordered that Chile respond within a very short time to deploy its forces, a situation that required considerable effort and served to evidence the rapid deployment capabilities of Chile's standby forces, its joint planning capability, and, more importantly, the quality of the training being provided by its recently inaugurated Joint Training Center for Peacekeeping Operations.

Later, the mandate of April 30, 2004, that generated MINUSTAH, ordering an additional deployment of forces for 6 months starting June 1, created the conditions to relieve the forces from the United States, Canada, and France, and replace them with other, mainly regional, forces. These forces are under the military command of a Brazilian general, and their political leader is a Chilean civilian. This fact, which might seem unimportant, had historical significance since it entailed the added value of cementing better foundations for regional cooperation and integration and better political and military understanding between the Latin American countries that are participating in the operation.

With respect to both UN missions, there is no doubt that to date they have been successful and that the varied experiences gained should be followed fully and in detail by the regional and international community as the operation progresses. Among the preliminary conclusions that can be drawn from this case, the following can be stated:

- The United Nations Stabilization Mission in Haiti is the first UN peacekeeping operation carried out in Haiti with such extensive participation by regional forces.
- The forces from the regional countries have varying degrees of experience in this type of operation, but the case of Haiti will certainly increase that experience and at the same time improve interoperability with a view to future operations of this type.
- The decision to participate with forces in Haiti is legitimate because it is a response to a UN mandate. For Chile, the decision to participate is an act that reflects the full exercise of its sovereignty and the defense and foreign policies of its government.
- In the recent past, Haiti has been the subject of repeated UN peacekeeping operations that have not achieved satisfactory and stable results in matters of internal order; nor have permanent solutions been reached to improve the quality of life of its population, not to mention the conditions necessary to better the country's future development.
- To date, the Haitian population has demonstrated an adequate degree of acceptance of the participating regional forces, or at least has been more receptive than in previous interventions. This acceptance inspires some degree of optimism about the possible permanent benefits the operation could bring to the country.
- Everything seems to indicate that this peacekeeping operation will have to be expanded over time by a new mandate. It is estimated that the new time period established could extend for several years if there is a desire to substantially improve the living conditions of the population and create the foundations for social and economic development that is sustainable over time.

NOTES
[1] Michelle Bachelet Jeria, National Defense Minister of Chile, speech to Chilean contingent of UN Interim Peacekeeping Force to Haiti, Santiago, March 3, 2004.
[2] Michelle Bachelet Jeria, *Diario La Tercera*, September 8, 2004.

3 Juan Carlos Salgado Brocal, Division General, National Defense Chief of Staff, "Experiences of a Challenge and Lessons Learned," seminar on Haiti at the Army War College, Santiago, July 14, 2004.

4 Maria Soledad Alvear, Foreign Affairs Minister of Chile, speech in *La Nacion*, October 29, 2002.

5 1980 Political Constitution of Chile (Santiago: Editorial Jurídica de Chile, January 12, 2000), 44.

6 Ibid., 31, 35.

7 National Defense Ministry, Under Secretariat of War, Supreme Decree No. 94, 1996.

8 Ministry of Defense, *Book of National Defense of Chile* (Santiago: Navy Press, 1997), 46.

9 Claudia Fuentes, "The Human Security Network from Lysoen to Santiago," in *Seguridad Humana: Conflict Prevention and Peace* (Chile: Flacso, 2002), 101–104.

10 See the full text of Supreme Decrees No. 94 of November 6, 1996, and No. 68 of October 14, 1999, from the National Defense Ministry's Under Secretariat of War, which state the national policy for the participation of the Chilean State in peacekeeping operations.

11 National Defense Staff, press release, "Ambassador Valdes met with the National Defense Minister," Santiago, August 11, 2004.

12 National Defense Ministry, Under Secretariat of War, Supreme Decree No. 2200/114, creating the Joint Center for Peacekeeping Operations of Chile, July 15, 2002.

13 National Defense Staff, Report Number 1, Executive Summary, Chile Haiti Report, Santiago, September 2004.

14 "Lagos and Lula point out the Region's presence in Haiti," *Diario la Nacion*, August 23, 2004.

15 Ministry of Defense, *Book of National Defense of Chile* (Santiago: Morgan Impresores, 2002), 84–86.

16 See the beginning of this chapter (section entitled "Chile and Peacekeeping Operations: A Brief History") for a discussion of the economic importance that international security aspects have for Chile.

17 See the Secretary-General's April 16, 2004, report to the Security Council, S/2004/300.

Chapter Six

Brazil: Peacekeeping and the Evolution of Foreign Policy

Eugenio Diniz

T he purpose of this chapter is to explain and analyze from available sources some aspects of the United Nations Stabilization Mission in Haiti (*Mission des Nations Unies pour la Stabilisation en Haïti*, or MINUSTAH).[1] The factors selected for analysis here are those that the author feels have not received sufficient attention, those whose weightier consequences have not yet been realized, or those on which the author disagrees with the prevailing view.

The first section addresses Brazil's decision to approve, participate in, and lead the MINUSTAH. Looking at this decision in the overall context of the evolution of Brazil's foreign policy, instead of doing it as a separate issue, provides a different view of the reasons that led Brazil to such decisionmaking. This is therefore the longest section of the paper.

The political process followed to implement this decision is then described, emphasizing the controversial points raised in the National Congress. The description reveals a clearly hierarchical, top-down decision, but one that was made democratically through the appropriate channels.

The third section reviews some other objectives of the mission itself, not necessarily of the Brazilian government, once again emphasizing the most controversial points. A fourth section analyzes a point that the author regards as very important and poorly highlighted, which could be a key innovation in the conduct of military operations in Brazil. Lastly, the final comments summarize the results yielded by the research.

UNDERSTANDING THE DECISION

At first glance, Brazil's decision to participate in and lead MINUSTAH, created by United Nations (UN) Resolution 1542 of April 30, 2004, may appear easy to understand. The Brazilian government has a clear desire to obtain a permanent seat on the UN Security Council and, although Brazilian diplomatic officials do not publicly associate Brazil's participation in the mission and the goal of a permanent seat on the council, diplomats from other countries have stated in the press that participation is the litmus test of Brazil's candidacy for the permanent seat.[2] On the other hand, military authorities and defense ministry officials are less reluctant to connect the two issues.[3] And in the national congress, leaders such as Deputy Professor Luizinho, the government's leader in the chamber of deputies, clearly and explicitly do associate the two issues.[4]

In addition, Lins da Silva states that in 2000, Brazilian exports to Haiti amounted to $17.2 million, while total imports stood at $46,000. In view of the initial cost estimate of approximately $50 million to $70 million for the mission, the idea of an economic motivation is obviously not consistent. Moreover, to make the mission financially feasible, the Brazilian government had to amend the law on Brazilian soldiers' pay in missions abroad, to bring it in line with the amounts paid by the United Nations.[5] The Brazilian government, however, was clearly expecting to minimize the financial loss entailed in the mission, which refutes any expectation of immediate or direct economic gains. Therefore, both the size of the Haitian economy and the initially expected costs obviously belie the assumption that Brazil aimed to achieve *direct* economic gains from its participation in MINUSTAH or that this expectation could have prompted Brazil's decision.

Brazil's decision would therefore appear to be a direct, linear, and consistent consequence of a general objective of Brazil's foreign policy. Nevertheless, a more thorough analysis reveals a delicate series of comings and goings, seemingly inconsistent decisions, and enhanced emphasis on interpretive subtleties suggesting that the decision was far more complex than it appeared at first glance. For instance, although Brazil had voted in favor of Resolution 1529 of February 29, 2004, which created the Multinational Interim Force, it did not agree to participate in that force, apparently because it felt that the resolution would have created a peace *enforcement* mission (under Chapter VII of the United Nations Charter); Brazil would only agree to participate in a peace*keeping* mission (one under Chapter VI of the UN Charter) at a later time[6] to be established by Resolution 1542. The trouble is that in this resolution, too, the Security Council says it is acting under Chapter VII. The interpretation of the Brazilian government is that there is no inconsistency. In Resolution 1529, the reference to the fact of the Security Council "acting under Chapter VII" of the Charter is already made in the preamble to the Resolution, whereas in Resolution 1542 this reference to Chapter VII of the Charter is made only in paragraph 7 which would indicate, in the interpretation of the Brazilian government, that only this paragraph of Resolution 1542 is based on Chapter VII and not the whole resolution. According to this interpretation, therefore, MINUSTAH would not be based on Chapter VII and would be a peacekeeping operation.

On the other hand, looking at the decision in the broader context of Brazilian foreign policy suggests that although there are no expectations of economic benefits *directly* deriving from its participation in MINUSTAH, this decision is perfectly consistent with a redefinition of Brazil's foreign policy that took place in the late 1980s and the early 1990s, in order to face the economic problems prevalent at that time.

It is argued here, however, that Brazil's decision to participate in and to lead the United Nations Stabilization Mission in Haiti must be understood in the general context of the evolution of Brazil's foreign policy and its redefinition beginning in the 1990s. The remainder of this section will provide a brief retrospective of Brazil's multilateral insertions, including peacekeeping missions, and an equally brief overview of Brazil's reshaping of its international economic relations, and particularly the challenges in the Americas. The continuities and changes introduced by the government of President Luís Inácio Lula da Silva will be identified, and the conclusions about Brazil's objectives in connection with MINUSTAH, which to a certain extent differ from the position of Brazilian officials and the current understanding in Brazil, will be explained.

Brazil: Diplomacy, Multilateralism, Peacekeeping Missions

Regarding multilateral arrangements and institutions, Brazil's diplomatic posture is characterized over time by ambiguity and ambivalence, in an attempt to reconcile rival parameters, and also in historical terms by a fluctuation between conflicting positions and viewpoints.

Since the early 20th century, Brazilian diplomacy has been dictated by efforts to improve the country's scope of international operations. Since that time, the predominant position in Brazilian diplomatic circles has been that Brazil would benefit vastly from the effective implementation and effect of international law. In addition to the defense of international law, other traditional principles of Brazilian diplomacy may be related to this position: nonintervention in the domestic affairs of states, the defense of the peaceful settlement of international disputes, and emphasis on general disarmament. Although it is admitted that general disarmament cannot be expected soon, Brazilian diplomacy is reluctant to accept initiatives that in its view would push it even farther into the future. For a long time, there was still an emphasis on decolonization, which for obvious reasons was abandoned, and has more recently been replaced by an emphasis on democracy.

Another permanent aspect of Brazil's diplomatic posture that has survived many administrations is the effort to emphasize concern for involvement in the international political agenda, which is easily understandable for a medium-sized country that sees itself as having great potential and has so many social problems to be faced and solved. There is a persistent concern about exposing what are regarded as international political obstacles to the development of poor countries, as well as mechanisms, institutions, or behaviors that tend to perpetuate underdevelopment.

However, there was not a single way to implement these concerns. So, since the early 20th century, Brazil's foreign policy has been fluctuating between two postures, which some analysts identify as *Americanist* and *globalist*. The *Americanist* posture is characterized by the perception that an increase in Brazil's scope of international operation and the solution of its constant concerns would be maximized by a closer political rapprochement to the United States, except for obvious differences on specific issues. At times, political and academic debate rather inappropriately called this posture an "automatic alignment" with the United States. The *globalist* posture is characterized by the opposite belief: that Brazil's scope of action and international interests would be more easily achieved through a broad diversification of its political relationships. It is this combination of elements that generates the aforesaid ambiguity concerning multilateral arrangements and institutions: on several occasions, it was felt that they would sanction situations that would depart from Brazil's international objectives.

When the United Nations was created, Brazil's demand for a permanent seat on the Security Council was blocked by opposition from the United Kingdom and the Soviet Union. However, it was a nonpermanent member of the organization's first Security Council. Between January 1946 and December 1968, Brazil was a nonpermanent member of the Security Council 5 times and was a member for 10 of the Council's 22 years.[7]

After that, Brazil was absent from the council for nearly 20 years. This period coincides with the climate of distrust that prevailed in Brazilian diplomatic circles toward multilateral organizations, which were seen as instruments of the "freeze of world power,"[8] in the words of influential ambassador Araújo Castro. Brazilian involvement in international organizations during this period was also characterized by a strong emphasis on development and the reduction of inequalities between countries. Brazilian diplomacy was then seeking to maximize its international autonomy and influence by distancing itself from the superpowers and from organizations that it felt contributed to preserving their contrasting situation, and by implementing a very active international posture, particularly toward developing countries. Brazilian foreign policy analysts usually refer to this period as the search for "autonomy through distance,"[9] with the general topic of the defense of international law always permeating all of Brazil's diplomatic activities.

In the late 1980s, this posture began to change. Events in the former Soviet Union and soon after in Eastern Europe were signaling a substantive shift in the international political dynamic, and eventually in the international political structure itself. This perception coincided with the gradual awareness of the phenomenon of globalization, and in the domestic political sphere with the awareness of the weakness of a development policy characterized by strongly protectionist features. Thus began the rethinking of Brazil's international involvements.

A first noticeable shift in Brazil's foreign policy took place in the 1990s in the form of intensified Brazilian action in multilateral organizations, which had ceased to be seen as instruments to perpetuate the political dominance of the powers and came to be viewed as an opportunity to increase Brazil's scope of operations, including with regard to the powers—a posture that analysts called "autonomy by participation"[10] or "autonomy by integration."[11] In fact, one of the first signs of this posture shift was Brazil's return to the UN Security Council in January 1988 through December 1989. Since that time, Brazil has returned to the Security Council for three more periods: January 1993 to December 1994, January 1998 to December 1999, and January 2004 to December 2005. Moreover, since the early 1990s, Brazil has reiterated its aim of obtaining a permanent seat on the Security Council in the wake of a UN reformulation process, which at that time had begun to be seen as necessary.

However, this new presence in the United Nations does not take place uncritically, nor does it imply any abandonment of the traditional reservations of Brazilian diplomacy. Two points in particular are worthy of note: continuing opposition to any posture or attitude implying any degree of relativization of the principle of nonintervention in the domestic affairs of other countries; and insistence that the issues of development and the reduction of inequalities between countries should be dealt with inside the United Nations, like peace and security issues.

These reservations can be seen in the reactions of some diplomats to the "Agenda for Peace" of Secretary-General Boutros Boutros-Ghali. On the one hand, there were statements in favor of an "Agenda for Development."[12] On the other hand, Brazil expressed strong reservations about the idea of peace enforcement operations based on Chapter VII of the UN Charter, preferring peacekeeping operations with the consent of the parties. In the case of the former, Brazil has always insisted that they be set up multilaterally, with a broad consensus, emphasizing that such a peace would be fragile if the issues that, according to Brazilian diplomacy, were the causes of the conflict—underdevelopment, poverty, and social and economic inequalities—were not dealt with. Even with all this in view, there is still concern about improper intervention in domestic affairs and the potential use of such mechanisms by a major power, in particular the United States, as instruments of unilateral policies.[13]

These considerations explain an apparent paradox. As pointed out by Brigagão and Proença Jr.,[14] although up to 2002 Brazil had participated in 26 of the 54 UN peacekeeping missions since 1956—including the first, in Suez—

it only participated in 11 out of 37 since 1989. In other words, between 1956 and 2002, Brazil participated in 48.15 percent of the UN peacekeeping missions; between 1956 and 1989, Brazil participated in 15 of 17, or 88.24 percent. But between 1989 and 2002, exactly during the period when Brazil resumed a strong and intense commitment to the UN, even demanding a permanent presence on the Security Council, it participated in only 29.73 percent of peacekeeping missions.[15] Naturally, the theory that this reduced commitment to peacekeeping missions could have weakened Brazil's claim for a permanent seat on the UN Security Council cannot be discounted.

The fact is that the increased number of UN peacekeeping missions since 1989 coincides with the appearance of enforcement-type actions based on Chapter VII of the UN Charter, which Brazil intensely opposes. In fact, Brazil only began participating in missions with an enforcement mandate starting in 1999, in East Timor. This is indeed symptomatic: in fact, mainly since 1989, one characteristic of Brazil's participation in peacekeeping missions is that they take place in Latin American or Portuguese-speaking countries. Brazil clearly prefers participation in areas it considers to be a priority for foreign policy.

Of course, this preference cannot be directly tied to economic or trade interests, at least not exclusively. Although economic and trade relations with Angola, for example, have intensified, this intensification can hardly be attributed to Brazil's presence in UN missions in that country. The scale of the economies involved would in no case justify the effort; moreover, the effort to create markets for Brazilian products and services has been made at the global scale—except, as stated above, for the strong emphasis on Latin America. Even in this latter case, there does not appear to be any parallel between Brazil's trade balance and the countries where Brazil has participated in peacekeeping missions (basically Central American countries, in addition to Peru and Ecuador).

Looking at the process of rapprochement to the aforesaid countries, which was accelerated in the 1990s, one can see the clear relationship to Brazil's long-term trade and economic goals and the connection, albeit indirect, between Brazil's participation in peacekeeping operations—including MINUSTAH—and its other foreign policy priorities.

Trading Pressures and Rapprochement with Latin America

Another key feature of Brazil's new international posture since the 1990s has been its accelerated and intense political rapprochement with Latin America. Aware of the need to open up its markets to international competition, but afraid to do so in a disorderly way detrimental to the country's economy; pressed by the Americas Initiative (AI) launched by President George H.W. Bush, which would later become the proposal for a Free Trade Area of the

Americas (FTAA); and in line with the provisions of the Brazilian constitution stating that Brazil "shall seek the economic, political, social, and cultural integration of the peoples of Latin America, aiming at the formation of a Latin American community of nations,"[16] Brazil initiated an intensive process of rapprochement with the countries of that region, in a highly proactive exercise of political initiative.

Actually, this rapprochement process had earlier roots. In 1979, after the dispute of the Corpus and Itaipu hydro powerplants was settled, and following the Falklands/Malvinas War in 1982, a rapprochement process began between Brazil and Argentina, formerly historical rivals on the continent.[17] This process, which involved accelerated mechanisms to create mutual trust on issues such as defense and security and particularly on nuclear matters, resulted in several bilateral cooperation treaties and a multilateral leap with the 1991 Treaty of Asuncion, which created the Common Market of the Southern Cone (MERCOSUR), that originally included Brazil, Argentina, Paraguay, and Uruguay.[18]

The accelerated creation of MERCOSUR reflected the movement required of Brazilian diplomacy in the early 1990s. The awareness of the failure of the previous development model demanded a new opening to foreign trade—which implied the urgent creation of new markets for Brazilian products in order to prevent an anticipated growth of imports from leading to disastrous deficits for Brazil's trade balance. At the time, Latin America seemed to be the most obvious and promising area, since as Vaz pointed out, in the 1970s and the early 1980s, the growth rate of interregional trade was higher than the growth rate of international trade.[19] However, the Americas Initiative announced by President Bush in June 1990 could destroy this opportunity because the promise of better access to the U.S. market could be very tempting to Brazil's Latin American neighbors, which would reduce Brazil's trade negotiation capabilities. In fact, the proposal for a Free Trade Area embedded in the AI was seen as a set of bilateral agreements between the United States and each individual country of the region.[20] This concern was reinforced by the almost simultaneous occurrence of the announcement of the AI and the negotiations between Mexico and the United States (which, with the inclusion of Canada later, would lead to the creation of the North American Free Trade Agreement, which took effect on January 1, 1994).[21]

The Americas Initiative did not succeed, but the idea of a Free Trade Area of the Americas resurfaced at the first Presidential Summit of the Americas held in Miami in December 1994. Once again, the proposal was coldly received by Brazil. Over time, the FTAA would become one of the most intense issues of all time in Brazil's public debate on foreign policy. Large national entities, such as the National Conference of Bishops of Brazil, supported informal plebiscites on the FTAA, and then-presidential candidate Luís

Inácio Lula da Silva said in 2002 that the FTAA would be more like a form of annexation than integration.[22]

The general belief that the FTAA would be detrimental to the country's interests led to a delay in its creation and implementation, and to joint initiatives that would improve Brazil's negotiation capabilities. The intensification of the creation of MERCOSUR was instrumental in this process, as was the signature of a Framework Interregional Cooperation Agreement between MERCOSUR and the European Community in December 1995.

However, this attitude of postponement underwent a change at the third Presidential Summit of the Americas held in Quebec in 2001. It began to become evident that Brazilian postponement would not affect the progress of the negotiations, so the worst situation for Brazil would not be the creation of the FTAA, but the creation of the FTAA without its presence, or without Brazil being able to ensure some of its interests in the negotiation. Moreover, it was beginning to be felt that not all segments of economic activity would be hurt by the creation of the FTAA; on the contrary, some of them would clearly benefit, as the costs of imported raw materials would drop. In the end, the alternatives that were considered throughout these years proved less promising than they appeared at first glance.[23]

So the new position in relation to the FTAA required Brazil to renew its negotiating effort and attempt to rebuild its bargaining power for the negotiations. It was no accident that the end of President Fernando Henrique Cardoso's administration was characterized by a newly intensified rapprochement with Latin America.

President Lula: Continuities and Changes

When President Luís Inácio Lula da Silva took office on January 1, 2003, Brazil's foreign policy seemed to be reiterating practically the same points of the immediately preceding period, but with a renewed assertiveness, in an attempt to leave behind what was seen as a defensive foreign policy posture of President Cardoso.[24]

First, in his inaugural address, President Lula stated that his foreign policy would be "guided by a humanist perspective," would be an "instrument for national development," and should "contribute to improving the living conditions of Brazilian women and men." Referring to the negotiations over the FTAA between MERCOSUR and the European Union and in the World Trade Organization, the president confirmed the fight against protectionism and the pursuit of the elimination of the "scandalous" farm subsidies of the developed countries, and of restrictions against exports of Brazilian industrial products, in that order. Then, he clearly stated that his government's top priority would be "to build a politically stable, prosperous, and united South America based upon ideals of democracy and social justice," emphasizing that this would call for "resolute action to revitalize the MERCOSUR," explicitly affirmed as "essentially a political blueprint" built on economic-trade foundations. Starting from MERCOSUR, and "provided we are invited and to the extent of our responsibilities," Brazil would be willing to contribute to various South American neighbors experiencing difficult situations "in order to find peaceful solutions to those crises based on dialogue, democratic principles, and the constitutional standards of each country." He extended this "commitment to concrete cooperation and permanent dialogue" to all the countries of Latin America.

Moreover, President Lula said that he intended to have a "mature partnership, based on reciprocal interest and mutual respect" with the United States; an interest in enhancing understanding and cooperation with developed countries, such as the European Union and its member countries and Japan; and the forging of closer ties with "large developing countries" like China, India, Russia, and South Africa. He also reaffirmed ties with the African continent.

Lastly, the president stated his intention to "stimulate the incipient elements of multipolarity of modern international life," defending the "democratization of international relations without hegemonies of any kind," giving value to multilateral organizations, "especially the United Nations," stating that Security Council resolutions must be fully complied with and, last of all, defending "a reformed Security Council, representing modern-day reality, with developed and developing countries of all the regions of the world among its permanent members."[25]

In general, the same points were reiterated in the inaugural address of foreign affairs minister Celso Amorim, also on January 1, 2003. Some emphases are worthy of note. First, the foreign minister said that Brazil would have "a foreign policy aimed at development and peace," in that order, thereby highlighting the importance of the issue of development. When referring to Africa, he expressly mentioned Angola and Mozambique, and in the same paragraph emphasized that he would promote "cooperation within the Community of Portuguese Language Countries, including its newest member, East Timor."

There are, therefore, clear signs of continuity—though stated in a very assertive way—and some significant nuances. The priority of the trade negotiations and intensive political activity stemming from MERCOSUR with the countries of Latin America is clearly stated, now with special emphasis on the closest neighbors in South America. Although the expression is not included in the inaugural addresses, after President Luís Inácio Lula da Silva took office, even "Brazil's leadership in South America" is clearly mentioned without eliciting any significant signs of displeasure from the neighbor countries. Ties with African and Portuguese-speaking countries are reemphasized as traditional areas of Brazil's political presence. And lastly, there is a reaffirmation of the political priority of the United Nations and its Security Council, reformulated to include "developing countries of all the regions of the world among its permanent members"—the Brazilian "code word" to claim a permanent seat on the council.

Brazil's Agreement to a Mission under Chapter VII

In the light of this retrospective, Brazil's decision to participate in—in this case, to lead—the United Nations Stabilization Mission in Haiti is easy to understand and almost perfectly consistent with the recent course of action of Brazil's foreign policy. Brazil understands that active participation in the United Nations is a core element in its quest for more political autonomy in the international arena, so much so that it asked for a reorganization of the UN in order to become a permanent member of its Security Council. This claim would have been weakened due to the reduction of Brazil's participation in the organization's peacekeeping missions, particularly in the period when Brazil's presence in the council was intensified—which critics might view as meaning that Brazil is seeking prestige but is not accepting responsibilities. From that point of view, Haiti would appear to be a unique opportunity: it is a situation with high political visibility in a region of high priority for Brazil's foreign policy, which could leverage, or at least in a certain way legitimate, the desired Brazilian leadership in South America. By leading forces in the service of the UN, Brazil would coordinate the South American continent's response to a crisis in a neighbor region. As explained above, this recognition of Brazilian leadership in South America is perceived as crucial to the effort of political coordination on trade negotiations, particularly in the case of the FTAA.

Argentina's acceptance of Brazilian leadership in MINUSTAH is thus not without significance. Argentina also aspires to a presence and a more active participation in the UN and in the Security Council and opposes the idea of Brazil being granted a permanent seat on the council. By expressing its consent to Brazilian leadership and agreement to send troops, Argentina could be signaling a policy shift in the direction of the Brazilian position. Although it cannot be confirmed, this Argentine acceptance could be regarded as a significant political result of the Brazilian government accepting the leadership of MINUSTAH.

So, contrary to what has been said, a clear link can be seen between Brazil's leadership of MINUSTAH and Brazilian economic interests. It is mathematically obvious that, when considered separately, the operation in Haiti represents more losses than gains; there could, however, be *indirect* economic gains, to the extent that the eventual recognition and acceptance of Brazil's political leadership in South America would permit or facilitate an effort of political coordination at the continental scale aimed at multilateral trade negotiations, mainly in the case of the FTAA. At least for the time being, though, it is not clear whether that consideration was effectively involved when the Brazilian government made the decision to join and lead MINUSTAH, or if it effectively impacted the decisionmakers' calculations.[26]

However, there is some inconsistency in Brazil's decision, having to do with the problems of the characteristics of MINUSTAH with respect to the degree of internal consent in Haiti. In fact, the frequent statements of former president Jean Bertrand Aristide that he was forced to leave, as well as recent armed actions attributed to the former president's supporters in the Lavalas Family party—with some soldiers in UN service being hit—together with Gerard Latortue's interim government's obvious difficulty in containing or repressing such actions, contradict the notion that MINUSTAH is a peacekeeping operation; it looks more and more like a peace enforcement mission. It was no accident that Resolution 1542, which created MINUSTAH on April 30, 2004, says that it is establishing the mission's mandate "under Chapter VII of the United Nations Charter." Clearly, this entails difficulties for the Brazilian government, which is strongly reluctant to accept operations based on Chapter VII. However, in spite of this difficulty, not accepting the leadership or not agreeing to participate in MINUSTAH could perhaps deal a deadly blow to Brazil's desire to obtain a permanent seat on the Security Council.[27]

It should be noted how potentially embarrassing this situation is for Brazil. On July 31, 1994, Resolution 940 was voted in the Security Council and was approved by 12 votes against 2 abstentions, Rwanda being absent. The abstentions were by China and, ironically, Brazil. The Brazilian government felt that the resolution should be based on Chapter VI.[28] This tense situation forced Brazilian authorities to make a significant rhetorical effort that systematically links the presence of UN forces in Haiti to a concomitant international commitment to face the causes of the Haitian conflict: hunger, poverty, and the fragility of democratic institutions.[29] Moreover, at least at the domestic level, the interpretation is being affirmed that MINUSTAH would be acting under Chapter VII only with respect to security provisions. Brazil's effort to differentiate Resolution 1542 from Resolution 940 is therefore quite clear.[30]

Brazilian diplomatic authorities therefore symptomatically tended to evade embarrassing questions, trying to justify participation based on regional solidarity and on humanitarian issues, distancing themselves from any political objective and discounting criticisms based on the former Haitian president's allegations that he was deposed. The Brazilian ambassador to the United Nations often referred to threats of bloodbaths before the departure of the former president and never referred to any advantage for Brazil resulting from approval of the resolutions or participation in the mission.[31] Even those who allude to possible political benefits insist on shading them, saying that nothing is guaranteed.[32] Moreover, Brazil also insists on the need to confront poverty, underdevelopment, and social inequalities in Haiti, and even manages to make its participation contingent on this confrontation.

The interpretive subtleties and the refusal to acknowledge possible benefits deriving from participation in MINUSTAH only seem to hide, although involuntarily and unconsciously, the feeling that in the Haiti episode, traditional principles of Brazil's diplomatic posture were given up or at least relativized—in the name of immediate political pragmatism and indirect trade pragmatism. From that standpoint, Brazilian participation and leadership in MINUSTAH could set an important and significant precedent for Brazilian diplomacy. We may be in the presence of a further shift in Brazil's foreign policy.[33]

THE DECISIONMAKING PROCESS[34]

Officially, Brazil's participation was the result of an invitation from French President Jacques Chirac on March 4, 2004. President Lula supposedly made the phone call to discuss his request to the French president to consider a proposal to make the International Monetary Fund's rules more flexible for emerging countries. However, on that occasion, President Chirac reportedly brought up the subject of the Haitian crisis and told President Lula that he would like to see Brazil assume the command of a UN peacekeeping force to be created in around 3 months. President Chirac supposedly also said that that was the wish of UN Secretary General Kofi Annan. President Lula reportedly then said that he had 1,100 available troops[35] who could participate in the future mission.[36]

Yet 3 days before that, on March 1, 2004, Brazil had already expressed interest in participating in the mission that would be characterized as a peacekeeping mission to replace the Multinational Interim Force created by Resolution 1529 of February 29, 2004—although on that occasion there was not a public statement of the interest in commanding the mission. At the time, it was said that the final decision would be taken by the foreign ministry and the defense ministry "in the next few days."[37] The invitation of President Chirac, therefore, seems to have stemmed from a prior Brazilian statement—especially since President Lula was able to immediately inform President Chirac of the availability of 1,100 troops, which indicates that the defense ministry and the foreign affairs ministry had already been consulted.

This distinction is important because it shows that Brazil's decision was not the result of any embarrassment that could have resulted from a refusal to participate in the mission from the very party seeking a more active role in the UN Security Council. On the contrary, the process seems to reveal a prior Brazilian initiative, a clear interest in participating, in spite of the difficulties discussed above, especially regarding the Chapter VII problem.

The defense ministry calculated the costs of the operation, while the ministry of planning, budget, and management evaluated the release of an extraordinary credit to cover the expenses—even with the expectation of a partial reimbursement of expenses by the United Nations.[38] On the other hand, although there is no public reference to consulting the finance ministry, it is almost impossible for that consultation not to have taken place. Both the political centrality of the finance ministry in the current administration and the top importance given to macroeconomic stability practically make it impossible for decisions of such magnitude to be made without consulting the finance ministry. It is also highly probable that there were consultations with the justice ministry and/or the attorney general on legal aspects of the issue, although there are no public references to the subject.

The proposal met with resistance even in some sectors of President Lula's Labor Party. Some lawmakers and intellectuals emphasized the accusations made by Haiti's former president and said that Brazil would be legitimizing "Bush's imperialist interventionist policy."[39] Nevertheless, on May 6, 2004, President Lula sent the Chamber of Deputies a presidential message (MSC 205/2004) requesting authorization to send 1,200 troops to Haiti.[40] The message was debated in a joint session of the foreign affairs and national defense committees and the constitution and justice committee and sent to the plenary session for voting. Before the debates and voting, on May 12, 2004, Foreign Affairs Minister Celso Amorim and then-Defense Minister José Viegas Filho held a public hearing in a joint session of the foreign affairs and national defense committees of the chamber of deputies and the federal senate.[41] During the debate, the opposition raised criticisms of the fact that Brazil was going to help keep the order in a foreign country, because Brazil also had serious public security problems; it was also theorized that Brazil was going to be used to defend U.S. and French interests; and displeasure was expressed about the fact that the UN colors were painted on the equipment before approval by the congress.[42]

Soon after, the plenary session voted on the request for urgent status for the presidential message. On the first vote, urgent status was rejected due to a request for a quorum check by deputy Fernando Gabeira, who opposed sending a contingent because Haiti would be in the area of influence of the United States, Canada, and France and the money to be spent in the mission should be spent in Brazil.[43] However, in the following session on the same day, urgent status was approved.[44]

On the following day, the matter passed a symbolic vote—without recording individual votes—after an agreement between party leaders. The Liberal Front Party, the Brazilian Social Democracy Party, the Democratic Labor Party from the opposition, and the Socialist Popular Party and the Green Party from the government political group voted against approval of the measure based on the arguments stated above.[45] After approval by the plenary session, the message was converted into chamber of deputies bill 1280/2004 and forwarded to the federal senate. After being reviewed by the foreign affairs committee and the national defense committee of that legislative body, and already converted into (senate) legislative decree bill 568/2004, the bill was voted at the senate plenary session on May 19, 2004, and was approved by 38 votes in favor and 10 against. Thus, legislative decree 207 of May 19, 2004, was enacted, authorizing the sending of the contingent of 1,200 Brazilian troops to MINUSTAH.[46]

This is clearly a *top-down* decision of the Brazilian government, which faced and still faces opposition in political sectors and from Brazilian public opinion, particularly from some sectors within the president of the republic's party. However, it was a decision made according to absolutely normal procedures and following the proper institutional channels. Brazilian decisions on foreign policy are usually initiated in the executive branch and approved by the legislative branch, usually with little follow-up from areas of public opinion or even from the business world. From that point of view, sending a contingent to Haiti involved more attention and follow-up than usual. In other words, it was not an initiative generated outside of the federal executive branch.

OBJECTIVES OF THE MISSION[47]

The objectives of the mission, and particularly the military objectives, are in principle a result of the mandate established by Resolution 1542 and are stated in it. At any rate, the Brazilian troops were expected to perform routine patrol tasks, protecting hospitals and public places and protecting and supporting humanitarian activities.[48] The most controversial objective was the need to disarm groups and militias. The Brazilian press revealed an estimate of 25,000 armed Haitians who either were or were not linked to political groups.[49] In view of the precarious situation of the security services provided by the interim Haitian government, as reported by UN Secretary-General Kofi Annan on August 30, 2004,[50] the possibility of confrontation was high, and in principle it would increase with the approach of the deadline set by the national senior police council of the interim government for armed groups to cease to represent themselves as security forces. This deadline period would end on September 15, 2004, and if this activity did not cease, the interim government, backed by MINUSTAH, was expected to act.[51] Although the Secretary General had stated in his report that the Haitian authorities had been distancing themselves from this deadline, in late September and early October, armed violence was in fact seen at several locations in the country.

Finally, the Secretary-General's last report of November 18, 2004, pointed out a deterioration of the security situation, particularly in Port-au-Prince—where the Brazilian contingent was on duty. Members of MINUSTAH, including one Brazilian, had already been targets of hostile action. The creation of joint patrolling activities between MINUSTAH and the Haitian police could stir things up even more, and there may be confrontations where Brazilians cause Brazilian and Haitian casualties.

In any case, these were the tasks to be expected by the Brazilian contingent. In order to perform these tasks, Brazilian forces were deployed in Port-au-Prince, with a detachment in Hinche.[52] It is conjectured that participation in MINUSTAH might even serve as a kind of training for the Brazilian army for eventual action in public security emergencies in Brazil, which could be a sort of subsidiary and secondary military objective of MINUSTAH.[53]

UNITS FROM DIFFERENT FORCES UNDER A SINGLE COMMAND?

In the case of Brazil, the most interesting and potentially innovative point regarding the use of its armed forces in Haiti seems up to now to have escaped commentators. Since the forces are very sensitive about their mutual balance, the simultaneous use of two or three of them is an issue that shocks political sensibilities. This is reflected in a peculiarity of Brazilian military jargon. While the English term *combined* is generally used for operations involving allied armed forces, in Brazil the term *combinado* refers to the use of two or more Brazilian armed forces under a single command—which is more often expressed in English by the term *joint*. On the other hand, the term *conjunto* (joint) refers to the simultaneous use in a given military operation of two or three Brazilian armed forces, without the existence of a unified command.[54] This latter situation is the most frequent in the Brazilian forces except situations where a single force is used alone—and in fact there is a certain resistance to use of the term *combinado*.[55]

However, the composition of the Brazilian contingent in MINUSTAH is not ruled by the logic of the *conjunto* (joint) use (in the Brazilian meaning). That contingent is composed of the following:

- the Haiti Brigade (967 troops), basically composed of the 19th Motorized Infantry Battalion—which participated in the East Timor mission—plus two engineer squads from the 3d Combat Engineer Battalion, one communications squad from the Electronic Warfare Training Center, and one command company from the 8th Mechanized Cavalry Squadron.
- the Haiti Marine Corps Operating Group (245 marines), mainly composed of the 3d Marine Infantry Battalion (Paissandu Battalion), but also involving the Marine Corps Special Operations Battalion (Tonelero Battalion) of the Marine Corps Engineer Battalion, the Marine Corps Armored Battalion, and the Rio de Janeiro Marine Corps Command and Control Battalion.

So the Haiti brigade is composed of units of the Brazilian Army, while the Marines belong to the Brazilian navy. Nevertheless, the entire contingent will be under the command of Brazilian Army Brigadier General Américo Salvador de Oliveira. Although the possibility of there being some informal arrangement—with the Marine forces in practice being detached to a given area or position and operating there under autonomous command and planning—the possibility of an effectively *combinado* (combined) use (in the Brazilian meaning) of the Brazilian armed forces would for them be one of the most interesting results of MINUSTAH. The information available to date also indicates that the Brazilian army planned the land operations. This point should be highlighted for follow-up and assessment of the Brazilian contingent's performance in Haiti.[56]

FINAL COMMENTS

Brazil's decision to participate in and to lead the United Nations Stabilization Mission in Haiti reflects the difficulty of reconciling the historical parameters of Brazil's diplomatic posture. This difficulty is clearly manifest in the Brazilian government's creative interpretation of the relationship between Resolution 1542 of April 30, 2004, and Chapter VII of the United Nations Charter. Brazil's decision seems to be a break from the traditional understanding of Brazilian diplomacy, which was opposed to peace enforcement operations, in favor of the positive impacts expected from the activity in Haiti: first, with respect to an essential objective of current Brazilian foreign policy, a permanent seat on the United Nations Security Council; and second, Brazilian leadership in South America and the eventual impacts on the important trade negotiations that Brazil is involved in, which are perceived as crucial to the Brazilian economy. This decision would weaken the doctrinal, juristic image of Brazilian diplomacy and therefore requires a rhetorical effort of justification that does not appear to be entirely convincing, at least in some political circles. Eventually, leadership of MINUSTAH could reveal a shifting point in Brazilian foreign policy, but it is still too early to confirm this.

Although the sending of Brazilian forces was approved by the congress, the debate that took place there was more intense than usual when foreign policy issues were discussed. This indicates that, contrary to the conventional understanding, the congress is far more attentive to foreign policy and defense issues than usually imagined. Therefore, if Brazil's decision to lead MINUSTAH was in fact the first step in a more assertive Brazilian international posture concerning the use of force, and particularly regarding peace enforcement operations and greater tolerance with actions based on Chapter VII of the UN Charter, it is possible that in the future, the Brazilian government would face increasing difficulties with the legislative branch.

However, first of all, the very composition of the Brazilian contingent points to a significant innovation in the operation of the Brazilian armed forces, which is the existence of a single commander for units belonging to different and separate forces—the Army and, in the case of the Marine Corps, the Navy. This type of use—*combinado* (combined) in Brazilian jargon—may be in the process of being tested in Haiti. The result and the evaluation of this experience could entail significant consequences for the organization of Brazil's armed forces.

NOTES

1   I wish to express my thanks to Jorge Ramalho Rocha for his commitment in collaboration on this work, and also to John Fishel, Andres Saenz, Salvador Ghelfi Raza, Domício Proença Jr., Tiago Campos, Érico Esteves Duarte, Rafael Ávila, Mauro Mosqueira, Paulo Brinckmann, Jacqueline Muniz, Wilson Lauria, and Marco Cepik for having read and commented on it. I also wish to express my thanks to Mrs. Jaci Teixeira Caetano de Almeida, from the Under-secretariat of Information of the Senate General Secretariat, for her speediness and attention in providing information on the handling of the Presidential Message in the Federal Senate.

2   See, for example, Jamil Chade, "Missão no Haiti pode ajudar País no CS da ONU," *O Estado de São Paulo*, May 5, 2004, A–16.

3   See Dorival Bogoni, "Brazilian Participation in MINUSTAH," presented in Washington, DC, on December 3, 2004. In the answer to question 1, this objective is clearly mentioned.

4   Agência Câmara de Notícias, "Câmara analisa envio de soldados para o Haiti," *A Semana*, May 10, 2004. Available at: <http://www.camara.gov.br/internet/agencia/materias.asp?pk=49862&pesq=Haiti|>.

5   See Eduardo Scolese and André Soliani, "Brasil usa soldo para pagar missão no Haiti," *Folha de São Paulo*, May 13, 2004, A–15; Provisional Measure 187 of May 13, 2004, converted into Law 10.937 of August 12, 2004.

6   Eliane Oliveira, "Forças brasileiras só irão num segundo momento," *O Globo*, March 2, 2004, 27.

7   This ambiguity may also be observed in the sphere of the League of Nations. Brazil was involved since the first discussions of the League in 1919; but it was also the first country to abandon it in 1926, as a result of the admission of Germany; however, Brazil continued cooperating with it in several situations, even after having left. Similarly, Brazil opposed the criteria used to compose the League's Executive Council, considering that it would create a legal inequality between the states, contrary to the principles of international law; on the other hand, it yielded in order to become a provisional member of the first group that would make up the

council because of the prestige it would entail and the possibility of defending its interests; but it also attempted to become a permanent member of that council, thus acknowledging and sanctioning the very inequality that it had previously denounced. On Brazil in the League of Nations, see Eugenio Vargas Garcia, *O Brasil e a Liga das Nações (1919–1926): Vencer ou não perder* (Porto Alegre/Brasília: Editora da Universidade UFRGS/ Fundação Alexandre de Gusmão, 2000).

[8]   See J.A. Araújo Castro, "O Congelamento do Poder Mundial," in Rodrigo Amado (org.) and Araújo Castro (Brasília: Editora da Universidade de Brasília, 1982), 197–212.

[9]   See Gelson Fonseca, Jr., "Alguns aspectos da Política Externa Brasileira Contemporânea," in *A legitimidade e outras questões internacionais: poder e ética entre as nações* (São Paulo, Paz e Terra, 1998), 353–374; Tullo e Oliveira Vigevani and Marcelo Fernandes, A política externa brasileira na era FHC: um exercício de autonomia pela integração. Trabalho apresentado no 4º Encontro Nacional da Associação Brasileira de Ciência Política, 2004. Accessed on August 4, 2004 at <http://www.cienciapolitica.org.br/ RI4-Tullo%20Vigevani%\20e%20Marcelo%20Fernandes%20de%20 Oliveira.pdf>.

[10] Fonseca, Jr.

[11] Vigevani e Oliveira.

[12] For example, see Fonseca, Jr.

[13] About the Brazilian vision on peace and security in the United Nations, see Valérie de Campos Mello, "Paz e Segurança na ONU: a Visão do Brasil" in Clóvis Brigagão and Domício Proença Jr., *O Brasil e o Mundo: Novas Visões* (Rio de Janeiro: Francisco Alves, 2002), 163–185.

[14] Clóvis Brigagão and Domício Proença Jr., *Concertação Múltipla: a inserção internacional de segurança do Brasil* (Rio de Janeiro: Francisco Alves, 2002), 118–125.

[15] Ibid.

[16] Article 4, sole paragraph of the Constitution of the Federal Republic of Brazil.

[17] On the rapprochement between Brazil and Argentina, see Sonia de Camargo and José Maria Vazquez Ocampo, *Autoritarismo e Democracia na Argentina e Brasil: uma década de política exterior (1973–1984)* (São Paulo: Convívio. Col. Política e Estratégia, 1988).

[18] On the creation of MERCOSUR, see Alcides Costa Vaz, *Cooperação, Integração e Processo Negociador: a Construção do Mercosul* (Brasília: Instituto Brasileiro de Relações Internacionais—IBRI, 2002).

[19] Ibid., 74.

[20] See José Augusto Guilhon Albuquerque, "A ALCA na política externa

brasileira," *Política Externa* 10, no. 2 (September/October/November 2001), 7–20.

[21] Vaz, 103.

[22] This argument changed after President Luís Inácio Lula da Silva took office.

[23] In general lines, we follow the explanation of Albuquerque, 15–18.

[24] See, for example, Alcides Costa Vaz, *O Governo Lula: uma nova política exterior?* Brasília, 2003.

[25] Inaugural address of President Luís Inácio Lula da Silva, January 1, 2003.

[26] For a different view, compare with the answer to question 4 as stated in Bogoni, "Brazilian Participation in MINUSTAH."

[27] As President Luís Inácio Lula da Silva said in his speech at the 59th UN General Assembly on September 21, 2004: "This is the way Brazil and other countries of Latin America have responded to the call of the UN to contribute to the stabilization of Haiti. Those who defend new paradigms in international relations could not be left out in the face of a concrete situation."

[28] See Carlos Eduardo Lins da Silva, "Futebol, paz e riscos para o Brasil no Haiti," *Política Externa* 13, no. 2 (September/October/November 2004), 79.

[29] See, for example, "Speech of President of the Republic Luiz Inácio Lula da Silva at the commencement ceremony," given at Palácio do Itamaraty on April 20, 2004; "Speech of President of the Republic Luiz Inácio Lula da Silva at the farewell ceremony of the troops participating in the Haiti peacekeeping mission," given at Brasilia Air Base on May 31, 2004; and the "Speech of President of the Republic Luiz Inácio Lula da Silva at the opening ceremony of the XVIII Group of Rio Summit," given in Rio de Janeiro on November 4, 2004.

[30] See, for example, Ronaldo Sardenberg, "Política Multilateral e Nações Unidas." A lecture presented at the Institute of Advanced Studies of the University of Sao Paulo, on August 17, 2004. Transcription available at <http://www.usp.br/iea/sardenberg.html>.

[31] See Sardenberg; and also Helena Celestino, "Corpo a corpo: Ronaldo Sardenberg," *O Globo*, March 10, 2004, 33.

[32] See, for example, statements of General Augusto Heleno: Tânia Monteiro, "Batalhão gaúcho comandará missão no Haiti," *O Estado de São Paulo*, March 6, 2004, A–20.

[33] Compare the position stated here with Bogoni, "Brazilian Participation in MINUSTAH," response to question 4.

[34] A general discussion of the Brazilian decisionmaking process for peace-keeping operations can be found in André Matheus e Souza and Beatriz Zaccaron, A participação do Brasil em missões de manutenção de paz: o

caso do Haiti. Work presented at the II Interinstitutional Meeting of International Conjuncture Analysis, held in Rio de Janeiro on November 9–10, 2004. Bogoni's answer to question 2 can be found in the relevant legislation; see Bogoni, "Brazilian Participation in MINUSTAH." It should also be mentioned that the text of Complementary Law 97 of June 9, 1999, was amended by Complementary Law 97, of September 3, 2004.

[35] In the presidential message sent to the Chamber of Deputies on May 6, 2004, President Lula requests authorization to send 1,200 troops—100 more than originally proposed.

[36] See Martha Beck and Eliane Oliveira, "Brasil pode comandar missão no Haiti," *O Globo*, March 5, 2004, 38; Tânia Monteiro, "Brasil deve comandar força de paz no Haiti," *O Estado de São Paulo*, March 5, 2004, A–14; and Ricardo Westin, "Brasil poderá comandar força de paz no Haiti," *Folha de São Paulo*, March 5, 2004, A–12.

[37] Eliane Oliveira, "Forças brasileiras só irão num segundo momento," *O Globo*, March 2, 2004, 27.

[38] See Roberto Godoy, "Brasileiros devem entrar em combate no Haiti," *O Estado de São Paulo*, May 6, 2004, A–20.

[39] Klécio Santos, "Missão do Brasil no Haiti enfrenta resistência no PT," Zero Hora, April 21, 2004, available at <www.defesanet.com.br>.

[40] Agência Câmara de Notícias, "Câmara analisa envio de soldados para o Haiti," *A Semana*, May 10, 2004, available at <www.camara.gov.br>.

[41] Agência Câmara de Notícias, "Ministros defendem envio de soldados para o Haiti," *Tempo Real*, May 12, 2004, available at <www.camara.gov.br>.

[42] Eduardo Scolese and André Soliani, "Brasil usa soldo para pagar missão no Haiti," *Folha de São Paulo*, May 13, 2004, A–15.

[43] Denise Madueño, "Câmara rejeita urgência sobre envio de tropes," *O Estado de São Paulo*, May 13, 2004, A–18.

[44] Agência Câmara de Notícias, "Deputados aprovam urgência para tropas no Haiti," *Tempo Real*, May 12, 2004, available at <www.camara.gov.br>.

[45] Fernanda Krakovics et al., "Câmara aprova envio de soldados brasileiros ao Haiti," *Folha de São Paulo*, May 14, 2004, A–10; Denise Madueño, "Câmara aprova o envio de tropas ao Haiti," *O Estado de São Paulo*, May 14, 2004, A–15; Agência Câmara de Notícias, "Deputados aprovam envio de tropas ao Haiti," *Tempo Real*, May 13, 2004, available at <www.camara.gov.br>.

[46] I hereby publicly express my sincere gratitude.

[47] In Bogoni's answer to question 4, even more objectives are reported. See Bogoni, "Brazilian Participation in MINUSTAH."

[48] Jamil Chade, "Militares vão proteger hospitais e prédios públicos," *O Estado de São Paulo*, March 6, 2004, A–20; Roberto Godoy, "Brasileiros devem entrar em combate no Haiti," *O Estado de São Paulo*, May 6, 2004, A–20.

[49] Eduardo Nunomura, "'Aos poucos, eles se aproximam de nós,'" *O Estado*

de São Paulo, July 11, 2004, A–16.

[50] United Nations, "Interim Report of the Secretary-General on the United Nations Stabilization Mission in Haiti," August 30, 2004.

[51] Ibid., paragraph 11, page 3.

[52] In accordance with the last report of Secretary-General Kofi Annan, the Brazilian detachment in Hinche was replaced by a Nepalese detachment. See United Nations, Report of the Secretary-General on the United Nations Stabilization Mission in Haiti, November 18, 2004, paragraph 4.

[53] André Soliani and Eduardo Scolese, "Haiti é treino para ação no Rio, diz Exército," *Folha de São Paulo,* May 16, 2005, A–25. The news report brings the following comments of General Américo Salvador de Oliveira, the commander of Brazilian forces in Haiti: "As regards that [sending of troops to Haiti] entirely to guarantee law and order, it is an objective I would say is achievable." However, the text of the news report is of poor quality, sometimes distorting the understanding of statements that are, at best, ambiguous.

[54] In this respect, compare Domício Proença, Jr., and Eugenio Diniz, *Política de Defesa no Brasil: uma análise crítica* (Brasília: Ed. da UnB, 1998), 77–79, note 6.

[55] On June 23–28, 2003, Operation Timbó was conducted within the Amazon Combined Command, addressing the training of the armed forces in combined operations (in the Brazilian meaning of the term). However, it was not actually a combat operation. On Operation Timbó, see <http://www.exercito.gov.br/03Brafor/operacoes/op_timbo/timbo.htm>.

[56] Not even for this was the logic of *conjunto* (joint) use (in the Brazilian meaning) omitted. In fact, except for the presence of the Haiti Marine Corps Operating Group, the actions of the Navy and Air Force were focused on the transportation of troops, supplies, ammunition, and equipment to the theater of operations, thereby avoiding the need for a unified command.

Chapter Seven

Argentina: An Integrated View of Participation in Peacekeeping

Luciana Micha

O ver time, and after processes of internal adjustment and review, United Nations (UN) peacekeeping missions have become an effective instrument for the organization to accomplish its original mandate of keeping and strengthening peace and international security, primarily based on two main methods: peacekeeping operations and multinational and regional coalitions. Argentina has contributed in both ways by being an active participant.

Argentina's role in UN peacekeeping operations (PKO) began in 1958 with the deployment of the first national military observers in the United Nations Observer Group in Lebanon. Since the early 1990s, this participation has increased considerably, becoming a constant and one of the pillars of Argentina's foreign policy, and in general being consolidated into a state policy that has permitted greater inclusion of the country in the international agenda, particularly in the countries involved in such operations.

To date, approximately 24,000 Argentine nationals have participated in these operations, mainly members of the armed forces and the national gendarmes, as well as representatives of the naval prefecture and the federal police. Argentina has participated in 35 of the more than 50 peacekeeping operations created since 1948 and has been one of the major contributors of manpower. Its current presence in missions such as those in Haiti, Cyprus, Kosovo, the Middle East, the Democratic Republic of Congo, the Western Sahara, and East Timor, with more than 1,000 military and gendarme personnel, places Argentina among the top 15 contributors of troops for peacekeeping missions (see table 7–1).

UNITED NATIONS MISSION IN HAITI

After an electoral process of dubious validity for many national voters, tensions in Haiti triggered an armed conflict in late February 2004. The epicenter of the armed confrontations was the locality of Gonaives in northern Haiti, in

TABLE 7–1. ARGENTINA'S DEPLOYMENT IN PEACEKEEPING MISSIONS (AS OF
SEPTEMBER 30, 2004)

Mission	Argentine Deployment
UN Truce Supervision Organization, Middle East	3 military observers
UN Mission for the Referendum in Western Sahara	1 military observer
UN Peacekeeping Force in Cyprus	407 troops (task force of troops from the army, navy, and air force, staff offices, and an air force helicopter unit) 80 foreign troops included in the Argentine contingent
UN Mission in Kosovo	115 troops from the National Gendarmerie Special Police Unit 27 civilian police personnel from the National Gendarmerie (Pristina) 1 military observer
UN Mission in the Democratic Republic of the Congo	2 civilian police personnel from the National Gendarmerie
UN Stabilization Mission in Haiti	614 troops consisting of a joint Argentine battalion of: 454 troops from the Argentine army and the Argentine army's marine infantry, 6 staff liaison officers 8 contingent staff officers 57 personnel with an air force traveling hospital 41-member crew with the UN air contingent (UNFLIGHT) with 2 helicopters 85-member crew with a transport boat

later days expanding to other cities on the island. The armed groups were occupying several positions and threatening to take the capital, Port-au-Prince.

Dr. Boniface Alexandre, president of Haiti's Supreme Court of Justice, took over the leadership of the internal administration of the government after the resignation of President Jean-Bertrand Aristide on February 29, 2004. The same day, the United Nations received a petition from the Republic of Haiti requesting aid. Security Council Resolution 1529 authorized the deployment of the Multinational Interim Force (MIF).[1] The transitional government of Haiti was created on March 17.

The Multinational Interim Force was gradually transferring the conduct of operations to a new multinational mission: the United National Stabilization Mission in Haiti (*Mission des Nations Unies pour la stabilisation en Haïti*, or MINUSTAH). On April 30, 2004, Security Council Resolution 1542 established a new UN mission in Haiti for an initial period of 6 months. Acting under Chapter VII of the UN Charter, MINUSTAH became effective June 1, 2004.

The key points considered as principal objectives of the mission to be conducted are listed in the MINUSTAH mandate, and could be summarized as follows:

- provide support for Haiti's constitutional and political process by maintaining a stable and secure environment
- assist the transitional government in monitoring and reforming the Haitian national police consistent with democratic standards
- assist the Haitian police with the development of a sustainable disarmament, demobilization, and reinsertion program for all the armed groups
- provide support for the conduct of national, legislative, and municipal elections
- promote and protect human rights.

The mission will therefore be multidimensional and will endeavor to help Haiti give a sustainable response to its many complex demands. The objectives emphasized in its mandate are to achieve peace and stability, to build and strengthen democratic institutions, to support the reinstatement of a state of law, and to promote economic and social development and governability. The mission must conduct these activities in cooperation and coordination with the Haitian national authorities, officials at the regional and local levels, and civilian society.

FIGURE 7–1. ARGENTINE PARTICIPATION IN PEACEKEEPING OPERATIONS

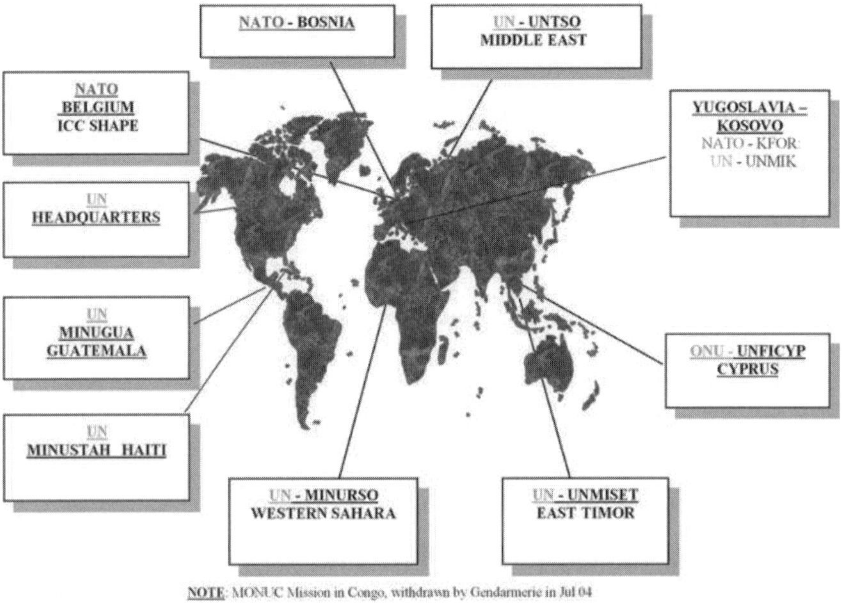

NOTE: MONUC Mission in Congo, withdrawn by Gendarmerie in Jul 04

ARGENTINA'S PARTICIPATION IN MINUSTAH

Article 3, section 1 of Chapter 7 of the United Nations Charter says:

> All Members of the United Nations, in order to contribute to maintaining peace and security, undertake to make available to the Security Council, at its request and in accordance with the special agreement or special agreements, the armed forces, the aid, and the facilities, including right-of-way, that are necessary for the purpose of maintaining international peace and security.

In spite of this, participating in a peacekeeping operation is a sovereign political decision for each state, and it is the responsibility of the political authorities of each member to analyze on a case-by-case basis their participation or non-participation in each of the UN initiatives. In the case of Argentina, many factors had to be considered at the time of the analysis, as well as when the final decision was made to authorize the participation of military forces for the national contribution to the peacekeeping mission in Haiti.

It could be said that acquired capabilities, prestige, and a sense of obligation were the three factors most considered in the national analysis to determine the country's participation in the peacekeeping operation in Haiti. The tradition of Argentina's military forces in peacekeeping operations in different scenarios of international armed conflicts, added to the experience already acquired in previous missions in Haiti by troops from the armed forces and the national gendarmes, was fundamental as a factor of influence: "The experience of the Armed Forces and security forces and the possibility of being used as a tool for the foreign policy of Argentina was a very important factor."[2]

Another important factor considered was the inescapable commitment to the Republic of Haiti and the well-being of its population. It should be noted that in the current crisis, Argentina was involved first in the international humanitarian aid forces by sending the "White Helmet Commission" to the area of operations.[3]

It is also important to emphasize previous participations in Haiti. Argentina actively contributed to the reestablishment of the political and humanitarian situation in the United Nations Mission in Haiti from 1993 to 1996 and the United Nations Civilian Police Mission in Haiti from 1997 to 1999.

Hemispheric solidarity and the participation of regional countries in the operation in Haiti were determining factors in the analysis for joining the conflict. The fact that Brazil and Chile had evidenced a clear commitment and will to provide military forces in the United Nations operations in Haiti generated a degree of regional cooperation that facilitated the decisionmaking process. According to one military official, "I am inclined to think that the predominant factor was the international policy of 'don't stand on the side-lines,'" with respect to the participation of Brazil and Chile.[4]

A national senator emphasized that:

> this is a decision taken along with countries that are members of MERCOSUR [Southern Cone Common Market] and felt this decision was important because integration does not just have to do with free trade agree-ments, but also the integration of the most varied factors, including the military. This will give the region a system for strengthening itself. The forces of the MERCOSUR are contributing to helping a country of the region that is in the throes of misery.[5]

In the words of Argentina's defense minister, "It's time for Latin America to show that it has put on long pants."[6]

Several sectors of the government saw the act of participating in a joint action with countries of the region such as Chile, Brazil, Paraguay, and Uru-guay, among others, as highly beneficial, pointing out that "this would be the first joint action of the MERCOSUR."[7] The fact that Argentina's troops are incorporated in a Latin American force and under UN mandate demonstrates its inclusion in international affairs and its active effort in favor of cooperation and peace.

Regional cooperation in specific activities such as those conducted in peacekeeping operations is a factor that must be carefully analyzed, since it entails different possibilities of interpretation. The interesting thing that can be found here is the different perceptions that exist about *cooperation* and its opposite, *competition*. The key is to understand that competition and coop-eration are not mutually exclusive, and that the two coexist in a single activity. This coexistence and conjuncture of the two perceptions generates positive results because they both stimulate the pursuit of excellence and bring posi-tions together. On the one hand, they create feelings of identification, and on the other they generate a need for continuous betterment for each state, without a zero result: the actors do not cancel one another out. The vocation of coop-eration is obvious in the macro view, concerning state political decisions. But in the micro view, there is a certain degree of competition that stimulates the state agencies involved. Peacekeeping operations generate centripetal forces that encourage both competition at technical levels and interstate coopera-tion at political levels.

In this respect, it can be said in general terms that the competition en-tailed in this type of activity is due to the "competition for prestige and inter-national recognition" associated with it. According to one military official, "In the 1990s, a lot was gained in experience but lost in presence, to the point that we were surpassed by Chile and Brazil in the size of the contingent, and that took away political weight from our participation."[8]

Some national voices contended that the delay in approving the law authorizing participation in Haiti created an advantage for the other countries of the region, particularly with respect to the contingent's placement in the theater of operations and the candidacies for key positions in the MINUSTAH mission. One senator complained on June 2, 2004, that the forces were not yet in Haiti. He even intimated some rivalry with Brazil when he said that if quick action had been taken, perhaps the national troops would have been at the head of the multinational troops, a role that Brazil is playing.[9]

Furthermore, it was perceived by public opinion that while the legislative bill for authorization was stuck in the labyrinth of Argentine state bureaucracy, President Lula da Silva sent a formation of soldiers from his country that would take command of the peacekeeping forces on June 1, 2004.

In reality, and after analyzing the consequences of the delay, it cannot definitively be said that it determined the distribution in the field or the key positions within the overall plan of the mission. The command of the military force in many UN missions goes to the country with the greatest contribution of troops. In this case, the force commander of MINUSTAH is General Augusto Heleno Ribeiro Pereira from the Federative Republic of Brazil, which is represented by more than 1,000 men in the field.

On the other hand, the delay in passing the authorization law did affect other important areas. In order to achieve deployment in the shortest possible time (as requested by the United Nations), for example, it was necessary to shorten the lead time for contracting and public tenders for the purchase of materials. This meant that the armed forces joint chiefs of staff had to act urgently, and the necessary predeployment quality control was not applied to recently purchased equipment. This situation resulted in a redesign of strategic transfers to the theater of operations because the materials purchased were delivered in stages. In summary, the time needed for decisionmaking exceeded the time needed to deploy the mission in due time and form, as military planning required.

In spite of the fact that the decisionmaking process was lengthy, it was done systematically and within the strict framework established by the law: at the proposal of the president and with the final approval of the legislative branch.[10] In both branches, the direct advice of the foreign affairs ministry, the defense ministry, and the armed forces joint chiefs of staff is required. Both ministers, with their direct advisors, were called to the national congress to express their reasoning, provide explanations, and attend the debates.

A joint session between the defense and foreign affairs committees in the national congress was attended by the chairman of the armed forces joint chiefs of staff, General Jorge Chevalier, with Colonels Mariano Menedez and Carlos Candia. A media source described their participation: "A careful explanation was given yesterday by two Colonels from the Argentine Army on the technical and operational scopes of the mission. Assisted by video screens on which the Senators and advisors could see the full scope of the operation, the officers described the steps and time frames that will apply once the National Congress makes the Bill a Law."[11]

In spite of the technical consulting provided and the proper methodology used, the decisionmaking process was slow, especially with respect to the parliamentary debate. As was publicly known, several government sources had openly opposed Argentina's participation. This resulted in some heated debates on the floor of the legislature. This also revealed that there is still no close cooperation between the foreign affairs and defense portfolios, in spite of the great efforts made by the two ministries in issues as specific as peacekeeping missions.[12] The decisionmaking was slow and serious narrow-mindedness was visible, with significant delays.

The decisionmaking process also revealed that there is still no state policy on participating in peacekeeping operations. According to one official, "One shortcoming of Argentina is that we do not have a national policy on peacekeeping missions. We had the feeling of having to explain once again why Argentina has to participate in peacekeeping operations; we felt all kinds of resistance."[13] In spite of Argentina's long tradition in this activity and the fact that it is considered a state policy due to its continuation over several administrations in spite of internal political changes, legislative obstacles and some budget restrictions sometimes put this perception in doubt.

The parliamentary debates can be found in the records of the nation's congress. It should be noted that they evidence an internal battle, which in a way was unnecessary when we realize that participation in peacekeeping operations should be a policy of consensus not subject to the ups and downs of partisan politics.[14] But there were arguments for and against, demonstrating incredible "childishness" or a total lack of knowledge of the issue, but easily absorbable by public opinion. For example, one deputy defended his opposition by arguing that the logistics support boat that would be used—indispensable for the logistics support of a Chapter VII operation—was in fact send to prevent Haitian refugees from fleeing to the United States; another deputy argued his vote in favor of authorization by saying that the weapons would only be used for self-defense, which does not coincide with the type of Chapter VII operation to be carried out. In a Chapter VII peacekeeping operation, weapons are used not only for self-defense but also for the defense of the lives of others and when the accomplishment of the mission is obstructed. But they must be in a position to use force if the parties in conflict do not stick to agreements. Otherwise, it would be a Chapter VI operation.

It was even suggested that the mission for Argentina's participation in Haiti, which is called for under Chapter VII, should follow the parameters set forth in Chapter VI. Aside from being unthinkable and impractical, this could even be dangerous if the methodology now existing for this type of operations permitted it. Fortunately, this does not agree with any of the rules established for these missions.[15]

Various statements showed a lack of technical knowledge and a great deal of confusion, which always gets to public opinion. In many cases there was confusion between the UN chapters and a poor understanding of the implications and features of each of them. There was a debate between the concepts of peacekeeping and peace enforcement missions.[16] It should be noted that the difference between Chapters VI, VI and a Half, and VII continues to be one of the most heated debates among academic fields and the peacekeeping missions experts themselves arriving at such totally different positions between chapters, even positions that leave no room for this type of divisions because they are not considered so obvious in the development of a conflict situation.[17]

The parliament ignored the central theme of the rules of engagement (ROEs), the authorization of the national government to use the deadly force of the weapons of Argentine soldiers. The ROEs that prevail in a peacekeeping operation must be approved by the parliament of each country. It is a mistake to say that the ROEs of one country are those of the United Nations for this mission: "It must be clear that the Rules of Engagement are national and must not be signed by military authorities because they have no legal validity if not concretely approved by those by whom the law is made in a Republic: The Congress."[18]

The debate in congress centered on semantic questions about chapters more than on concrete realities and future projections. Basic themes such as the ROE were not questioned, the UN pull-out strategies (if established) were not analyzed, nor were emergency evacuations due to renewed hostilities or an extreme escalation of violence. Nor were there questions about the estimated time Argentine troops would be in the field, their replacement by other contingents, or what the reaction would be to possible Argentine casualties. There is a possibility that force may have to be used, since this is a Chapter VII operation. This increases the probability that casualties will occur and that Argentine nationals who fall in MINUSTAH will be repatriated. At this time, public opinion is not prepared for this because, given the case, possible casualties do not influence the decision to remain in the mission. It is not now known whether the government in fact has an official position on this question.

Finally, the law was passed on June 18, 2004, authorizing the participation of Argentina with personnel and resources to contribute to the MINUSTAH mission. The problems brought up by the passage of the law were quite varied. On the question of the budget, some representatives of the budget committee of the national congress were upset that they were not included in the debates. The mass media indicated some general numbers that varied from one publication to another, and it was not clear whether the country or the United Nations would cover the costs of the operation. A figure of 10 million pesos was mentioned, but it was not clear if it was for transportation, resupply, or monthly or annual maintenance of the deployed troops. The lack of accurate and clear information on budgeting emphasized the lack of concrete political objectives. It is also felt that the scarce information on the subject creates a feeling of uncertainty with respect to public opinion.

In general terms, it should be noted that each troop contributing country (TCC) for UN peacekeeping missions has its own financial responsibilities, with quotas for reimbursement by the international organization. The UN reimbursement system has changed over time, and is now very specific on the system used for the calculation of reimbursements to be given to the TCCs. (See chapter VI of the Journal of Lessons Learned: "Argentina's Experience in Peacekeeping Missions" published by the Foreign Service Institute of Argentina, in which there is a summary of the current United Nations reimbursement system.)

The defense ministry and the joint chiefs of staff emphasized the need to have accurate, detailed budgeting. The need for vertical and horizontal accountability was stressed. The budget and finance analysis was successful to a large measure due to the experience acquired and the high level of technical knowledge of the general UN reimbursement system for peacekeeping missions. For that reason, there was insistence on the need to have national funds in time and form to commission and ready the forces to be deployed, which continues to be the responsibility of the contributing country.

As for the financial problems of covering the expenses of participation, some logistical problems were also added. Readying the personnel and equipment to be deployed required an enormous effort of coordination, not only by the forces but mainly by the joint chiefs of staff, which under Directive 02/99, "Directive from the Chairman of the Joint Chiefs of Staff of the Armed Forces for the Organization, Oversight, Command, and Control for the conduct of Peacekeeping Operations and other related actions," is the Argentine agency responsible for national command and control in all peacekeeping operations in which Argentina participates. This command and control was delegated by the national executive branch by decree 864 of August 11, 1999, and defense ministry resolution 861 of September 28, 1999.

Note that the participation and deployment of forces in the Haiti operation involved having the means necessary to transport the personnel and equipment, and an additional force: self-support in the field. To that end, participation in the Haiti mission is the first integral joint deployment effort contributed to by Argentina. The best solution to relieve this problem would be investing in the armed forces in advance, and not when the United Nations requires their contribution urgently. This would make it possible to keep at least three rotations of contingents properly organized, equipped, and trained. In the final analysis, this would certainly lessen the costs of deployment.

It is the inescapable responsibility of the state contributing troops to peacekeeping missions to ready and train all its personnel. For instruction and training, Argentina has an excellent resource, specifically since 1995, when the Argentine Joint Training Center for Peacekeeping Operations was created. The center provides predeployment instruction at the national level for the Argentine contingents to be used in peacekeeping operations. It also provides training at the international level since, at the request of the United Nations, it partners in training staffs for various peacekeeping missions. The center has a long history, a highly trained teaching staff, both civilian and military, and instructors and graduates from several countries interested in the subject of peace and conflict resolution.[19]

As for readiness, it was evidenced in the preparation of the forces for the MINUSTAH mission, although Argentina had not managed to have, or to convince political decisionmakers of the need to have, a prepared logistics structure in accordance with the specific requirements of participating in this type of mission. The UN standards have been increasing with each mission. In addition, at the international level, more emphasis is being placed on the need to have interoperability among the various contingents present in peacekeeping missions. For that reason, personnel and equipment readiness is essential when deploying troops on such a complex mission with the climatic and infrastructure requirements involved in participation in Haiti.

ANALYSIS OF THE EFFECTIVENESS OF COMBINED FORCES IN PEACEKEEPING OPERATIONS

At this time, it would be hasty and almost rash to draw any lessons about the variables that have a decisive impact on the effectiveness of combined military forces in the MINUSTAH mission. A series of questions could be listed about how the combination of multinational military forces, police forces, and civilian agencies in international missions can achieve and maintain law and order. In light of the above, in the final analysis, a study could be made of the extent to which they can support the process of reconstructing institutionalism and governability in fragile states, which is clearly the case of Haiti.

On the first point, it is necessary to signal that each conflict has its own characteristics, so each peacekeeping mission has had elements distinctive and specific to it. However, an analysis can be made of some variables that influence the effectiveness of military forces, security forces, and civilian agencies in achieving order and keeping the peace. These variables do not just depend on the conduct of the mission in the field; they also involve different levels of action: strategic, operational, and tactical. Specifically, in missions under the UN umbrella, the actions of the Security Council, the Secretariat, the agencies and programs, the elements deployed in the theater of operations, and the TCCs influence the effectiveness of the combined forces in carrying out a specific mandate.

To summarize, the elements that would influence effectiveness can be listed as follows:

- international commitment that is maintained over time
- presence of clear objectives and mandate consistent with the stated objectives
- necessary human, material, and financial resources available on time and in the proper form
- rules of engagement defined and known to all elements deployed on the mission. It is important that they be solid and designed in accordance with the needs of each mission so that they are compatible with the national ROEs of the TCCs.
- leadership by a country or group of countries that implicates their prestige in achieving the mission and the stated objectives. (In theory, leadership would tend to come from the UN Security Council; in practice, it is appropriate for the countries involved in the peacekeeping mission to have a more active role committed to the success of the mission's objectives.)
- assurance of constant and adequate contribution by the TCCs. It is very important for this that the United Nations make timely reimbursements of the TCCs' contributions, particularly self-support reimbursements.
- importance of the rapid deployment of military units during the initial process of a PKO.[20] The deployment capabilities of the TCCs must be strengthened, and this requires an agreement (more comprehensive than the United Nations Stand-by Arrangements System) that enables the United Nations to have reliable and flexible reserve units for rapid deployment in new operations. In the case of the MINUSTAH operation, the initial deployment was in mid-2004. In spite of this, it does not have the total forces stipulated by the mandate to achieve the assigned mission.
- clarity in the chain of command and control. Unity of command is an indispensable requirement for the conduct of a peacekeeping operation. The Special Representative of the Secretary-General must achieve unity of action in the field, so he must have the authority to conduct and coordinate the military, police, civilian, and humanitarian support activities. Local authorities should not be permitted to interfere with the UN chain of command.

- cooperation and coordination among the various elements present in the field. It is imperative to achieve what is known as *unity of purpose.* It is also necessary to establish cooperation and smooth communications with any NGOs present in the area. (This requires supplying accurate public information, integrating elements, and coordinating actions.)
- creation of favorable public opinion of the mission (at the international level, in the countries sending troops, and in the country where the peacekeeping mission is stationed)
- adequate instruction and training for all the elements present in the mission, including the international civilian component. There must be support from the international community for the member states whose participation is relevant, to establish regional partnerships for training forces in peacekeeping operations. Training civilian police forces at the regional level would promote a common level of preparation in accordance with the guidelines and standardized procedures for peacekeeping operations and the efficiency standards issued by the United Nations. As for the combined training of military forces, Argentina has worked in that direction along with the United States and several countries of the region, which conduct drills to strengthen regional cooperation. Examples of these are the Cabañas exercise and the South and North PKO seminars.
- interoperability of the various international elements. It would be appropriate, as mentioned in the Brahimi Report,[21] to conduct joint training through collective training programs including field exercises to strengthen interoperability. One example is the Nordic Coordinated Agreement for Military Peace Support initiative, which involved countries with longtime prestige and outstanding participation in peacekeeping missions, such as Denmark, Sweden, Norway, and Finland.
- equality of legal status of the military and police elements present in the mission.

The success of military forces and civilian police forces in conducting a peacekeeping mission will be influenced to a great extent by:

- political and legal backing from their country of origin
- logistical capability. This implies that military and police units must properly deploy the necessary equipment as established to perform their mission. It is very important to have the right individual and major equipment. To that end, the need must be emphasized to invest in the armed forces in advance, and not when the United Nations makes an urgent request for their participation in a peacekeeping

mission. It would be extremely beneficial for Argentina's proper participation in current peacekeeping operations to consolidate a medium-term equipment resupply program to achieve a minimum rapid deployment capability (particularly considering the UN recommendations and requirements for rapid deployment capability).[22] Having personnel organized, outfitted, and trained in advance, with properly readied equipment and materials, would greatly relieve the nation's predeployment costs.

- coherent internal organization
- possibility for TCCs to deploy organic elements on the mission. In that respect, the minimum force to be deployed for Chapter VII operations is the unit (regiment), because that is the force that, according to retired general Evergisto de Vergara, has the "esprit de corps" to face danger: "Combining soldiers of different origins but belonging to the same force, not to mention different forces, is not appropriate for facing the dangers inherent to a Chapter VII Operation. Having 600 men united under a part-time leader is not the same as having an organic regiment. The difference is that the organic regiment has 'esprit de corps' and a mutual knowledge of its men, and works as a team."[23]
- maintaining the unit's esprit de corps and morale, which is easy to say but difficult to do, especially in such adverse circumstances as those in the case of Haiti.[24]

A more inclusive analysis could be made of the effectiveness of combined action in supporting governability and institutionalism in fragile states, taking into consideration the objectives stated for the MINUSTAH mission.

The challenge of Haiti lies in being able to find and implement an effective and durable solution. This requires a holistic approach to the term *peacekeeping*, which goes beyond military and security priorities and the response to problems of governance, political legitimacy, social inclusion, economic development, institution building, and respect for the state of law and human rights.

In this vein, the first challenge is political. The mission leader (Special Representative of the Secretary-General of MINUSTAH, Ambassador Juan Gabriel Valdez) must consolidate a strategy for achieving a political solution to the conflict. Economic, social, and military aid will only be palliatives if a political solution to the Haitian problem is not achieved. To do this, it is imperative to promote political dialogue between the actors in conflict in order to reach solid agreements that establish the starting point for the reconstruction of the political system, and from there, institutional and economic reconstruction.

In this sense, it is obvious that the military component, the civilian police component, and the humanitarian branch are palliatives until a solution sustained over time is achieved, and that solution is intrinsically political. According to General de Vergara, "Independently of how well or poorly the components of the mission are performing, what is happening in Haiti is that the State is absent, since it is fragmented into factions disputing the exercise of power. This is a cultural problem that cannot be resolved using goodwill or force. What is missing is national identity. Until the State is reconstructed in Haiti, instability will continue and the [international] troops will have to stay to preserve the peace."[25]

In spite of this, in addition to the effort to build a strategy for achieving a political solution to the conflict, it is indispensable that the mission have the economic and financial aid to go ahead with the activities to be conducted immediately after the minimum reestablishment of peace—especially those involved in reconciling opposing factions and ensuring economic reestablishment. This is why Ambassador Valdez emphasized that "an international military presence must be maintained in order to maintain security, in addition to economic support, so that the poorest country in Latin America can stabilize in the long term."[26]

At the international political level, a satisfactory response must be given to the mission's basic requirements, and this effort must be coherent, constant, and long-term. In general (and this applies to most of the current missions), work must be done in the Security Council on the discrepancy between the activities financed voluntarily (generally reconstruction and development) and those charged to the regular PKO fund (usually allocated to security issues). The success of a mission depends on both forms of financing; peace cannot be assured by promoting order, disarmament, and demobilization without tasks of reintegration and the rebuilding of institutions.

To that end, the legislative bodies of the United Nations must consider including reintegration programs in the prorated budgets of peacekeeping operations for the first stage of an operation, in order to facilitate the rapid dissolution of the combatant factions and reduce the probability of renewed conflicts.

In summary, it is indispensable to strengthen and coordinate the work of all the elements present in peacekeeping operations. This must include international agencies, programs, and funds to provide an integral and comprehensive response to the problems existing in the zone of conflict and to work jointly with civilian society to consolidate a coherent strategy that is in keeping with the special needs of that society and is self-sustainable.

GENERAL RECOMMENDATIONS

The central question presented to us is: What are the most important recommendations for political decisionmakers that would make it possible to strengthen Latin America's capabilities for peacekeeping operations and other integrated operations within the framework of the regional cooperation in security matters?

From the analysis done in this project, some points can be highlighted to establish recommendations aimed at strengthening the national policies implemented in each state participating in peacekeeping missions. The recommendations in the area of political decisionmaking are to:

- establish a state policy for the participation of military and security forces in peacekeeping operations. Establish clear and comprehensive policies on national participation, which would include a sufficient legal, administrative, and financial framework.
- establish a clear and accurate communications strategy that includes and provides for interaction among the various institutional actors that play roles in preparing and conducting peacekeeping missions.
- strengthen current mechanisms for coordination among the agencies involved in making the decisions on participation in each peacekeeping mission. Relations must be improved among the most involved agencies (defense, foreign affairs, interior, and economy, including agents under their command such as the armed forces joint chiefs of staff, the controller general, and the Permanent Mission to the United Nations).
- create favorable national public opinion concerning this type of activity.
- invest in advance in the armed forces for proper engagement, and not when the United Nations makes an urgent request for the participation of national contingents. This investment would reduce the initial deployment costs (particularly training activities and personnel and equipment readiness).
- determine the financial basis for sustained participation in accordance with national potential. The expenditures for a peacekeeping operation must not be extrabudgetary. They must be constant and be available in time and in form, since otherwise the result is problems with medium- and long-term planning. It must be remembered that for any national deployment of units for a UN mission, the TCC must communicate with it at least 6 months in advance.

With respect to the military, and based on the information gathered by this research, the planning was done in accordance with the needs stated in the "Guidelines for TCCs in the MINUSTAH mission." From the analysis made by military decisionmakers, they are considered to have taken account during the planning period of most of the points to be analyzed for sending troops, in spite of the restrictions discussed above due to delays in the decisionmaking process. The points of analysis for sending troops to PKOs include:

- main summary of the events that motivated the UN request
- historical overview of the conflict; current situation
- regional repercussions
- UN action and the mandate prepared by the Security Council
- analysis of the legal documentation (Status of Forces Agreement, if there is one) establishing international participation in the conflict
- legal framework for action by military and security forces outside the national territory
- outline of the mission; duration
- level of equipment required to perform the task to be assigned
- participation of other countries in the mission; interoperability with other forces
- outline of the rules of engagement; compatibility with the national ROEs
- initial logistics, transportation, and sustained operations; budget; self-support required by United Nations
- creation of a technical group charged with negotiating memoranda of understanding and letters of assistance with the United Nations; integral analysis of regulations for UN reimbursements and short- and medium-term consequences of any delays in reimbursements owed.

CONCLUSION

Internal conflicts in fragile states such as Haiti are increasingly affecting a large number of people throughout the world. Peacekeeping operations are a tool of the international community to face this type of problem. They are a singularly advantageous way of approaching conflicts: their universality strengthens their legitimacy and limits the consequences for the sovereignty of the host country. The United Nations, in spite of its deficiencies or current crises, continues to be the multilateral security agency with the highest level of legitimacy for the prevention, handling, and resolution of conflicts.

However, its operational and response capability will primarily depend on contributions from member states. The major challenge today for the states participating in this activity is being able to provide a quick, efficient, and committed response based on a regional conception of conflicts. Accordingly, it is necessary for all UN member states to be committed to the development of a coordinated strategy for achieving international security. Both the United Nations and regional organizations must respond to these crises in a quick and effective manner.

Whether the operations are conducted by the United Nations or by regional blocs, the nations will continue to be responsible for supplying military and security forces. For that reason, each state that wants to participate in a peacekeeping operation must prepare its elements to conduct that activity in a professional manner and within the strict framework of the law.

In the regional context, the Latin American states have been increasingly committed to contributing to peacekeeping operations. In the case of the MINUSTAH mission, this American commitment is consolidated, and must be supported and intensified.

From a strategic standpoint, it is necessary to contribute to peacekeeping operations with systemic and self-sustaining elements. To that end, we agree with the idea outlined in the Brahimi Report on the proposal to create brigade-sized multinational forces (standby), stressing the feasibility of training and consolidation on a regional basis.

From an operational standpoint, regionally based forces are easier to establish, involve lower costs, and facilitate interoperability and convergence of training and equipment standards. The support and consolidation of different regionally based response mechanisms would mean a greater commitment by Latin American states seeking common defense and an effective response to regional challenges. So the success of the MINUSTAH mission lies in finding an effective solution to the Haitian problem and strengthening the capacity for regional action in the area of peacekeeping missions.

NOTES

[1] As of March 18, 2004, the Multinational Interim Force was composed of U.S. (1,813), French (554), Canadian (331), and Chilean (330) troops.

[2] Interview with the Chief of the Peacekeeping Organizations Department of the Joint Chiefs of Staff, Col. Eduardo Horacio Cundins, September 15, 2004.

[3] See B.O. 04/03/04, Humanitarian Aid, (Decree 280/2004), ordering the participation of resources, personnel, and volunteers of the White Helmet Commission in the Republic of Haiti.

[4] Interview with General (Ret.) Evergisto de Vergara. Former Chief III of Operations of the Joint Chiefs of Staff and former Force Commander of the UNFICYP mission, among other relevant positions in connection with peacekeeping operations.

[5] The senator's statements to *La Prensa*, June 7, 2004.

[6] Statements of Defense Minister Dr. José Pampuro to *La Nación*, June 6, 2004.

[7] Statements of Senator Miguel Angel Pichetto, *Clarín*, June 4, 2004.

[8] Interview with Retired General Evergisto de Vergara, August 25, 2004.

[9] Statement from Senator Eduardo Menem in *Pagina 12*, June 2, 2004.

[10] It should be noted that during past administrations, the decision on Argentina's participation in peacekeeping missions was made directly by

the Executive Branch, to a large extent obviating the approval of the Legislative Branch (with the case of Kosovo as a possible example).

11 Information excerpted from *En Diario BAE*, June 2, 2004.

12 It is important to stress the great efforts made in Argentina to achieve a better and more extensive approach between the various government agencies that are part of the peacekeeping mission's activity. For over 5 years now, there has been a direct connection between members of the Foreign Affairs Ministry, International Trade and Education, the Joint Chiefs of Staff of the Armed Forces, the Army, Navy, Air Force, the Argentine Center for Joint Training in Peacekeeping Operations (CAECOPAZ), the National Gendarmerie, the National Foreign Missions Training and Education Center (CENCAMEX), the National Controller, and the Argentine Council for International Relations, among others, in order to coordinate tasks, to consolidate lessons learned, and to make an intrinsically multidisciplinary task systematic.

13 Interview with the Chief of the Peacekeeping Organizations Department of the Joint Chiefs of Staff, Col. Eduardo Horacio Cundins.

14 Some advisors belonging to the House of Deputies expressed their perception of how little political consensus there was before the discussion entered the National Congress. The Executive Branch, they said, did not give clear signals and did not lay the groundwork in advance for the formal discussion in Congress. (Information excerpted from informal conversations with advisors belonging to the House of Deputies of the National Congress.)

15 "Senator Bonaerense . . . outlined the idea of modifying the bill to bring the mission under UN Art. 6. The motion was defeated." Reported in the Buenos Aires newspaper, *Económica* (BAE), May 27, 2004.

16 In spite of the fact that, in that very same room, Colonel Menedez very clearly explained Chapters VI and VII and the current differences and incompatibilities that do not necessarily define the precise division between peace enforcement and peacekeeping.

17 "Most of the mandates for new Peacekeeping Operations have included references to Chapter VII of the Charter. Accordingly, it is erroneous to use the 'Chapter VI–Chapter VII' distinction to try to differentiate between Peacekeeping Missions that do not involve the right to use force and those that do. This is because all types of Peacekeeping Missions, in particular PKOs, always entail the right to use force, at least in defense of the personnel participating in the mission (legitimate self-defense), but never the use of force of an aggressive nature." Excerpted from the Third Journal of Lessons Learned, Argentine International Relations Council, to be published by the CARI (DIC 04).

18 Interview with Retired General de Vergara.

[19]   Also note the task being done by the Argentine Training and Instruction Center for Foreign Missions (CENCAMEX) for the instruction of forces belonging to the National Gendarmerie.

[20]   "Rapid and efficient deployment capability" must be understood from an operational perspective. The Brahimi Report says within 30 days after approval of the mandate for a conventional mission, and within 90 days for a complex operation.

[21]   Comprehensive Review of the Whole Question of Peacekeeping Operations in All Their Aspects, Document No. A/55/305-S/2000/809, August 21, 2000. Commonly known as the Brahimi Report.

[22]   In this respect, consideration could also be given to other possible alternatives, such as acting in combination with other Latin American nations in order to contribute to UN peacekeeping operations with a multinational brigade with rapid response capability. Another option to consider could be what is known as the "triangular arrangement," which is established among countries that contribute contingents, others that supply equipment, and the UN which provides reimbursements for personnel and equipment deployed in a PKO.

[23]   General (Ret.) Evergisto de Vergara.

[24]   It is important to note the inclement weather conditions of the theater of operations. The Haiti mission experienced the tragic passage of Hurricane Jane in mid-September 2004, which seriously affected the localities of Gonaives (the area of responsibility for the Joint Argentine Battalion), among other areas.

[25]   General (Ret.) Evergisto de Vergara.

[26]   Statements of Ambassador Juan Valdez published in *Clarín*, November 14, 2004.

Chapter Eight

Uruguay: Meeting the Challenges of Modern Peacekeeping Operations

JORGE W. ROSALES

T his chapter examines the factors that shape the design and use of integral capabilities for peacekeeping operations (PKO) in a set of Western Hemisphere countries at the start of the 21st century, with the following objectives:

- develop recommendations for policymakers concerning the improvement of capabilities for PKO and other integrated operations within the framework of cooperation for regional security
- identify and evaluate factors that impact the effectiveness of combined military and police forces and civilian agencies in international missions that support the exercise of authority and law and order in the creation of institutions in fragile states
- use performance measures that help evaluate the effectiveness of combined forces conducting integrated operations in international peacekeeping missions in the Western Hemisphere or under the conduct of Western Hemisphere countries.

To achieve these objectives, an analysis was made of the experiences and lessons learned from the United Nations (UN) operations in Latin America, the current regional situation, international and regional political-military trends, and Uruguay's extensive past participation in peacekeeping operations. In addition, conclusions were drawn from Uruguay's current participation in Haiti that made it possible to formulate specific recommendations in support of the overall research project.

LATIN AMERICA AND INTERVENTIONS

In the 1980s, many countries of the South American continent experienced a transition from authoritarian governments to more democratic societies and are now in the process of building them, without yet having been able to completely heal wounds that were sustained in events dating back three decades. This affects the delicate balance necessary in civilian-military relations, and is of prime importance for participation in peacekeeping operations. In spite of this, there is more confidence today in the capability of democratic institutions to deal seriously with internal as well as regional security problems.

In fact, the region today shares several aspects that should be cited because they are directly related to the subject involved:

- The nations of Latin America have a tradition of support for the principles of nonintervention in foreign domestic matters and share a common belief in democratic principles and respect for human rights.
- The responsibility of protecting the population in the hemisphere has improved in the short term through diplomatic, economic, and other nonmilitary means. In the long term, action must be taken to deal with the primordial causes of conflicts, including poverty and the gap between the wealthy and poor in the hemisphere.
- It is preferable to use prevention to forestall conflicts than to use force once conflicts have broken out.
- Although military interventions are considered exceptional in some cases, it is impossible to ignore the specter of possible regional reactions to the humanitarian crises caused by civil war, the collapse of nations, or governments that are unable or unwilling to protect their citizens or that permit or perpetrate active and massive violations against the rights of their citizens. Even though regional military intervention is the last resort, this possibility may give more credibility to the forces of prevention.
- The United Nations Security Council has the primary obligation to act in a timely manner to authorize any intervention.
- Any multilateral force acting in the region must carry out interventions preferably using troops from the continent.

CHALLENGES OF MODERN PEACEKEEPING OPERATIONS

As the subject is directly related to effectiveness and efficiency in carrying out these activities, it is appropriate to review the complex and delicate work and tasks that personnel participating in PKO may currently be called upon to perform during the discharge of their mission.

One of the big differences between conventional peacekeeping operations and modern peacekeeping operations is that the risks now involved are much greater. Conventional peacekeeping basically deals with interstate conflicts in which the United Nations is called upon to separate the warring states by establishing a neutral zone to buffer conflicts between them. Some of the major activities of these forces—now called first-generation peacekeeping forces—involve monitoring, patrolling, and reporting cease-fire violations. Examples of this type of PKO include the following: acting between Israel and Egypt during the 1956 Suez crisis, the United Nations Operation in the Congo (1960), and the UN Peacekeeping Force in Cyprus (1964). However, more and more intrastate conflicts have had to be dealt with, whose prolongation over time has resulted in failed states with ineffective or nonexistent judicial, criminal, and police authorities.

Participants in modern peacekeeping operations must frequently face an environment in which there are often no official boundaries separating the warring factions. Instead of being faced with professional soldiers from sovereign states, they may encounter mercenaries and combatants who do not pay much attention to the law on armed conflict and other internationally recognized laws of war.[1] As a result, among other consequences, there is an increase in the number of these peacekeepers who are illegally detained and even taken hostage. The proliferation of small subversive groups and nonstate unconventional agents such as mercenary leaders and child soldiers increases the tension in the environment in which peacekeepers must perform. Conflicts are becoming increasingly complex, unleashing humanitarian crises when large numbers of local displaced persons and/or refugees become a major part of the crisis itself.

A UN intervention has a complex range of activities to manage in order to respond to the growing demands of the international community. Military observers now work and live among the factions. In addition to the local population, military personnel will also have to interact with the press, local political leaders, and other humanitarian actors. The modern peacekeeper is expected to be capable of reporting any form of human rights violation, to be a good negotiator with communications skills, and to be able to operate sophisticated equipment such as computers and other communications equipment.[2] The various duties that "peacetime soldiers" may be called upon to discharge include the following:

- guard borders or demilitarized zones
- conduct air, river, and land security, intelligence, or reconnaissance patrols
- mediate at the signature of peace agreements between warring states or groups
- negotiate cease-fires
- administer human and economic resources in territories affected by a state of hostilities on a temporary basis until the reinstatement of local authorities
- limit and control the arsenals of states that are in a compromised situation with a developing conflict or in a situation of armed peace

- verify the effective application of peace agreements, collaborate with international human rights and refugee organizations and various non-governmental organizations
- create favorable conditions for the conduct of elections
- provide security for United Nations civilian officials for the normal discharge of the specific tasks of their duties.

In the words of UN Secretary-General Kofi Annan: "It is no longer enough to just implement accords or separate the antagonists, the international community now wants the UN to draw boundaries, control and eliminate heavy arms, stifle anarchy, and guarantee the distribution of humanitarian aid in war zones."

In summary, today's challenges are greater, but so are the many resources we have available to us. In the case of Uruguay, we can avail ourselves of a background of experience accumulated during more than 20 years of continuous participation with various components throughout the world in a climate of professionalism, mutual trust, and security. In addition, for years, classroom work has been done with regional assistance (PKO South) and various military exercises (such as Cabañas). This work has made it possible to develop a regional "common language" in a series of areas that permits integration and facilitates the important factor of interoperability.[3] *Interoperability* is the ability of two or more systems or components to exchange information, operate together, and use the same forces to conduct a joint mission. There are two general cases of interoperability.

Strategic interoperability results from the ability and capability of the actors to give and/or accept support from other actors that facilitates their integrated action and makes it possible to procure benefits that are difficult to achieve alone.

Interoperability in peacekeeping missions is the result of combining, exchanging, and integrating the combat strength (human and material resources) of the military factors of two or more nations (combined framework) under a single command, whose specific objective is the conduct of a specific mission, such as peacekeeping and humanitarian assistance operations.

Interoperability can be implemented through several methods:

- exchange and knowledge of the doctrine used
- integrated personnel education, training, and improvement exchanges, making it possible to reduce costs and minimize risks to personnel
- unification of combat and support processes and procedures in catastrophic situations (rules of engagement)
- knowledge and use of other languages
- incorporation of material resources compatible with those of other

armed forces between the weapons and services of a force and between the various forces. The region also shares a series of principles on states of law, market economy, and other factors that have a favorable impact.

There are also some experiences in progress, such as the case of Cyprus, in which components from Chile, Paraguay, and Uruguay are participating as part of the Argentine Battalion.

DISMANTLING ARMIES

There are various predictions about the coming downfalls of countries desperately involved in civil wars, genocides, and border confrontations, in which it will be unavoidable to resort to professional forces to reestablish peace. According to Yale University historian Paul Kennedy:

> Most of the world's armies are lamentable. They have little combat experience, low morale, and poor equipment. They are full of soldiers who are patiently awaiting retirement or who enlist for only two years. This was the flaw of the "coalition of the willing" so extolled by U.S. Defense Secretary Donald Rumsfeld. How could Filipino, Latvian, and Salvadoran troops be expected to fight solidly in Baghdad?

There are only about eight armies in the world that have the esprit de corps and the combat capability required in a world torn by civil war: India (Gurkhas included), France, Turkey, Australia, perhaps Russia and Poland, and the U.S. and British armies. No one is frightened under fire. Pride does not permit it.

A June 22 report in *The Guardian* of London said that Prime Minister Tony Blair asked the foreign affairs and defense ministries to draw up plans for some type of military assistance (or intervention) in Darfur, where murders, mutilations, and rapes by Arab militias against Christian animist tribes are horrifying the world. However, the British Army, like the U.S. Army, is deployed in Iraq, Afghanistan, the Balkans, Cyprus, and two dozen other places. At the same time, everybody knows that the UN Secretary-General's office is brimming with omens and fear that the next social crisis in Africa will not generate any positive response in the world's richest countries.

Other reports argue that, in future decades, large regions of the world will become failed societies that will seek help from the international community, especially from the United Nations. However, who will Kofi Annan or his successors appeal to for the necessary professional military security?

Without making a value judgment on these statements and questions, one need only analyze the worst fears of the World Bank and the UN Population

Fund to be prevented from making very optimistic predictions. By the year 2050, the current world population of 6 billion (2 billion of whom are below the poverty line) will probably reach a total of 9 billion (4 billion of whom will be below the poverty line). In nearly all the Latin American countries where the economic and political forces require adherence to the economic standards of the World Trade Organization and the political standards of the United Nations, the respective governments place priority on dealing with severe social problems (health, housing, education), with unequal consideration to the problems inherent to defense. This is resulting in budget cuts for the armed forces, a reduction in personnel, and negative impacts on the levels of readiness, equipment, and professional level of the members.

In contrast, and according to the above excerpt and various updated information, the growing need to have countries willing to contribute troops for peacekeeping missions seems very clear, particularly when the armies of the powerful nations are involved in other kinds of operations. It is appropriate to note the risks involved in the dismantling of armies in this context and in relation to the statements with respect to the new challenges. The question immediately arises: Will the countries of the region be capable of maintaining sufficient troops at the performance levels required to conduct these missions effectively?

LATIN AMERICAN MILITARY STRENGTH

The possibility of forming a combined military structure in the region appears to have begun to be considered in South America. The military dimension of the Southern Cone Common Market (MERCOSUR) has been discussed nearly since the group was founded. In 1993, General Gleuber Vieira, second assistant chief of staff of the Brazilian Army, said, "The current integration . . . of the four members of the MERCOSUR could lead us to build a collective security system. However, I think that a geopolitical understanding of the Southern Cone makes it advisable for all the countries in that subregion to participate."

In 1996, addressing his armed forces, Argentine President Carlos Menem mentioned the possibility of a common defense agreement of MERCOSUR. It was put on the official Argentina-Brazil agenda in a meeting of foreign affairs and defense ministers and service heads in Rio de Janeiro in July of that year. Representatives of the cabinet of the Brazilian government of President Lula who participated in the 2003 Latin American Forum meeting in Brazil stated the need to have a permanent military structure in the region. And on March 16, 2004, the Socialist Party of Chile proposed the formation of a Latin American military force as multilateral "logic" in order to take action in the crises in the region that need it and "to avoid the logical intervention of the United States."

The reality is that the nationalist sectors and even the political left in South America with influence in most of the governments of the region have come to accept and even push for this type of project. As University of Brazil professor Luiz Alberto Moniz Bandeira said recently, "An integration that would be important is the formation of a joint military force within the MERCOSUR."

A change of attitude has been occurring in the governments, and one example is that starting on July 1, the peacekeeping force in Haiti was formed with the predominant inclusion of MERCOSUR members and associates. This brought new life to the debate on whether MERCOSUR should advance the adoption of a common defense policy.

The force that is acting under the UN resolution has a Chilean as the Secretary General's representative, and the military component is commanded by a Brazilian general, the second in command being an Argentine general. Brazil is contributing the largest contingent (1,400 men), then Chile with more than 1,000, Uruguay with 570, and Argentina with 450.

Both the political-ideological debate and the formation of a peacekeeping force in Haiti demonstrate that in South America in general, and in the MERCOSUR countries and Chile in particular, having a permanent military force in the region to act in PKO has begun to be a policy objective. This trend is consistent with the proposal made by the members of the Brahimi commission in the well-known report of the year 2000, on the formation of "coherent forces made up of regional type brigades." Later reports relating to the subject mention this, too, particularly referring to requests for joint training.

German vice minister of defense Hans Georg Wagner visited countries of the Southern Cone in April. His visit was an opportunity to introduce reflection on what could be the content of a defense agenda between South America and Europe, and in particular the axis made up of Germany and France, at a time when these new proposals were beginning to be seen in this region.

In this situation, in terms of formulating hypotheses, the experience of the Eurocorp (a permanent land combat unit made up of Germany, France, Spain, Belgium, and Luxembourg) is a model that could perhaps prove useful (except for the different logics), particularly knowing about the experience of its process and the characteristics of its operation. Another integration model specifically for handling peacekeeping missions that could also be enormously useful is that of the Multinational Standby High Readiness Brigade for United Nations Operations (SHIRBRIG).

Perhaps at this stage, a concrete project could be formulated among the countries of the region, and by other countries that are part of any of these combined forces, to define basic questions, such as viability, objectives, forces to be included, and finalization dates. It could begin with a combined military commission made up of a few dozen officers who would be charged with planning the project. As for the location, consideration could be given to the Argentine province of Corrientes, which borders on Brazil and Uruguay and is near Paraguay, where there are unused barracks. In addition, this region is very close to the tri-border region between Argentina, Brazil, and Paraguay, where there is also a vulnerable zone for possible support bases for international terrorism.

At the UN level, the importance of regional organizations and other alliances was demonstrated by the International Force for East Timor, the UN Multinational Interim Force in Haiti (UNMIH), and the role of the African Union in Darfur, among others.

In summary, the visit of the German vice minister of defense introduced the appropriateness of developing a concrete agenda of cooperation and possibly learning from existing experiences, for the design of a multinational military force in the region, which appears to be the political trend according to the facts already related. Enormous contributions could be obtained from the analysis of a model in order to improve the current PKO capabilities in areas such as identifying relevant common aspects or factors; establishing means of control, training, and preparation in general (psychology, health, and mission-related); and identifying materials and equipment, performance measures to evaluate efficiency, and others.

UN PARTICIPATION IN LATIN AMERICA

To understand the UN Stabilization Mission in Haiti (MINUSTAH), it is useful to review briefly other UN operations in the region:

- Mission in the Dominican Republic, 1965. Purpose: Monitor the situation caused by rival governments in the Dominican Republic. Ended in October 1966.
- UN Observer Group in Central America, 1989. Purpose: Monitor the cease-fire in Nicaragua. Ended in January 1992.
- UN Observers in El Salvador, 1991. Purpose: Enforce the cease-fire in El Salvador. Ended in April 1995.
- UN Mission in Haiti, 1993. Purpose: Stabilize Haiti after the coup d'état. Ended in June 1996.
- UN Support in Haiti, 1996. Purpose: Modernize the police and army of Haiti. Ended in July 1997.
- UN Inspection in Guatemala, 1997. Purpose: Monitor the cease-fire in the civil war. Ended in May 1997.
- Transitional UN Mission in Haiti, 1997. Purpose: Help stabilize Haiti. Ended in November 1997.
- UN Civilian Police Mission in Haiti, 1997. Purpose: Modernize Haiti's police forces. Ended in March 2000.

- UN Stabilization Mission in Haiti, 2004. Purpose: Restore stability in Haiti. In progress.

Between 1915 and 1934, Haiti was occupied by the United States, with a significant expansion of the national infrastructure and various social improvements. When the United States withdrew, the infrastructure began failing, and local leaders became dictators in the absence of institutions that supported governability.

In 1986, after a coup d'état, Jean Claude Duvalier left Haiti, thereby ending 30 years of his family's dictatorial government. The violence that was unleashed then resulted in a succession of two military governments.

In 1993, the International Civilian Mission in Haiti was installed, and the United Nations decreed the total embargo of oil and arms to Haiti, later leading to the creation of the UNMIH. When that mission failed, the sanctions were reinstated, while claims of human rights violations increased.

The UN authorized the creation of a multinational force independent of UNMIH to reestablish a "stable and secure" environment. Operation *Restore Democracy*, led almost exclusively by U.S. troops, reinstated Jean Bertrand Aristide to the presidency in September 1994. In November 2000, international observers did not endorse the election, and the United Nations ended its mission in Haiti.

In late 2003, gangs acting as a political police force covered the streets of Haitian cities suppressing dissidents with complete impunity. By January 2004, political tensions throughout the country worsened, Haiti was without a parliament, demonstrations proliferated with dozens of dead, and repression was again on the rise.

In summary, throughout the history of UN participation, it appears clear that the military factor was preponderant, basically aimed at stability, with short-term interventions that did not properly address the roots of the conflicts or the reconstruction of the affected countries. The feeling is that this should be considered a "lesson learned" to be seriously considered before taking future action, as is apparently the case with the current mission in Haiti.

MINUSTAH: THE UNITED NATIONS STABILIZATION MISSION IN HAITI

When Aristide resigned as president on February 29, 2004, the leadership was taken over by Boniface Alexandre, who immediately requested international support to restore peace and security in the country. Hours later, the UN Security Council approved Resolution 1529 authorizing the immediate deployment of a Multinational Interim Force for a period of 3 months to contribute to securing and stabilizing the country.

On April 30, the Security Council approved Resolution 1542/2004, establishing the United Nations Stabilization Mission in Haiti. The resolution ordered that it act under Chapter VII of the UN Charter and be made up of a maximum of 1,622 members of the civilian police and a military component with a maximum of 6,700 soldiers. The electoral process was scheduled for the year 2006.

Considering the arrival time of the military contingents, three stages were planned for their arrival, deployment, and use. The first stage was transfer of responsibility from the MIF (June 25–July 30, 2004). The next stage called for redesign of the limits of stage one (July 30–August 7, 2004) and, with the arrival of Nepal, Paraguay, and Sri Lanka, growth of the area of responsibility of the center and support activities by various command, engineer, air, and hospital units. In the final stage, a sufficiently secure environment would be established to permit the achievement of the political and human rights objectives of MINUSTAH (August 7–final stage).

Highlights of Uruguay's Participation in UN Missions

- More than 15,000 Uruguayan troops deployed to date
- 70 years of collaboration with peacekeeping processes throughout the world
- Presence in 11 out of 16 existing UN missions
- Presence for 25 years in the Multinational Force and Observers Mission in the Middle East
- Of 100 contributing countries currently providing 44,000 troops, Uruguay has more than 2,500 troops in operations outside the country
- Of the 1,837 casualties since 1948, only 12 were Uruguayans
- Uruguay has deployed troops on all the continents
- Currently operating on three major fronts in Africa, Central America, and the Middle East

---

URUGUAY IN PKO

Uruguay, with a population of 3 million inhabitants, has a surprising rate of participation in these missions, and is currently in seventh place among troop-contributing countries; and, if we consider the ratio between participating troops and the population (0.9 percent of the population has participated), Uruguay is in first place.

Table 8–1 shows the number of Uruguayan troops participating in various missions around the world.

TABLE 8–1. NUMBER OF URUGUAYAN TROOPS IN UN MISSIONS

Country	Mission	Troops
Democratic Republic of the Congo	MONUC	1,789
Afghanistan	UNAMA	1
Cyprus	UNFICYP	4
Ethiopia/Eritrea	UNMEE	2
Ivory Coast	MINUCI	3
Georgia	UNOMIG	1
India/Pakistan	UNMOGIP	1
Western Sahara	MINURSO	2
Sierra Leone	UNAMSIL	7
Sinai	MFO	87
Haiti	MINUSTAH	572
	United Nations Headquarters	2
TOTAL		2,471

ORGANIZATION OF THE "URUGUAY I" JOINT BATTALION

On June 16, 2004, the Uruguayan parliament approved Law 17,785 ordering the members of its armed forces to participate in the United Nations Mission in Haiti. This joint battalion was initially composed of 47 officers and 516 soldiers from the three branches of the armed forces (basically Army). On June 23, 2004, a commission traveled to Haiti to view the future area of operations, and most of the battalion arrived starting August 11. On August 17–18, the president of Uruguay visited, accompanied by the commanders-in-chief of the army, navy, and air force, and held meetings with his Haitian counterpart, Boniface Alexandre. In September, the Uruguayan public health minister visited Haiti and offered support with more potable water units and groups of medical personnel covering four basic specialties (surgery, general medicine, gynecology, and pediatrics).

In the purely operational context, the assigned tasks were carried out normally, and contributions were made in the area of humanitarian aid by evacuating civilians, distributing food and water, and maintaining peace and security following the disasters of hurricanes Jeanne and Ivan, which lashed the island. In the face of the damage caused, troops were deployed to Gonaives in the northern part of the country, in support of the Argentine contingent. In security missions, Uruguayan troops escorting convoys of vehicles carrying humanitarian aid and in providing security at distribution points, had to fire shots in the air and throw tear gas grenades to disperse the population, with no wounded.

Since a large part of the content of the UN mandates considers it a primary objective to protect civilians and to encourage and promote universally accepted human rights, the Uruguayan troops' mission was not only to provide a secure environment to permit the work of the other UN components and other organizations, but also to protect them, as well as civilians, especially the most vulnerable groups (women, children, and the elderly).

Another facet that must be considered in the new generation of PKO is the fact that in the absence of local agents or UN civilian police for maintaining law and order, troops may be assigned to police work, which in fact happened in Bunia. This work included detention and arrest, searches, and the confiscation of weapons and munitions, all in accordance with the host country's law and in coordination with local judicial authorities for due process. In this last area, the Uruguayan troops deployed in Haiti are also capable of acting as police elements to control civil disturbances.

Currently, the Uruguay battalion is in Les Cayes, carrying out foot, motorized, and mechanized patrols, and the situation is calm. In Uruguay, additional resources—a company plus a subunit for logistical support (an increase of 200 in MINUSTAH forces)—are in the final phase of readiness for departure to Haiti.

GENERAL CONCLUSIONS

The nations of the hemisphere share a common belief in democratic principles and respect for human rights, which is an advantage in approaching difficult subjects such as regional security, including participation in peacekeeping missions. This part of the hemisphere begins the 21st century as the least militarized region of the world in terms of the percentage of labor and funding devoted to state preparations for conflicts, and is also the region that provides the most support per capita to UN peacekeeping forces.

Latin America is a region that has the capability of conducting a serious and professional conversation at any time among the representatives of its component countries on any security issue, particularly the so-called new challenges (international terrorism, the war on drugs, human trafficking, PKO), or promptly participating in a campaign for humanitarian aid to the victims of an earthquake, flood, or other disaster in a neighboring country (such as the recent fire in Asuncion).

In general, Latin American countries have armed forces that, in spite of being subjected to rigid budget restrictions and reduced forces, are professionally educated and backed by well-informed civilian personnel with the professional capability for the formulation and implementation of honest and feasible bilateral or multilateral policies.

There is a trend toward forming a permanent multinational military force in the region, without yet having a concrete model to follow.

Short-term UN interventions that did not contribute solutions to the roots or basic reasons for conflicts or properly attend to the reconstruction of the affected country were useless, as is demonstrated in the history of Haiti.

Modern PKO are much more complex than the conventional variety and demand a high level of professionalism on the part of the participants.

Finally, it should be noted that the attacks of September 11, 2001, gave birth to a new context of discussions on matters of security, which must not be confused with the problems posed by humanitarian and other crises that result in PKO.

RESEARCH CONCLUSIONS AND RECOMMENDATIONS

The following conclusions address the specific points of the research questionnaire provided by the Center for Hemispheric Defense Studies.

1. What factors influenced your country's decision to participate in peacekeeping operations for Haiti?

All the powerful factors that carry any weight in international and, obviously, military policy, were influential in Uruguay's decision to participate in this operation. Aside from the normal factors that were considered for participation in previous missions such as support for foreign policy and the prestige they entail, in the particular case of Haiti, emphasis is placed on the principle of hemispheric solidarity and the majority participation of contingents from the southern subregion of South America. This decision enables Uruguay to continue to honor its commitment to the international community by participating in peacekeeping operations as a major tool of the United Nations for contributing to peace and international security, by being a regional actor of international prestige, and by remaining consistent as the region's biggest contributor of personnel in these operations.

2. How was the decision made?

Uruguay has an agency at the national level called the National Peacekeeping Operations Support System (SINOMAPA) that was created by a law from the executive branch in 1994 (Decree 560/94). The agency's mission is to coordinate with state and international agencies, plan these operations, advise the executive branch on the subject, and instruct the personnel who will participate in each approved mission, proposing the respective teaching programs.

The director general of this system is the army chief of staff under the national defense ministry. In addition, regulations state that the SINOMAPA will have a national peacekeeping operations support board permanently composed of delegates from the ministries of foreign affairs, the interior, and economy and finance, the national civil service office, the commands of the army, navy, and air force, and the national armed forces directorate. One of its duties is to advise the director general on any aspect necessary to determine the appropriateness of participating in a peacekeeping mission.

In the case of Haiti, while this procedure was followed, there was special involvement of the executive branch supported by the military factor with respect to the need to participate in the mission due to the above-stated aspects of hemisphere solidarity and majority subregional participation. Once participation was decided by the executive branch, the legislative branch approved it as provided in the national constitution. So we can say that it was a combination of processes from the top down and vice-versa.

3. How was the mission designed and planned? By whom? And to what extent was it shaped by outside influences?

Design and planning were generally assigned to the Army Peacekeeping Co-ordination Center (CECOMAPA), in this case the 1st Joint Battalion. There was also active participation by the Navy CECOMAPA. Advice followed the normal channels to the executive branch through the national defense ministry. There was no known impact of outside influences.

4. What are/were the political objectives of the mission? Economic objectives?

We can point out the following political objectives:

- favorable international standing due to cooperation in a humanitarian crisis and teamwork with various regional contingents and other UN components
- participation in the fight for the defense of human rights, demonstrating the high priority of this subject on our nation's scale of values
- expression of its agreement that the specific political objectives of the mission are in keeping with Uruguay's foreign policy and with the United Nations Charter, and the provisions of the respective mandate drawn up by the Security Council. This includes stabilization and security in the operations to permit the functioning of the electoral process, while the indispensable tasks for building and consolidating a durable peace are added in the medium term.

There are no specific economic objectives in the short term, apart from normal reimbursement by the United Nations.

5. What were/are the military/national security objectives?

- protect UN personnel and facilities and ensure freedom of movement
- comply with the mission's rules of engagement
- work jointly with other military contingents, particularly those of the subregion

- support the Haitian police in restoring and maintaining order and public safety
- maintain a deterrent presence through proactive patrolling and reconnaissance
- comply with the provisions of the mission mandate relating to the protection provided by international agreements on universally recognized human rights and the additional agreements and protocols concerning international humanitarian law by the members of the UN and the parties in conflict.

6. Have the objectives changed over time? In what way? Why?

In the short term of the conduct of the mission, it is seen that before initiating peace-building tasks with development projects, it is necessary to achieve a stable and secure environment. This relates to the existing conflict between two different viewpoints. The first concerns the peace enforcement–peacekeeping–peacebuilding cycle that is simplified above.

The second relates to the theory that reconstruction or peacebuilding operations must be present in all the stages of conflict resolution because they contribute to eradicating the causes of the conflict. This entails the need to provide security for the components performing those tasks.

7. What independent variables influence the effectiveness of combined military forces, police forces, and civilian agencies in international missions to support governability, the respect and maintenance of law and order, and the institutionalism of fragile states (PKO)?

We can cite several factors:

- language differences
- differences in military terminology, standard procedures, and decisionmaking processes at tactical and operational levels
- differences in predeployment training processes
- different degrees of knowledge of local culture and different perceptions of the host country's cultural environment among the various contingents, especially if they come from different continents
- different objectives between the participating international organizations, nongovernmental organizations, and others, above all in the medium and long terms, mainly due to the differences between their mandates, funding, chains of command, operating procedures, degree of training, impartiality, and degree of independence from the members of the UN Military and Police components. To these are added the personalities and powers of those heading these groups in the mission area.

- lack of coordination among the agencies involved. This goes up to the mission level in the person of the Officer for the Coordination of Humanitarian Assistance. In many cases, the coordination of this office is only through periodic meetings, generating obstacles for the reasons stated above.
- differences of priorities between civilians and the military, with respect to the tendency of the one to favor development and the other to favor security
- different approaches to the subject between the troop-contributing countries and the UN civilian police corps.

8. What performance measures can be used to evaluate the effectiveness of combined forces conducting integrated operations in international peacekeeping missions either in the Western Hemisphere or conducted by nations of the Western Hemisphere?

- Take advantage of joint exercises at the chiefs of staff level (example, the South and North PKO organized by the U.S. Southern Command) to increase the standardization of procedures for planning and conducting operations.
- Take advantage of field exercises, such as Cabañas, aimed at standardizing procedures in the field. It should be noted that although they are organized by the United States, the performance of their troops is far from what really must be done in the various PKO because the United States does not consider them a typical operation when shared with the rest of the countries of the region.
- Make evaluations and learn lessons from existing experiences in combined units such as the Argentine Battalion in Cyprus, or other models that could be observed such as SHIRBRIG, discussed above.
- Strengthen and broaden the formation of brigade-level units composed of battalions and logistics support units and other support (helicopters, river units, gendarmes) from countries of the region, with careful monitoring and evaluations. This would make it necessary to develop joint standby agreements, presented and agreed on with the UN's Force Generation Service.
- Regionally centralize training for these missions, and use the extensive experience of many regional countries (such as Uruguay).

9. What are the most important recommendations for policymakers to enhance the capabilities for peacekeeping operations and other integrated operations within the framework of regional security cooperation?

Policymakers need to define the real need to strengthen global, regional, and subregional organizations to deal with armed conflicts and other problems that put populations at risk. Although there are trade agreements in the region, they never involve joint military operations because the basic missions the armed forces have in the various countries predominate. In spite of this, there is cooperation in some areas that involves security.

In the current context, and in view of the possibility of forming a large regional unit to conduct PKO, a means of consensus must be adopted with solutions that permit joint international action with due attention to the specific features of all members.

Negative policy positions generally cite reasons of sovereignty. In the case of the MERCOSUR, those opposing this idea say that it is a trade agreement, not a policy agreement. If any project materializes in this sense, the possibility of any of the member countries exercising any kind of unquestioned leadership due to its predominance in other areas (economic or military) must be avoided from the beginning. It must be balanced in all aspects, and respect fair and equal proportionality for all those involved, from command, to the numbers of personnel, to participation in the preparation and instruction processes.

Policymakers should stress the risks involved in dismantling armies, asking the question: Will the countries of the region be capable of maintaining sufficient troops at the performance levels required to efficiently carry out these missions?

Policymakers should promote the organization of and participation in international meetings dealing with these subjects, with true national representatives who know the possibilities and the limits of policy, in order to make real and timely contributions to sharing pertinent information and keeping up to date on existing trends in the region in this complex area of action.

Any intervention must follow these rules: It must have a transparent and genuine humanitarian purpose and established objectives that define references to success. Authorization to intervene must be followed immediately by implementation. It must be militarily sustainable. It must be accompanied by a strategy for the reestablishment of the country after the conflict that includes preventing renewed conflict, and deal with the basic causes of the conflict. It must be proportional to the goals. It must be sensitive to the social and economic impact, especially on women and children. The entire international community must bear the costs. It must not have an indirect effect on neighboring countries. The participating troops must respect human rights.

In sum, the Haiti peacekeeping operation is an opportunity for the region to seek a new convergence of principles and methods for integrating and achieving interoperability, including laying some foundations in other areas that help consolidate peace and justice throughout the hemisphere.

NOTES

[1] The Law on Armed Conflict and other internationally recognized laws of war include the following:

- Regulations relating to the laws and customs of land war (H.I.V.R.) CICR, 1996
- International Convention on the recruitment, use, financing, and training of mercenaries (December 4, 1989)
- Convention on the Rights of Children (November 20, 1989); Protocol of the Convention on the Participation of Children in Armed Conflicts (May 25, 2000)
- The 1949 Geneva Conventions and the 1977 additional protocols. Nearly all states are signers of the four Geneva Conventions of August 12, 1949, which are treated as international law. They contain provisions on the protection of wounded and sick troops, prisoners of war, and exposed civilians. Of particular interest is the subject of Article 3, common to the four Conventions, on the proper treatment of prisoners of war, ordering the application of a series of provisions, some of which prohibit the following at any time and place: a) attempts on life and bodily integrity, especially homicide in all its forms, mutilation, cruel treatment, torture, and torment; b) hostage-taking; c) attempts against personal dignity, particularly humiliating and degrading treatment; and d) sentences and executions without prior judgment before a legitimately constituted court, with the legal guarantees recognized as indispensable by civilized peoples. It is also stated that the wounded and sick are to be picked up and assisted. More on this subject can be found at <http://www.icrc.org/spa>.

[2] The various duties that "peacetime soldiers" may be called upon to discharge include the following:

- guard borders or demilitarized zones
- conduct air, river, and land security, intelligence, or reconnaissance patrols
- mediate at the signature of peace agreements between warring states or groups
- negotiate cease-fires
- administer human and economic resources in territories affected by a

state of hostilities on a temporary basis until the reinstatement of local authorities

- limit and control the arsenals of states that are in a compromised situation with a developing conflict or in a situation of armed peace
- verify the effective application of peace agreements, collaborate with international human rights and refugee organizations and various non-governmental organizations
- create favorable conditions for the conduct of elections
- provide security for United Nations civilian officials for the normal discharge of the specific tasks of their duties
- perform humanitarian aid tasks.

3 *Interoperability* is the ability of two or more systems or components to exchange information, operate together, and use the same forces to conduct a joint mission. There are two general cases of interoperability. *Strategic interoperability* results from the ability and capability of the actors to give and/or accept support from other actors that facilitates their integrated action and makes it possible to procure benefits that are difficult to achieve alone. *Interoperability in peacekeeping missions* is the result of combining, exchanging, and integrating the combat strength (human and material resources) of the military factors of two or more nations (combined framework) under a single command, whose specific objective is the conduct of a specific mission, such as peacekeeping and humanitarian assistance operations.

Interoperability can be implemented through several methods:

- exchange and knowledge of the doctrine used
- integrated personnel education, training, and improvement exchanges, making it possible to reduce costs and minimize risks to personnel
- unification of combat and support processes and procedures in catastrophic situations (rules of engagement)
- knowledge and use of other languages
- incorporation of material resources compatible with those of other armed forces
- integrated instruction and training with other armed forces (exercises)
- active participation in peacekeeping missions, integrating the international community or participating in multinational coalitions, sharing and exchanging common objectives.

Chapter Nine

Bolivia: Responding to International Commitments

Rolando Sánchez Serrano

The first condition of non-violence is justice spread to every area of life.
Perhaps that is asking too much of human nature. However, I do not think so.
No one should dogmatize about the capability of human nature for degradation
or exaltation.

—Mahatma Gandhi

This chapter discusses Bolivia's participation in the combined peace-keeping operations in Haiti and examines the motives behind and objectives of the decision to send a contingent of police forces. This discussion is presented in the context of the sociopolitical situation in the region combined with the uncertainties and complexities of the social and historic processes of the world and the Western Hemisphere. In these circumstances, having the capability to forecast, and in the last resort to react to, possible outbreaks of conflicts and wars becomes an issue of prime importance for all the countries of the hemisphere.

The new threats[1] to peaceful coexistence among the peoples of Latin America and the Caribbean come from inside nations and extend across borders due to the favorable conditions existing in some societies for the emergence and expansion of such threats. Violent conflicts and confrontations find fertile ground in social environments with high levels of poverty, social inequality between the privileged classes and marginal society, socioeconomic unrest, and social exclusion among the various classes. In other words, the poor and excluded classes tend to be willing to be involved in acts of political violence and with illegal businesses (drug trafficking, terrorism), criminal organizations, guerrilla groups, or fundamentalist ideologies fragmenting the political community. For these reasons, the task of preventing outbreaks of political violence in the countries of the region must be taken on with seriousness and responsibility by governments and international organizations.

It is precisely in this sociopolitical context of instability, distrust, insecurity, recklessness, and potential violence that the project of *building* capacities to prevent and respond to threats of violence becomes relevant for the countries of the region. From this perspective, the need to create or strengthen elements favorable to peacekeeping, international security, the institutionalization of sociopolitical behaviors and actions, the deepening of democracy, and the reinforcement of the social commitment to peaceful coexistence become obvious to these nations and among the various social sectors and cultural identities. Furthermore, in addition to the tasks of pacifying societies embroiled in violent conflicts, it is also important to pay attention to the causes for such conflicts. One example of this is the enormous inequality between those who are privileged by the system and those who are excluded by it. It is one thing to face the disastrous consequences of violence and internal wars, and another to prevent and reduce the possibilities of outbreaks of armed conflicts.

Bolivia's participation as a member of the United Nations (UN) in the joint peacekeeping operations in the Republic of Haiti was above all a response to commitments and agreements aimed at responding resolutely to the requests of international agencies in global events in order to gain greater trust among the world community.[2] To that end, the state entities such as the armed forces and the national police that are involved in the peacekeeping tasks have made a significant effort to represent the country in a worthy and efficient manner. According to the senior advisor to the National Defense Ministry, "When the United Nations gives us the mission, we must perform these peacekeeping operations responsibly." For the uniformed and civilian personnel who participate in peacekeeping actions, this means a real achievement in their professional career and an honor to have contributed to the peaceful coexistence of humanity.

From this standpoint, the participating officers and civilians try to give the best they have to offer in their field in order to achieve the objectives and goals of the mission, with concern for the people who are suffering from the disasters of sociopolitical violence and for the country they represent. In terms of improving these operations, it is important to create a collective consciousness among countries and social sectors about a human existence based on ethical principles and values of respect, justice, solidarity, and mutual cooperation among nations and groups involved. The majority of the civilian population must be willing to cooperate with peacekeeping processes in keeping with the primary objectives of the United Nations. This chapter will attempt to contribute to the hemispheric effort to develop capabilities for peacekeeping in the countries of Latin America and the Caribbean where there may be the greatest possibilities for acts of violence. In these conditions, the effort made by the United Nations to establish a multinational force made up initially of the United States, France, and Canada, at the same time promoting the UN Stabilization Mission in Haiti in which several Latin American countries have participated, is justified.

BOLIVIA'S PARTICIPATION IN PEACEKEEPING OPERATIONS

After the Holocaust and the economic and human losses caused by World War II, the United Nations, among other international agencies, was formed with the basic purpose of jointly preserving world peace and international security.[3] To that end, the member nations made the commitment to cooperate in solving international economic, political, social, and humanitarian problems in order to bring human rights and freedoms to all, with no distinction as to race, sex, culture, or religion. In keeping with this commitment among the nations that really believe it is possible to achieve peaceful human coexistence based on mutual international cooperation, the member nations have participated in different peacekeeping operations called for by the United Nations Security Council. However, these interventions for the pacification of violent conflicts increased at the end of the 1980s as a result of the collapse of the socialist world and the former Union of Soviet Socialist Republics and due to problems of confrontation of an internal nature.[4] Battles between fundamentalist groups and religious sects, including the fight against drug trafficking and terrorism, have precipitated conditions for the United Nations to intervene with combined forces to facilitate peaceful settlements between groups involved in disputes in an attempt to maintain the security and sociopolitical stability of nations. As a result, the United Nations Security Council has called upon the member countries to form combined peacekeeping forces, which also permitted Bolivia to be called upon to participate in joint peacekeeping actions.

Since the middle of the 1990s, the United Nations has called upon Bolivia to be part of joint peacekeeping forces in violent conflicts and confrontations in the Republic of Haiti.[5] The state has also participated in upholding the peacekeeping operations in Angola and Congo since 1999; the process of selecting and readying the military and civilian personnel who were at the scene of the conflicts began in 1995[6] in order to send personnel trained to participate efficiently in peacekeeping operations. Bolivia has therefore participated in peacekeeping missions in three scenarios: Angola, Congo, and Haiti. In the first two cases, contingents from the armed forces supported by civilians (doctors, dentists, nurses, and technicians) were sent, while about 100 national police troops, senior officers, and graduates of the Senior National Police Academy's police administration and training course were sent to Haiti.

Specifically, requests for the participation of the Bolivian police in the operations to reestablish democratic order and peace in Haiti began in June

1994 after the UN Security Council authorized the use of force to reinstate democracy in Haiti. In September 1994, Bolivian Foreign Affairs announced the country's possible participation without making the deployment of police forces official. Later in September, the United Nations Security Council invited the Bolivian government to contribute to the actions to restore constitutional order in Haiti. Bolivia agreed to contribute a contingent of police instructors made up of staff and officers for a mission to advise, train, and monitor Haitian police personnel so that they could perform their duties efficiently in compliance with institutional standards.[7] The Bolivian police contingent became part of the Multinational Force of the International Monitoring Police from October 1994 to March 1995, carrying out the activities defined by the general plan drawn up by the Central Command of the International Police Monitoring (IPM)–Bolivia force. The Bolivian police contingent was assigned the northern part of the city of Port-au-Prince and Fort Liberté as its area of operations.

IPM–Bolivia was basically aimed at permitting a peaceful transition to democracy in Haiti by providing monitoring services for Haitian police forces and discharging the duties of prevention, assistance, and security for citizens through continuous patrolling; and scheduling courses on organization, police doctrine, patrolling, traffic control, community relations, operating procedures, and surveillance. The objective was to support the tasks of reorganizing and reestablishing an efficient public force in Haiti that would guarantee compliance with the laws and respect for human rights, as well as the defense of society and democracy.

Bolivia participated in these peacekeeping operations with a group of 106 police personnel in the first phase and 109 during the second phase (see table 9–1).

The Bolivian police conducted the tasks of controlling social order and compliance with institutional standards at the same time they conducted training programs, specifically handling 2,121 cases (see table 9–2).

TABLE 9–1. BOLIVIAN POLICE FORCES IN HAITI PEACEKEEPING OPERATIONS

Rank	Number in First Phase	Number in Second Phase
Colonel	1	1
Lieutenant Colonel	3	1
Major	52	5
Captain	49	79
Lieutenant	1	23
Totals	106	109

Source: National Police, Institutional Management Unit, "Report on Operation *Uphold Democracy*, Republic of Haiti," La Paz, 2004.

TABLE 9–2. SUMMARY OF POLICE CASES HANDLED BY THE IPM-BOLIVIA
(OCTOBER 1994 AND SEPTEMBER 1995)

Type of Action	Oct	Nov	Dec	Jan	Feb	Mar	Total
Felonies	39	112	199	164	111	51	676
Misdemeanors	22	68	130	98	81	40	439
Assistance	12	57	63	46	60	24	262
Special Services	21	61	120	137	114	84	537
Other events	15	39	60	29	35	29	207
Total Cases	109	337	572	474	401	228	2,121

Source: National Police, Institutional Management Unit, "Report on Operation *Uphold Democracy*, Republic of Haiti," La Paz, 2004.

In addition, preparations are ongoing to send a group of civilian police to support the UN Stabilization Mission in Haiti. This deployment is still in process.[8]

THE DECISION TO PARTICIPATE

Bolivia's decision to participate in the peacekeeping operations in Haiti mainly had to do with the country's accords and agreements with the international community as a member of the United Nations, which creates certain rights and duties for the Bolivian state with respect to that international agency. The decision to send military, police, and civilian contingents to the peacekeeping operations was therefore basically justified and substantiated in these international treaties and agreements. So the government authorities argue that Bolivia must accept the invitation of the United Nations Security Council without objections.[9] In addition, it is understood that the participation of the armed forces or the national police in peacekeeping tasks is an important acknowledgment by that international agency of the capability of the country's defense, security, and public order institutions. In other words, for most of the country's diplomatic representatives and government authorities, the invitations issued by the United Nations to participate in peacekeeping operations meant an important opportunity for the military, police, and civilians to broaden their experience and capabilities at the international level.

The process whereby the decision is made to send contingents to peacekeeping operations consists basically of the preeminence of the international agreements to which the country is committed. The arguments that defend this position maintain that the country cannot stay on the sidelines of these peacekeeping actions, as was stated by the Director of the Foreign Affairs Ministry's Directorate General of Multinational Relations in September 2004:

Since Bolivia belongs to the United Nations, which oversees international security, then one of its first missions is to support international peace and security. Bolivia supports all peace building actions that promote disarmament and are aimed at controlling the proliferation of all types of weapons, be they nuclear or chemical.

In addition, there are other motives that have to do with the standing of the Bolivian state in the world community. Since Bolivia is a small country without much weight on the international scene, it feels that the most appropriate thing is to take a committed position on the resolutions issued from international agencies by aligning itself with the countries that play a major role in the guidance of these agencies, either in the United Nations or within the Organization of American States.

The process of sending troops to joint peacekeeping operations and the return to democracy in Haiti began with the official invitation from the United Nations Security Council, through Bolivia's Embassy and Permanent Representative to the United Nations, to the Bolivian Foreign Affairs Minister, requesting the supply and deployment of a contingent of civilian police for tasks of controlling social order and the respect of institutional standards. Specifically, a police contingent was requested to perform tasks associated with prevention, assistance, and the security of the citizenry, involving activities such as patrolling and scheduling training courses for Haitian police forces.

Next, the Foreign Affairs Minister forwarded the invitation in an official letter to the Senior Commander of the National Police so that state institution could explore the possibility of forming a group of police personnel in accordance with the requirements and requests stated by the Multinational Force Command and the Central Command of the International Police Monitoring Force. When the police entity received the international agency's invitation to participate in combined peacekeeping actions, the information was distributed to the various police authorities so that interested personnel could apply for the selection process if they met the requirements. One of the primary requirements was that candidates—aside from meeting the police training requirements—have no negative incident in their record of service to the community. Accordingly, the travel of a total of 109 staff and officer graduates of the Senior National Police Training Center was authorized by a resolution of the Senior Command of the National Police.[10] After the candidates were selected at the level of the national police, the list of the police agents who met the requirements was sent to the international agency for evaluation and final selection.

However, the requirements set by the international agency did not define the decision for participation in peacekeeping operations and the selection of the officers. It was also contingent on certain factors associated with the policy of the police institution, such as its interest in recovering or increasing its prestige. The national police saw the possibility of participating in this type of international task as a favorable opportunity because its loss of trust among the population—due to some members of the police having been involved in illegal actions—was well known, and it thought it could recover that trust based on some recognition on the international scene. This depended on the level of the participating police personnel in the areas of community service professionalism, efficiency, and ethics in tasks with other combined forces.

Furthermore, decisions to send troops to the peacekeeping operations in Haiti did not pose many obstacles at the level of the executive branch. The problems began to arise at the level of the legislative branch, since the final authorization for the country's participation in international peacekeeping operations must be granted by the National Congress.[11] Objections to participation were minor when the majority of the legislators (two-thirds as most indicated) belonged to the political parties that were part of the governing coalition. Due to the broad support enjoyed by the then-current coalition government among lawmakers, there was not much discussion at the time of the congressional authorization for Bolivia to participate in the operations to keep the peace and reestablish democracy in Haiti between October 1994 and March 1995. In other words, the executive branch had secured a legislative "steamroller" for approval of the various laws and other legislative authorizations.[12]

Nor were there many stumbling blocks for the congressional authorization to send troops to Angola and Congo and their respective replacements every 6 months since 1999. This was favored because in the administration from 1997 to 2002 that ended up with two presidents (Hugo Banzer and Jorge Quiroga),[13] the governing coalition had the legislative majority in the congress. In other words, when the parties present in the government had a majority representation in the legislature, the decisions of the executive branch were endorsed by the congress without much difficulty. Among these authorizations was one to deploy military and police troops abroad. On this subject, a Movement Towards Socialism (MAS) legislator argued that the authorization to deploy troops abroad was

> fine until we—the Movement Towards Socialism, MAS—get to congress, because these authorization debates lasted fifteen minutes and were approved and ready. But the first time this request was made in our presence, it lasted two days. Then what did they do, the international agencies invited legislators to go to Congo, to go to Mozambique, of course not a single one of them was from the MAS. So the legislators from the traditional parties that until August 6, 2002, were used to saying yes without any argument had no response when we engaged the subject, and had to undergo our broadsides on the subject; and they coached the lawmakers

with arguments on the importance of participating in peacekeeping. And after they were coached those lawmakers argued that our dignity, that the Bolivian soldier and all that silliness, that they have not changed the condition of the Bolivian soldier or altered the capability and efficiency of the Armed Forces. So the debate was bitter.

The information in this interview shows that when a considerable number of lawmakers were opposed to the governing coalition in the legislature, as was the case of the MAS,[14] the decision to send contingents abroad was no longer so easy. For various reasons, the opposition attempted to demonstrate its leadership in the various legislative debates, and this became obvious when the opposition party was guided by ideologies based on certain radical leftist principles and "resistance" to the international policies promoted by first world countries such as the United States. It is important to note that since the September 11, 2001, attack, this country has consistently backed projects for the preservation of peace and security in the Western Hemisphere.

The decision to send police to the peacekeeping operations in Haiti was not easy to accomplish, especially in view of the fact that for the legislative authorization, many lawmakers from the opposition party (MAS) were voicing the rationale that the interventions promoted by the United States through the United Nations were merely disguised occupations of defenseless countries in keeping with the interests of U.S. "imperialism."

However, the legislators who do not share the ideology of the traditional left and are more left- or right-center argue that sending contingents to peacekeeping operations is important. These sectors feel that participation is beneficial to the armed forces and the national police in that they acquire new experience and capabilities in such operations. Similarly, the lawmakers who are in favor of troop deployments feel that it is important to increase the number of officers and civilians taking part in peacekeeping actions. This participation would result in favorable conditions on the international stage and in other aspects such as foreign cooperation for the country's socioeconomic development projects.

On the other hand, the possible effects that participation in these peacekeeping operations could entail inside the Bolivian state were not considered in taking this decision. This is because the political decision to deploy police contingents is made imperceptibly or subtly, and often the population only becomes aware of it at the time the group of military or police personnel is already leaving the country. Most of the citizenry is not interested in whether the country participates in peacekeeping missions. Actually, people pay more attention to the news about domestic problems such as the policy regarding oil, the referendum, the legislature, or the various sociopolitical protests that are constantly arising from the country's various social and regional sectors.

In view of the above, it could be said that the decisions on participation in peacekeeping operations are only dealt with at the level of the executive branch backed by the Congress, in which the major actors are the Foreign Affairs Ministry, the National Defense Ministry, the Armed Forces Joint Chiefs of Staff, the National Police Command, and the Congress.

OBJECTIVES AND PLANNING OF THE PEACEKEEPING MISSION IN HAITI

The motivations behind the decisions to send contingents to the peacekeeping operations in Haiti are mainly associated with the agreements the country has with international agencies such as the United Nations or the Organization of American States, which are the basis for initiating the process of selecting and readying police and civilian personnel for peacekeeping actions. In addition, there are other purposes linked to greater professionalization of the police, as well as economic incentives for participants. This view is not necessarily shared by the various political actors; for example, MAS leaders and legislators argue that the interests of U.S. "imperialism" are behind peacekeeping operations, with the aim of having the armed forces of Latin America and the Caribbean under its command and influence in order to use them against countries that show resistance to "imperialist" domination.

However, it is notable that the criteria cited by the political actors and police authorities who support and are in favor of peacekeeping operations are generally associated with the possible immediate benefits that can be obtained. On the other hand, the politicians opposed to peacekeeping tasks see this participation from an ideological standpoint, arguing that peacekeeping interventions in the Western Hemisphere are strictly to further the interests of U.S. "imperialism."

There is some lack of a broader vision among the hierarchical authorities of the government and politicians on the sociopolitical *meaning* of preserving peaceful coexistence among the countries of the hemisphere and among the various social and cultural identities within countries. These values reflect the central principles of the United Nations Charter to "achieve international cooperation in the resolution of international economic, social, cultural, or humanitarian problems and in the *development and promotion of respect for human rights and the basic freedoms of all, without distinction as to race, sex, language, or religion*" [emphasis added].

OBJECTIVES

The principal objectives considered for the deployment of police to the joint peacekeeping operations in Haiti were political goals, professionalization of the police, and economic objectives:

Political:
- the desire for Bolivia to have a presence in peacekeeping actions in an international environment favorable to the country; participation in international cooperation efforts that can assist or complement other projects
- support for all international efforts aimed at keeping or reestablishing peace in the world or among nations.

This also has to do with the perception of Bolivia as a pacifist country by definition. A Foreign Affairs Ministry official said in September 2004 that "Bolivia is a pacifist country by vocation, so our country supports all these initiatives, and is always going to work for the existence of peace anywhere in the world." In spite of this "pacifist vocation" projected toward the international community, recent events confirm the existence of sociopolitical conflicts of interest in the country that have frequently led to political violence, as occurred in the events of October 2003.[15]

Professionalization of the police:
- provide a good, efficient representation of the country in the combined peacekeeping forces
- use the police forces' experience and capabilities to the benefit of the institution; the Bolivian police who participate in peacekeeping missions can contribute new knowledge that can be spread throughout the police institution
- gain new knowledge in the area of combat and control in scenarios of violence and social upheaval.

Economic:
- gain additional economic income for the officers sent to the operations, since they receive monthly pay from the international agency in exchange for their participation, and their families continue to collect the wages of the absent police personnel.

With respect to this last objective, almost all the government authorities and lawmakers who are in favor of sending police forces to Haiti agree that the economic benefit for those who go to the operations is an important factor.

Specific Objectives
The purposes for participation of the Bolivian police contingent in the operations for peacekeeping and democratic reestablishment in Haiti between October 1994 and March 1995 included the following:

- the organization of police activities associated with Companies 19 and 22 located in Fort Liberté
- basic instruction for Haitian police personnel in police procedures and techniques and in observing and applying institutional standards
- recovery of the Haitian population's confidence in the police function by strengthening police work and working with the community
- investigation of felonies
- projecting an image of the Bolivian National Police in the international environment.[16]

To achieve these objectives, the Bolivian police contingent performed varied monitoring, advisory, training, and patrol tasks.

In any case, the objectives targeted by sending contingents to the peacekeeping operations in Haiti have more to do with honoring the country's agreements with international agencies such as the United Nations or the Organization of American States, in which Bolivia wants to have a presence by contributing to these peacekeeping actions. Added to this is the desire to increase the capability of the police through the preparation and experience obtained for participation, and to gain some economic benefits for the families of the officers sent to those operations.

Planning

The process of planning the deployment of police contingents to the peacekeeping operations in Haiti began when the United Nations issued the official invitation to the Bolivian government and therefore to the National Police Command through the Foreign Affairs Ministry. The invitation was then extended throughout the police institution, indicating the conditions and requirements for candidacy so that only those who meet the requirements could apply to participate in the selection process. This is possible at the time the national police authorities decide to participate, after a detailed analysis of the parameters and benefits the international agency offers to participants. These parameters and benefits would include the living conditions in the conflict area, responsibility for possible accidents and/or disastrous consequences (disability or death), the form of participation in joint actions, and the economic benefits. When the decision was made to participate in the mission, the officers and subordinate personnel were selected so the list could be sent to the international agency for the definitive appointment of participants. Once they were accepted as part of the mission, they began readiness and training activities with local and foreign instructors in order to achieve efficient performance in peacekeeping tasks. The planning process was completed by the national police in coordination with Foreign Affairs and the Central Command of the International Police Monitoring Command.

In planning to send police to the peacekeeping operations in Haiti, the police authorities tried to follow as well as possible the standards and the selection requirements stated in the request and observe their own institutional regulations. So the officers who met the various requirements were selected from among the students in the Senior National Police Academy. This enabled those selected to gain important recognition from the international agency and the Haitian population when they exhibited efficient performance in the various police tasks such as patrolling and the training of Haitian police forces.

On the subject of planning activities, it is important to note that the Armed Forces of Bolivia have already planned to create a military school to ready contingents for peacekeeping operations to be located in Camin, in the Department of Santa Cruz. This demonstrates the commitment on the part of the military to improve the training and instruction conditions for the forces to be sent to peacekeeping missions.

POSSIBILITIES OF EFFECTIVENESS OF COMBINED FORCES

The effectiveness of the police participating in the peacekeeping operations in Haiti is primarily related to the quality of preparation and the living conditions in the area of operations. The ability of these personnel to understand the problems of people in conditions of poverty and sociopolitical disorder and their degree of acceptance by the national or local society assisted by the combined forces have had a profound impact on the effectiveness of the police in conducting various tasks.

Furthermore, living conditions in the fields of operation impact the effectiveness of peacekeeping tasks, especially the way the communal living spaces are arranged, since this can generate a certain degree of motivation and responsibility among personnel that comes from socioeconomic, political, and cultural contexts different from the scene of the intervention. The participating countries that have a better economic standing and optimum defense capabilities offer their soldiers or police comfortable living conditions. For example, nations such as Argentina have the capability to transfer their troops in their own boats to the vicinity of the host country. This is not the situation of Bolivia, which only sends police forces without much support in terms of additional resources for troop transportation and logistics.

Those who have a better environment may not have the social and human sensitivity demonstrated by those who live with the bare essentials to understand people's problems, motivations, and inclinations. In addition, soldiers or police who do not have many resources often come from countries where the economic, social, and political situation is similar to the socioterritorial area of action.

It is also important to note a central issue associated with adaptation to the social environment. Police who have experienced social upheaval, political instability, guerrilla aggression, or drug terrorism first-hand in their own countries may be better equipped to adapt to the socioterritorial scenarios in conflict, since they know how sociopolitical problems work and develop because they have experience in controlling and handling conflictive and violent situations. This may not be true of contingents that come from developed countries.

With respect to the recruitment of staff and officers, it is by official invitation and not in terms of a mandatory call to participate in peacekeeping operations. In the case of Haiti, the decision to participate in such operations is essentially *free and voluntary*, so this decision to support peacekeeping actions takes on a *humanitarian quality and a sense of solidarity with one's fellow man*. In other words, the voluntary nature of the formation of the joint peacekeeping forces has a positive impact on the effectiveness and professionalism of the participating agents.

Similarly, the degree of acceptance expressed by national or local society toward the peacekeepers impacts the effectiveness of their actions. A sociopolitical context of acceptance of and cooperation with peacekeeping tasks conducted by foreigners is preferable to achieving peacekeeping objectives in a hostile environment that resists any type of foreign intervention.

PERFORMANCE OF COMBINED FORCES

Determining the performance level of the effectiveness of combined peacekeeping forces is not an easy task because it requires a very careful review of each case, identifying the various elements that could indicate the degree of effectiveness of peacekeeping missions. However, some factors make it possible to evaluate the effectiveness of peacekeeping operations, such as the increase or decrease of sociopolitical violence, the extent to which the behaviors and actions of political and social actors obey the democratic "rules of the game," and the recovery or maintenance of political stability. This means that an effective intervention must reduce conflicts and violent confrontations. If they increase or intensify, it means that the operations have not been of much value or have not been appropriate to the specificities of the sociopolitical and cultural context.

Similarly, compliance of the behaviors and actions of political and social actors with official standards and other rules of the game would indicate that the interventions were effective and had results favorable to strengthening democratic institutions. On the other hand, if the institutional guidelines are violated and the use of force becomes the preferred option for the groups in conflict, it could be said that the peacekeeping operations were not very effective.

In addition, the effectiveness of peacekeeping tasks can be evaluated by the degree of acknowledgment or gratitude the various social sectors and ethnic-cultural groups in conflict express toward the police forces that have taken various actions to mitigate the situation of violence and maintain sociopolitical order. For example, a participant in a peacekeeping contingent in Haiti related the gratitude of the host country population:

> The day when we were coming home, the only mission the people—the Haitians—cried to see leaving was the Bolivian mission, and that shows that we Bolivians were efficient in our work, because not only did we act as members of the combined forces, we have also experienced the consequences of poverty, the consequences of the lack of education.

This means that when the police demonstrate greater sensitivity and social commitment to those who are suffering the adverse consequences of social disorder and sociopolitical conflicts, the affected population shows an attitude of active acceptance of the troops and cooperation in peacekeeping tasks. If the peacekeepers demonstrate an intolerant and authoritarian attitude toward the civilian population involved in problems of social upheaval and sociopolitical violence, people soon take on an attitude of indifference toward peacekeeping work and can end up resorting to resistance and aggression toward the foreigners. This is what appears to happen with military or police forces that come from first world countries. These forces seem to be impacted by the situation of poverty, social disorder, and political violence faced by the host countries because these problems are nearly nonexistent in their countries of origin. As a result, their actions are not so appropriate to the specificity of the context, which in some cases results in attitudes of intolerance among the people. In any of these cases, the evaluation of the effectiveness of combined forces in peacekeeping missions basically has to do with the reduction of violence, the easing of social conflicts, the recovery of political and social stability, and respect for institutional standards, without loss of human life among the combined forces or the host population. If, on the other hand, these factors worsen, it means that the peacekeeping actions have not been effective.

RECOMMENDATIONS

Based on the arguments stated above, it is possible to set certain guidelines for improving peacekeeping operations in countries embroiled in violent conflicts and confrontations:

- Deepen and broaden the profile and preparation of the volunteers making up combined peacekeeping and international security forces in the Western Hemisphere.
- In peacekeeping operations, it is indispensable above all to emphasize

respect for human rights, so that the society and its social and political leaders value the true dimension and meaning of peacekeeping and the effort made by international agencies such as the United Nations or the Organization of American States.

- Spread the idea of the importance of enjoying peaceful coexistence among nations and among the various social sectors and ethnic-cultural groups in order to improve the living conditions of men, women, youth, and children, by holding seminars and forums in various environments and locations of the country in order to generate a social commitment to the human condition beyond national borders.

- Maintain contacts between former participants (military, police, and civilian) in peacekeeping operations in order to preserve a sense of unity and to be able to mobilize them rapidly in situations of pressing need.

- In the National Congress, promote the idea that debating on the deployment of troops to peacekeeping operations is a matter of importance for human coexistence in the world, since it involves the preservation of life itself, so it must not be confused with unilateral interests or radical ideological positions.

- Promote the creation in Bolivia of a specialized center for the discussion, training, planning, and preparation associated with making contingents available for peacekeeping operations.

CONCLUSION

Most of the countries of Latin America and the Caribbean are fragile states and likely to be involved in internal conflicts as a result of the persistence in the region of authoritarian and sectarian sociopolitical logics in certain circles of sectoral power. It is lamentable that they still think the violent imposition of the interests of oligarchic ultra-conservative groups or extremist ideologies is the best way to solve the burning problems confronting Latin American nations. It is in this context of social conflict and institutional weakness that acts of political violence break out, as in the case of Haiti, or internal wars such as those in Colombia, or the constant threat of guerrilla warfare in Peru.

The peacekeeping mission undertaken by the UN with regard to the critical situation now being experienced by the Republic of Haiti is of prime importance because it is the first experience in controlling armed conflicts in which the countries of the region are participating by contributing military, police, and civilian contingents. It also makes it possible to develop capabilities for joint action among the Latin American states to achieve a solid, committed, and efficient response based on a policy of reciprocal cooperation among nations that promote conditions for a more stable, peaceful, and integrated region by establishing a regional base of broad-based, rapid-response, multinational forces.

In this perspective, the UN's invitation to the Bolivian government to participate in the peacekeeping operations in Haiti was received with all the required seriousness and responsibility. Bolivia has a foreign policy of supporting UN actions aimed at preserving peaceful coexistence between peoples and among the various social sectors, and the tasks aimed at controlling armed conflicts. Accordingly, Bolivia did not delay in sending a police contingent to Haiti to perform patrol and control duties and to organize training courses for the Haitian police.

It is important to note that there are still some social and political sectors that do not necessarily share the policy of the Bolivian state to resolutely support the peacekeeping operations sponsored by the United Nations, arguing that certain interests of some developed countries hamper the free determination of the Latin American nations. However, both the authorities of the executive branch and the military and police demonstrate a very favorable attitude toward sending personnel on peacekeeping missions, realizing that Bolivia's participation in such missions fosters the peaceful coexistence of humanity and also makes it possible for the armed forces and the national police to gain new experience in the control of sociopolitical conflicts.

Furthermore, it is noted that the countries of the region demonstrate a remarkable commitment to contributing military and police contingents to the peacekeeping operations sponsored by the United Nations, which is very favorable to the consolidation of the democracies and the development of the societies of Latin America and the Caribbean. This becomes even more relevant with the realization that security, social order, and political stability are essential in overcoming the great social inequalities that often lead to violent conflicts.

NOTES

[1] Due to the fall of the Berlin Wall, the collapse of the former Soviet Union, and the rise of the so-called new democracies, analysts of world politics and ideological models of society said that one of the broad sociopolitical options, the socialist or communist scheme, had failed, giving free rein to capitalism in economics and liberal democracy in politics. As a result, it was felt that the Cold War between East and West, which had up to then defined the international policy of most countries of the world, was over, because it made no sense after the fall of one of the rivals. So the notion of national or international security took on a new meaning, and now the new threats, such as international terrorism, drug trafficking, drug wars, the spread of ethnic-cultural identities, the deterioration of the environment, the demographic explosion, and others, would be a greater danger

to peacekeeping and global security. A conception of security based essentially on political and military factors became a conception more associated with human qualities. Then the prophecy of the great danger presented by the new threats became a cruel and pathetic reality after the terrorist attack on the World Trade Center on September 11, 2001. The following works can be consulted on the subject: Adam Przeworski, *Democracy and the Market Political and Economic Reforms in Eastern Europe and Latin America* (New York: Cambridge University Press, 1991); Francis Fukuyama, *The End of History and the Last Man* (Agostini, Spain: Planeta, 1995); Samuel Huntington, *The Third Wave: Democratization at the End of the 20ᵗʰ Century* (Barcelona, Spain: Paidos, 1994); María Cristina Rosas, *Hemisphere Security and Global Insecurity: Between Interamerican Cooperation and Preventive War* (Mexico City: UNAM–Canadian Embassy, 2004); and others.

2   The various descriptive reflections and proposals made in the text are primarily based on a review of the literature on the subject of peacekeeping and security and the analysis of documents (reports, official notes, and conclusions of forums on sending contingents to peacekeeping operations), and interviews with Bolivian government authorities, lawmakers, and military and police personnel. The documents reviewed include: National Police, Institutional Management Unit, "Report on Operation Uphold Democracy, Republic of Haiti," La Paz, 2004; Permanent Council of the OAS, "Report on OAS Activities relating to Haiti," 2004; UN Security Council, Authorization of the use of force to restore democracy in Haiti, June 1994; Presidency of the Republic of Bolivia, Law approving the Memorandum of Understanding signed between the Government of Bolivia and the United Nations on the Contribution to United Nations Reserve Forces, April 28, 1999; Letter from the United Nations to Bolivia's Permanent Ambassador to the UN, April 1, 2004; Letter from Bolivia's Permanent Ambassador to the UN to the Bolivian Foreign Affairs Ministry, April 1, 2004; Letter from the Foreign Affairs Ministry to the Commander in Chief of the Bolivian National Police, April 19, 2004; Letter of Congressional Authorization to the President of the Republic for the deployment of 202 military troops, May 12, 2004; and Letter from the Commander in Chief of the National Police to the Ministry of Foreign Affairs.

3   The United Nations Charter, signed in June 1945 and put into effect in October of that year, states in Chapter I, Article 1, Paragraphs 1 and 2: "1. To maintain international peace and security, and to that end: to take effective collective measures to prevent and eliminate threats to peace and to suppress acts of aggression or other violations of peace; and to achieve through peaceful means, and in accordance with the principles of justice and international law, the settlement or arrangement of international

disputes or situations liable to lead to violations of peace; 2. To promote friendly relations between nations based on respect for the principle of equal rights and the free determination of peoples, and to take other appropriate measures to strengthen world peace."

4   Up until the end of the so-called Cold War between East and West, and as a result of the collapse of the socialist road taken by the former Soviet Union, peacekeeping interventions were mainly aimed at conflicts between nations, and only 13 operations occurred in that period. However, after the Cold War, peacekeeping operations rapidly increased in number and complexity, and 28 new operations have been undertaken since 1989, reaching the highest point in the mid-1990s with the participation of forces nearly 70,000 strong—between civilian and military personnel—from 77 countries. And most of these new conflicts involve intrastate wars between ethnic groups or between guerrilla groups. See <www.onu.org/temas/paz/misiones.htm>.

5   Bolivia's participation in the peacekeeping operations in Haiti was basically the result of the authorization by the UN Security Council in July 1994 on the use of force to restore democracy in Haiti, after the constitutional president of Haiti at the time, Jean Bertrand Aristide, was unseated by a coup d'état; this resulted in the Bolivian government being asked by the United Nations and the ousted Aristide to participate in the peacekeeping operations. See United Nations Security Council Resolution No. 362/94 of September 29, 1994; official letter from Aristide to the Bolivian government (September 28, 1994) requesting the deployment of police chiefs to assist the Haitian police in an advisory capacity, [Presidential Decree] DP 684/94.

6   The United Nations issued the formal invitation to the Bolivian state in 1995 to participate in the peacekeeping operations in May 1997; the Memorandum of Understanding between the United Nations and the Government of the Republic of Bolivia on contributing to the United Nations reserve forces agreements system was signed. And in April 1999 that agreement was made legal through a law promulgated by then-President Hugo Banzer, under which Bolivia participated in the joint peacekeeping actions in Angola and then in Congo on the African continent. See Carol Dick Richter, *The Bolivian Experience in Peacekeeping Operations* (Buenos Aires: CHDS, 2001); UN, Memorandum of Understanding between the United Nations and the Government of the Republic of Bolivia on contributing to the United Nations reserve forces agreements system, New York, May 22, 1997; Law Approving the Memorandum of Understanding between the United Nations and the Government of Bolivia, April 28, 1999. Under that law, Bolivia sent a contingent of 202 military and civilian personnel every 6 months. It is now in Bolivian Watch VI.

7   However, actually sending the police contingent was the result of the official request Aristide made to the Bolivian government. On September 28, 1994, Aristide requested the participation of Bolivia in the combined peacekeeping forces to perform advisory, training, and patrol duties in Fort Liberté and Port-au-Prince. See National Police, Institutional Management Unit, "Report on Operation *Uphold Democracy*, Republic of Haiti," La Paz, 2004.

8   From April to July 2004, correspondence was repeatedly exchanged between the Permanent Embassy to the United Nations, the Organization of American States, the Foreign Affairs Ministry, and the National Police, about the possible shipment of a contingent of civilian police to Haiti. However, the travel of a group of eight officers who were to participate in the training course for the establishment of a police unit in the city of Port-au-Prince was rejected. See letter from the Commander in Chief of the National Police to the Foreign Affairs Ministry, June 8, 2004, expressing a heated protest to the refusal for police personnel to participate in the course.

9   For example, in 1997, then-President Gonzalo Sanchez de Lozada granted full powers to Bolivia's ambassador and permanent representative to the United Nations to sign the memorandum of understanding between the Bolivian government and the United Nations, which resulted in the deployment of contingents to peacekeeping operations abroad. See Letter of Power of Attorney signed by then-President Gonzalo Sanchez de Lozada, May 14, 1997.

10   National Police Senior Command Resolution No. 362/94 of September 29, 1994.

11   Article 59 Paragraph 16, of the Constitution of the Bolivian State says that among the powers of the legislative branch are: "To authorize the deployment of troops outside the territory of the Republic and to determine the duration of their absence." So the final authorization to send contingents out of the country to foreign peacekeeping operations must be passed by the National Congress.

12   From 1993 to 1997, the government was run by a coalition made up of Gonzalo Sanchez de Lozada's National Revolutionary Movement party, Antonio Aranibar's Free Bolivia Movement party, and the late Max Fernandez's Civilian Solidarity Unit Party, as the principal parties of the government pact that gave the presidency to Sanchez de Lozada. The interparty coalition had a majority in the legislature for the approval of the various important laws—for example, the law on the capitalization of state companies.

13   The so-called "mega-coalition" running the government from 1997 to 2002 included many political parties to make the late Hugo Banzer

president; among the strongest were Banzer's ADN, Jaime Paz's MIR, Remedios Loza's Consciencia de Patria (CONDEPA), and Johnny Fernandez's Civilian Solidarity Unit, so the "mega" had steamroller strength in the legislature for the passage of the various laws. However, Hugo Banzer could not complete his term due to a terminal illness, which resulted in the institutional transition in August 2001, when then-Vice President Jorge Quiroga became president.

[14] The Movement Towards Socialism (MAS) came in second in the 2002 national elections, thereby becoming the country's second strongest political force; although in the post-electoral political negotiations the leaders of that party did not show much interest in running the government. This enabled the MNR party's Gonzalo Sanchez de Lozada to be elected for a second time as President, supported by the MIR and UCS. However, Sanchez de Lozada was forced to resign due to the social upheaval that broke out in October 2003, in which the MAS played a significant role in intensifying and expanding the social movement, calling for the resignation of the president and the defense of natural gas. Furthermore, in the December 2004 municipal election the only political party that had any national presence was the MAS, with the electoral support of around 18 percent of the entire country, since the other parties' votes had dropped dramatically, making the MAS the top political force in Bolivia. For the time being, the MAS has a remarkable influence on the country's politics.

[15] In October 2003, Bolivia experienced social upheaval and political violence without precedent since the democratic era began in 1982. The social uprising, especially in the vicinity of the city of El Alto, as well as confrontations between the military, police, and insurgents, resulted in more than 60 dead, hundreds wounded, and enormous destruction of public assets. Bloody days that finally ended with the resignation of then-President Gonzalo Sanchez de Lozada led to the institutional transition with the rise of then-Vice President Carlos de Mesa to the top office in the nation. On this subject, see OSAL, *The Gas War in Bolivia*, OSAL–CLACSO–ASDI, Buenos Aires, Year IV No. 12, September-December 2003; Alvaro Garcia, Raul Prada, and Luis, *Memories of October*, Muela del Diablo, La Paz, 2004.

[16] National Police, Institutional Management Unit, "Report on Operation *Uphold Democracy*, Republic of Haiti," La Paz, 2004.

Chapter Ten

Guatemala: Transforming Toward a New Mission

Guillermo Pacheco

I n recent years, we have witnessed a series of events in the international arena that confirm the onset of change and a review of policies
that seemed to be irreversible realities. Some of the concepts and ideas
that have contributed to defining this new cycle have arisen in a framework of
more rational international cooperation, distinguished in large part by the
definitive demise of East–West confrontation. However, these circumstances
are not sufficient to safeguard a transition free of obstacles or possible points
of conflict.

In these circumstances, the change in the relationship between the two
major military powers and the disappearance of a world divided by two military blocs have played a significant role in generating encouraging conditions
in which the United Nations finally can be fully operative.[1]

United Nations (UN) peacekeeping operations (PKO) began during
the historic period of the Cold War as a mechanism for resolving conflicts
between states. Unarmed or lightly armed military personnel from a number
of member countries under the command of the United Nations conduct and
deploy these operations. Peacekeeping personnel can be deployed when the
major international powers agree to entrust the United Nations with the task
of ending conflicts that could threaten international peace and stability, including some of the so-called proxy wars between client states of the superpowers.

The end of the Cold War therefore brought about important changes in
peacekeeping work and in the roles played by organizations such as the United
Nations and other multilateral coalitions. As a new spirit of cooperation develops and grows, the UN Security Council has been conducting peacekeeping missions with increasingly more visible and complex components, most
of them in cases aimed at enforcing peace agreements between protagonists
in conflicts inside states themselves. These missions have also gradually included new nonmilitary elements, which when included in the planning

process help to ensure the mission's sustainability. As a general rule, these missions are deployed when a mutual ceasefire has been achieved between the parties involved in a conflict. In such a case, UN troops observe the development of the situation in the field and report impartially on the observance of and compliance with the ceasefire and cessation of hostilities agreements between the parties. They simultaneously monitor the withdrawal of troops or other elements included in peace agreements, in an effort to provide the time and space necessary for diplomatic efforts to advance in identifying and attending to the basic causes of the conflict.

UN Security Council Resolution 1529 authorized the deployment of a multinational interim force in Haiti in response to its request for assistance in reestablishing a stable environment for the country's democratic and political process. That resolution was followed 6 months later by Security Council Resolution 1542, creating the United Nations Mission for Haiti in June 2004.

BACKGROUND

Guatemala does not have a long history of participation in peacekeeping operations, due in part to the fact that its armed forces have been involved in an internal armed conflict since the 1950s. Even so, Guatemala participated directly in Haiti in 1994 and 1995 with a contingent of more than 150 people. Similarly, it has participated as an observer in many missions at the invitation of other Latin American countries—for example, the invitation of the Argentine government to the mission in Cyprus in 2000. (See table 10–1 for a summary of the various peacekeeping missions in which Guatemala has been involved.)

Guatemala achieved peace after the Firm and Durable Peace Accord in 1996, after nearly 36 years of internal armed conflict. During that time, the army played a major role defending the state's interests against the revolutionary forces. Later, in peacetime, the country reached a transitional period in which it was imperative to define a new mission and role for the army. Changes included a significant reduction of the defense budget and of the existing forces, aimed at consolidating a more efficient army that was both highly flexible and modern. This process, part of the Guatemalan Army Transformation and Modernization Project, comprises at least five phases, which include the participation of troops in peacekeeping and humanitarian support missions.

Concurrent with these changes was a transformation of political-diplomatic leadership aimed at achieving mastery of the tasks expected of the armed forces and of matters associated with the conduct of peacekeeping missions. To that end, direct contacts were established between the Foreign Affairs Ministry and the United Nations, which made it possible to define legal

TABLE 10–1. GUATEMALA'S PARTICIPATION IN PEACEKEEPING OPERATIONS

	Mission	Country	Force size
Current	• MINUSTAH	Haiti	70 troops
(2005+)	• United Nations Department of Peacekeeping Operations	U.S.	1 senior officer
	• UNOCI	Cote d'Ivoire	3 military observers
	• UNOB	Burundi	3 military observers
Past	• UNMIH (1994-1995)	Haiti	3 military contingents, 6 military observers
	• UNFICYP (1997-1998)	Cyprus	2 staff officers
Planned	• Peace North Exercise	Dominican Republic	1 senior officer
	• United Nations Department of Peacekeeping Operations	U.S. and Haiti	3 officers
	• MONU	Congo	1 Special Forces contingent, 1 Military Police contingent
	• Peace South Exercise	Brazil	1 senior officer
	• Deployment	Sudan	11 military officers
	• Peacekeeping Operations Schools: CECOPAC and CAECOPAZ	Chile and Argentina	—

parameters for the participation of Guatemala's armed forces in peacekeeping operations.

INFLUENCING FACTORS

Influenced largely by a new vision and an environment allowing the exercise of a new national policy, the political-diplomatic leadership recognized the potential of the existing capacities to participate in peacekeeping operations. Civilian political-diplomatic capabilities combined with the military capabilities of the Guatemalan army were perhaps the determining factors at the time the decision was taken to actively participate in the peacekeeping mission in Haiti. The professionalism and resident capabilities of the armed forces helped determine the extent to which they could assist in an operation that in some aspects resembled the circumstances that Guatemala had experienced for more than four decades.

In addition, Guatemala's political-diplomatic leadership in the Central American region influenced the decision to participate in a PKO that—as in the case of Haiti—would at the same time provide an opportunity to recover military leadership. During the course of the internal armed conflict, the Guatemalan army demonstrated the military professionalism that allowed it to occupy a recognized position among the armies of the Central American region.

From the time peace was achieved, Guatemala's political and military authorities showed their support for peacekeeping missions in other countries by responding simultaneously to the challenges facing its armed forces and to a direct request from the United Nations. This is the first operation participated in under the Guatemalan flag. At the time, Guatemalan officers were also participating in missions in Burundi (three military observers) and in Ivory Coast (three military observers) with UN contingents.

Guatemala has supported each of the decisions issued by the United Nations Security Council. To make that support official, in November 2003 it signed a memorandum of understanding[2] with the United Nations in which Guatemala's participation in the UN Reserve Forces agreement system was legalized; the signature of a memorandum to specifically cover the support to be provided by Guatemala was pending. The latter memorandum indicates the numbers in which the Guatemalan government can support the United Nations in its operations. Some of these figures include 1 civilian affairs company (107 troops); 1 military medical corps company (42 troops); 1 infantry company (146 troops); and 1 company of military police (168 troops). All the troops are military, with a response deadline of 30 days for each request.

One determining factor in the selection of the support, as included in the memorandum, was the experience and specialty of the armed forces during the internal armed conflict, particularly in the area known as civilian affairs. The army effectively used civilian action in its relations with the population to strengthen the rejection of insurgent groups and break up their support bases. This direct relationship with the population was expressed by providing humanitarian aid for the victim populations and later organizing them into the so-called civilian defense patrols that helped increase military power and presence in the most remote and vulnerable areas of the country. This experience is very characteristic of the Guatemalan armed forces and could be applied in peacekeeping operations depending on the characteristics of the terrain and the population to be supported.[3]

Other specialties considered to support such missions are also the product of the experience gained during the years of the internal conflict. This is true of military health units, whose experience in accompanying troops on their operations and to distant, topographically complex locations allowed their doctors and specialists to work effectively in caring for troops in conditions very similar to those seen in populations where it is necessary to support PKO. The other specialties considered are mainly military support, such as infantry and military police.

Another deciding factor in participation in the PKO in Haiti related to the economic benefit Guatemala would obtain through the reimbursement provided by the United Nations for the personnel, weaponry, major equipment, and self-support used during the mission. These funds benefited the process of transforming and modernizing the army by providing funds for the procurement of new equipment.

As a member of various regional groups, Guatemala has been involved in the current processes associated with hemisphere solidarity. At the 6th Conference of Defense Ministers of the Americas held in November 2005 in Quito, Guatemala supported the inclusion in the Final Declaration of support for the Haiti process in the context of the Declaration of Security of the Americas (Special Conference on Security, Mexico City, 2003). In the Central American Armed Forces Conference (CFAC),[4] Guatemala led in forming a joint contingent of the countries making up the conference without yet defining under what flag the contingent would be represented.

In the case of the resolution to participate in Haiti, solidarity prevailed over the sway of the United States. When the attempt was made to exert influence in the case of Iraq, Guatemala decided, as a rule, not to take part if its participation was not covered under the UN flag. The United States has expressed its pleasure at being able to participate jointly with the member countries of the CFAC. This interest facilitated meetings with officials from various countries, including Defense Secretary Donald Rumsfeld, who visited El Salvador and Nicaragua in late 2004. At the Conference of Defense Ministers of the Americas, Defense Secretary Rumsfeld also invited all the ministers representing Central America to consider the option of joint participation in this type of operation.

There was also discussion at the Quito conference about the risks that jeopardize the values promoted by the Democratic Charter of the Americas, identifying the common and most critical threats to the security and stability of the states of the region. The threat most directly perceived by the political authorities was the threat to the democracy defended by the Democratic Charter of the Americas, which accepts the perception that the new threats can be destabilizing to a fragile state.

On the other hand, the representatives of the political sector played almost no part in the process that decided on the participation of troops in Haiti. The political leadership does not have a thorough knowledge of the subject and is not interested in opening up a space for a debate on the subject of peacekeeping missions in the specific committees of the Congress of the

Republic. Lawmakers did not provide any feedback on the subject, since the congress did not legislate for the participation of the troops in Haiti.

POLICY FOR PARTICIPATION IN HAITI

Guatemala based the decision for its participation on defense policy and the National Defense Book published in November 2003, which states that participation in such operations will be a basic component in the new vision and function of the armed forces, in response to the new threats posed throughout the world.

In the context of the national policy of PKO participation, making the decision to participate in Haiti was both a top-down and bottom-up process. It was a policy decision taken from the highest levels of government in solidarity with the problems of a friendly state whose democracy was threatened and was also due to a direct request from the United Nations. The decision was generated from the office of the president through the foreign affairs ministry, which negotiated the terms of participation after the call from the UN. The foreign affairs ministry, in turn, had advice from the national defense staff. From the bottom up, the decision was made by the national defense ministry in coordination with the national defense staff in line with the parameters defined by the National Defense Policy and the processes initiated to implement the transformation and modernization of the Guatemalan army through its participation in peacekeeping operations.

Participating Institutions

The foreign affairs ministry was in charge of the political-diplomatic negotiations with the United Nations after learning of its request. The ministry was the liaison institution for determining the political need to sign a cooperation agreement, and not only to include the country in the Haiti process. The ministry also sought to ensure that Guatemala's participation would be considered for other missions, as was done in the case of the Republic of the Congo.

The policy decisionmaking associated with the use of the armed forces was taken over by the national defense ministry. In the case of Guatemala, according to the legislation, the policy decision was combined with the military decision. The defense ministry has as an advisory and technical agency the national defense staff, which took the technical decision on the feasibility and design of the mission.

Since this participation is subsidized by direct funds from the UN through its payments system, the finance ministry took part in the approval of the advance funds for the preparation, deployment, and maintenance of the contingent in Haiti. It is expected that the funds can be used for that purpose when the UN payments system can reimburse them.

In addition, the Congress of the Republic did not issue any regulation or legislative decree to approve the departure of the contingent in the Haiti PKO, but it did so in 2004 to authorize the entry of troops from the United States to conduct humanitarian support exercises in some of the country's communities.

Decisionmaking Criteria

The prevailing criterion was the political-diplomatic factor. The policy decision based on the new defense policy determined that a priority function of the armed forces would be participation in peacekeeping operations. For that reason, they responded to the UN request and to what had already been decided, the actions to achieve the purpose of the aforesaid memorandum of understanding. Then, the national policy that had been delineated determined the participation of the armed forces in PKO.

Another factor considered in the decision was the experience the Guatemalan army has gained in other areas and activities in different parts of the world, in addition to the experience it had in participation with three contingents in 1994 and 1995 in the Republic of Haiti. This previous experience indicated that this was a very good opportunity, not only to answer the call of the UN, but also to acquire more experience in this type of operation and working with members of other armed forces.[5]

Concept

Recent trends regarding the new role of the armed forces, and the definition of the roles of the army in Guatemala as well, were also proof of the pressure from some social sectors that demanded that the army no longer play a part in internal security. So participation in peacekeeping operations is a feasible option for the international image of Guatemala and its armed forces.

GUATEMALA'S PARTICIPATION IN HAITI

After passage of Security Council Resolution 1542 and the request made by the United Nations, the political leadership ordered participation in the peacekeeping operations mission in Haiti through a memorandum to the foreign affairs and national defense ministries. The national defense ministry and the national defense staff designed and planned the mission, which was duly approved.

Mission Design

From a political-diplomatic standpoint, the foreign affairs ministry and the national defense ministry jointly designed the purposes of the mission after receiving a memorandum from the office of the president announcing the acceptance of the UN's invitation.[6] This invitation stated that the first task would be to support the protection and security of the other contingents using military police. The national defense ministry, along with the national defense staff, directly planned the military and security aspects of the mission with the support of UN officials.

In addition, the peacekeeping operations department of the national defense staff's operations directorate was directly in charge of the design and planning of the mission with advice from the agencies involved in the political-diplomatic and operations-military preparation. Similarly, the military authorities were charged with the preparation of the materials and equipment the contingent would use in the mission.

Two months before the departure of the contingent, the training and preparation of the selected troops (12 officers, 23 support specialists, and 35 military police) was begun based on the type of mission to be conducted. In addition, the contingent equipment was inspected. An induction was also held with the selected officers, which in the case of Guatemala would be a line of military police that would be predominant during its involvement.

The participation of the national defense staff in the design of the mission was decisive. Design and planning were the responsibility of commanders directly associated with the subject and of the operations and planning directorate, through the peacekeeping operations department. In the case of Guatemala, since there are no joint chiefs of staff, the design and planning were done in the national defense staff.[7]

The dominant role for planning and design fell on the army, since it was participating in the entire operation. The indications received from the United Nations based on the characteristics of the mission were also taken into account and centered solely on the subject of protection of the mission by the military police.

Officials from the United Nations Department of Peacekeeping Operations provided support and advice in mission design and planning. Since this was the first time the Guatemalan armed forces would participate with an independent contingent that would not be under the flag of the country conducting the mission, it was indispensable to have additional support in order to have a clearer view of the situation.

Political and Economic Objectives of the Mission

The primary political objective was to position Guatemala among the countries of the hemisphere that would respond to the call for solidarity from a friendly nearby country in peacekeeping operations according to the requests of world (UN) and regional (Organization of American States) agencies.

Another important factor was the position the political leadership was pursuing with respect to making decisions on the mission and functions of the armed forces. This came up in a conjuncture that entailed both the end of the internal armed conflict and the reassessment of an assigned mission based on current challenges, and made it possible to reduce the influence previously exerted by the army and to enable it to participate in other functions beyond the conventional missions assigned to the armed forces. This factor was considered when defining the defense policy as one of the alternative options of missions the army could perform. In these circumstances, peacekeeping operations became one of the most preferred alternatives.

The economic objectives that were prevalent in designing the mission were equally expressed both by the political-diplomatic and the operations-military visions. They centered on the policy of reimbursement of the UN–allocated funds in order to recover the investment and also to gain funds to support the transformation and modernization process and equipment purchases for the armed forces.

The objectives that determined the mission were closely related to the selected criteria. The political-diplomatic factor was decisive in taking the decision to participate and, in turn, the operations-military factor was decisive with respect to design and planning.

Military Objectives of the Mission

The stated military objectives were to honor the true functions of the armed forces and to order their action in a context of international standing in new ways of approaching a mission of this type.

These objectives are also associated with the type of unit deployed, which in this particular case is a unit of military police. Guatemala had been assigned as its primary objective the protection of the General Headquarters of the United Nations Stabilization Mission in Haiti, with other missions such as protecting dignitaries and convoys and maintaining discipline, law, and order.

The military objectives are congruent with the political objectives, since they used the same criteria and concept. The definition of the mission also had appropriate coordination from the policymakers, which permitted them to have the same objective.

Stability of Objectives

The political objectives have not changed. They have been consolidated with the preparation of a coming memorandum of understanding with the United Nations specifically for the mission in Haiti in order to delineate and expand the mission's action in the near future.

The economic objectives are also stable, since no variable has been added and we do not yet have reimbursements from the UN. The objective in this regard is the same, consisting of using the reimbursements for the purchase of equipment for the armed forces to assist in their modernization process.

The military objectives have changed, since the original proposal was not a military police contingent, but a special operations contingent. The UN request has been to enlarge the contingent from 70 to 160 troops and expand its duties to direct support for the mission and not only security tasks. Another factor that impacted the change of objectives is the joint action of the Central American member nations of the CFAC to send a joint force under the flag of the regional organization, with the support of the United States. This would impact the change of the objective of the mission in its original form.

LESSONS LEARNED

One major factor that impacts the effectiveness of the forces used, either armed or combined, is the cultural variable in interactions with the population or the competent authorities. These actors may have different views, and if these are not considered in the preparation of the contingents along with the planning and design of the mission, they can cause delays in the performance of the mission.

The degree of commitment among the parties involved to accept the presence of military forces, either combined or from a single independent country, that come into the territory under the UN flag could be a variable that impacts their effectiveness. Since they are combined forces, their training, preparation, and instruction are decisive factors when the mission is implemented, because they must pursue common and shared objectives in order to provide an optimum response to the required needs. In this vein, the historical view of the conflict and the current situation must be taken into account in the preparation of the contingent, so as to facilitate the troops' approach to the cultural issue.

A performance measure that can be used is the degree of integration, first within the contingents themselves, and then with the authorities and population with which they must interact. It is imperative that unity first be achieved in the forces so as to homogenize the objective of the mission, starting with their training and preparation and continuing with the actions taken to consolidate their basic objectives. Another important factor to consider as a performance measure is the achievement of the designed and planned objective. If that objective changes for any reason, the force's effectiveness may not be optimal.

CONCLUSIONS AND RECOMMENDATIONS

Policymakers, who are the main actors in deciding about the participation of armed and/or police forces in peacekeeping operations, may want to consider several recommendations, the most important of which may be the following:

- The decision of the political leadership to participate in peacekeeping operations must be based on a coherent national policy in close relation to the country's foreign and defense policy.
- Channels of communication among the ministries or institutions involved must be optimized, from the time the decision is made through the design and planning stage, encouraging horizontality in each of the decisions or actions taken on the matter.
- Political leaders must be aware that negotiation and participation are not only a military issue, but also a political-diplomatic issue, and the military is not the only component.
- Existing capacities for participating in a PKO mission, from political-diplomatic to operations-military capabilities, must be enhanced, particularly the military component, in order to shatter the paradigm that the military is part of the internal workings of a country.
- The legislature must be more active in approving the participation of the armed forces in actions outside the national territory—particularly in peacekeeping operations, whose purpose is to provide support and collaboration to another state that is having problems.
- In the case of small countries, the best option is joint or combined forces, which make it possible to strengthen existing resources, as expressed by the Conference of Central American Armed Forces in considering sending a multinational contingent.

NOTES

1   Dr. Roberto Garcia Moritan, "Peacekeeping Operations in a Changing World," Foreign Affairs Ministry, "Ser en el 2000," Argentina, 2001.

2   Memorandum of Understanding between the United Nations and the Government of the Republic of Guatemala, on Contribution to the United Nations Reserve Forces Agreements System, signed November 12, 2003.

3   Interview with Col. José Luis Barrientos Paau, Head of the Civilian-Military Cooperation Directorate of the National Defense Staff. Until the April 2004 reorganization, this department was called the Civilian Affairs Directorate, but due to the influence of sectors of society that remembered the presence of the army in communities affected by the conflict, the decision was made to change its name to the current designation.

4   The Central American Armed Forces Conference comprises Guatemala, El Salvador, Honduras, and Nicaragua.

5   Interview with Col. Roberto Aníbal Rivera Martínez, Operations and Planning Director of the Guatemalan Army National Defense Staff.

6   Interview with Ambassador Carla Rodríguez, Director General of Multilateral Relations of the Foreign Affairs Ministry.

7   Interview with Col. Roberto Aníbal Rivera Martínez.

Chapter Eleven

Peru: A Renewed Participation in International Peacekeeping

ENRIQUE OBANDO

The country of Haiti is no stranger to having United Nations (UN) peacekeeping operations conducted in its territory. Before the current action started in 2004, the United Nations had conducted four operations.[1] As a result of the September 1991 military coup that overthrew the democratically elected government of Jean Bertrand Aristide, a United Nations and Organization of American States (OAS) joint international civilian mission was deployed in February 1993. Haiti's political forces then agreed on a pact to reestablish the constitutional government, and in September of that year, the Security Council organized the first peacekeeping operations in the country. The United Nations Mission in Haiti (UNMIH), which lasted from September 1993 to June 1996, was created to support the modernization of the army and to create a new police force in Haiti. However, rebels prevented the deployment of the mission, and several efforts to pressure them to abandon power failed. Finally, in July 1994, the Security Council authorized the deployment of a multinational force of 20,000 members to reestablish the legitimate government. In the face of this situation, the rebels abandoned power, and in March 1995 UNMIH went into effect again to guarantee security and to create a new professional police force and generate conditions so that democratic elections could be held.

From July 1996 to July 1997, UNMIH was replaced by the United Nations Support Mission in Haiti in order to support the democratically elected Haitian government in consolidating the climate of security, continue the training of the new police force, reestablish institutions, and support national reconciliation and the rebuilding of the economy.

Between August and December 1997, the United Nations Transition Mission in Haiti was created with the specific purpose of training specialized units of the new national police force whose mission would be the protection of strategic buildings, the authorities, and other institutions in Haiti.

Finally, between December 1997 and March 2000, the United Nations Civilian Police Mission in Haiti was implemented to train the upper ranks and specialized police units in coordination with the United Nations Development Program. It was during this period that the first replacement of a democratic government by another legitimately elected government took place. However, the political and economic crises were not resolved, and this lack of stability caused a delay in the necessary democratic reforms.

In 2000, parliamentary and presidential elections were held, and President Jean Bertrand Aristide and his *Fanmi Lavalas* party proclaimed their victory with little more than 10 percent of the vote. Both the opposition and the international community questioned his victory and accused the government of manipulating the elections. After years of discontent and political instability, a new opposition alliance asked for the resignation of the president in late 2003. The Caribbean Community and Common Market (CARICOM) offered to mediate, and on January 31, 2004, it issued a priority action plan that was followed in February by an implementation plan supported by CARICOM, Canada, the United States, France, the OAS, and the European Union. Aristide accepted both plans, which called for urgent reforms and a new cabinet in exchange for permitting him to finish out his term of office as president. The opposition, however, rejected the plans, and armed action was initiated in the city of Gonaives that February. The violence then spread to other cities, which allowed the insurgents to take control of a large part of the northern area of the country. On February 29, Aristide resigned and left the country. Supreme Court president Boniface Alexandre was sworn in as interim president and requested the intervention of the United Nations. Security Council Resolution 1529 authorized the creation of a Multinational Interim Force (MIF) to be made up of troops from the United States, Canada, Chile, Argentina, and other countries of the hemisphere.

The Security Council then determined that the situation in Haiti was a threat to peace and security in the region, and in Resolution 1542 of April 30, 2004, acting under Chapter VII of the United Nations Charter, established the creation of the United Nations Stabilization Mission in Haiti (*Mission des Nations Unies pour la stabilisation en Haïti,* or MINUSTAH). Resolution 1542 transferred the authority of the Multinational Interim Force to the MINUSTAH starting on June 1, 2004. MINUSTAH had a mandate for a period of 6 months. Elections were to take place in 2005, and the new president was to take office on February 7, 2006. In Resolution 1576 on November 29, 2004, the Security Council extended the mandate of MINUSTAH to June 1, 2005, with the intention of renewing it for successive additional periods.

In order to achieve a broad political consensus enabling the transitional government to work, it signed a political pact with the various political groups and civilian society. Aristide's *Fanmi Lavalas* party denounced the pact.

Starting in October 2004, the security situation in Haiti began to deteriorate with acts of violence, mainly in the capital.

MANDATE OF THE MINUSTAH

The mandate of the United Nations Stabilization Mission in Haiti is as follows:[2]

Guarantee a Secure and Stable Environment

- support the transitional government to ensure a secure and stable environment in which the constitutional and political process in Haiti can be carried out
- assist the transitional government in monitoring, restructuring, and reforming Haiti's national police force in a manner consistent with democratic police standards, including the investigation and certification of personnel, consulting in reorganization and training, including gender training, as well as monitoring/consulting with members of Haiti's national police force
- assist the transitional government, particularly the national police force of Haiti, with comprehensive and sustainable disarmament and demobilization programs for all armed groups, including the women and children associated with those groups, as well as weapons control and public safety measures
- assist in the restoration and maintenance of the rule of law, public security, and public order in Haiti by providing operational support to Haiti's national police force and coast guard, as well as strengthening institutions, including reestablishing the corrections system
- protect UN personnel and their facilities and equipment, and guarantee their safety and freedom of movement, taking account of the transitional government's primary responsibility in that area
- protect civilians under the imminent threat of physical violence, within their capabilities and deployment areas, without prejudice to the responsibilities of the transitional government and the police authorities.

Support the Political Process

- support the constitutional and political process being developed in Haiti through good offices, promoting democratic principles and good government and institutional development
- assist the transitional government in its efforts to generate a process of national dialogue and reconciliation
- assist the transitional government in its efforts to organize, monitor, and conduct free and fair municipal, parliamentary, and presidential

elections as soon as possible, particularly through providing technical, logistical, and administrative assistance and permanent security with appropriate support for an electoral process with the participation of voters representative of the national demographic, including women
- assist the transitional government in extending the authority of the state to all of Haiti and support good government at local levels.

Protect and Monitor Human Rights

- support the transitional government and Haitian human rights institutions and groups in their efforts to promote and protect human rights, particularly those of women and children, so as to ensure individual responsibility for human rights abuses and reparations for victims
- monitor and report on the human rights situation in cooperation with the Office of the United Nations High Commission for Human Rights, including the situation of returning refugees and displaced persons.

The council asked MINUSTAH to cooperate and coordinate with OAS and Caribbean CARICOM in carrying out their mandate.

PERU AND UNITED NATIONS PEACEKEEPING OPERATIONS

Haiti is the first peacekeeping operation in which the Peruvian armed forces have participated with an autonomous contingent since the 1970s. From November 15, 1973, to August 15, 1975 after the Yom Kippur War, Peru sent a battalion of 497 men, first to the Sinai Peninsula to separate Egyptians and Israelis and then to the Golan Heights to separate the Syrian and Israeli forces. Officers, technicians, noncommissioned officers (NCOs), and troops participated in the operation and were even assisted by third-year students from the Chorrillos Military Academy, the Peruvian army's cadet school. However, during the 1980s and 1990s, the Peruvian armed forces were used for the internal war against the subversive forces of *Sendero Luminoso* and the Tupac Amaru Revolutionary Movement (MRTA)—which cost the country 30,000 dead according to official calculations and 69,000 according to the Truth and Reconciliation Commission—so it was unable to concern itself with missions beyond its borders. For some 30 years, Peru did not send autonomous units on peacekeeping operations. However, interest in participating was always maintained through the contribution of military observers to various UN operations.

Sending observers to peacekeeping operations dates back to 1958, when Peru sent 10 officers to Lebanon between June and December. In the 1980s and 1990s, internal war prevented the country from autonomously participating in these operations, and it resorted to sending observers as a strategy for maintaining a presence in the activity pending better times. Between September 12, 1988, and September 13, 1989, a Peruvian commission of three army officers, two navy officers, and two air force officers participated in the United Nations Iran-Iraq Military Observers Group mission for the observation, oversight, and control of the ceasefire between Iran and Iraq. In 1989, a delegation of observers made up of 10 army officers, 5 navy officers, and 5 air force officers sent to Namibia had the mandate of controlling the cease-fire and the security of the electoral process in that country. Between 1991 and 1992, in the Western Sahara, Peruvian army Brigadier General Luis Block acted as commander in chief of the UN force, with the support of 10 army officers, 3 navy officers, and 2 air force officers. The mission consisted of the ceasefire and the security of the referendum process. Five military observers from Peru (three army, one navy, and one air force) also participated in the Western Sahara in 1998. Observers also participated in Sierra Leone in 2000, and between 2001 and 2002, 8 officers and 28 technicians and NCOs participated in East Timor with an army MI–26T helicopter as part of the United Nations Temporary Administration Force.[3]

Peru currently has military observers in the following United Nations operations:[4]

- Democratic Republic of Congo: Since 2000, three air force officers and two female army officers have been participating as observers.
- Eritrea and Ethiopia: Three army officers have been there since 2001.
- Cyprus: Initially, one army officer and one NCO were assigned to the Argentine Task Force deployed on the island. Since September 2004, a section of 24 fusiliers has been participating in the Argentine force.
- Liberia: Two army officers, two navy officers, and one air force officer have been participating as observers since 2003.
- Ivory Coast: One army officer, one navy officer, and one air force officer have been present as observers since June 2004.
- Haiti: Two army officers and one air force officer have had chief of staff responsibilities in the MINUSTAH since May 2004.
- Burundi: Three armed forces officers, one from each branch, have been participating since June 2004.

In addition, since 1999, the Peruvian armed forces have been training in peacekeeping operations by sending personnel to training courses conducted abroad. In this manner, they have participated in the following activities:[5]

- In September 1999, officers from the armed forces conducted an orientation visit on peacekeeping operations to the United States Army's Institute of Peacekeeping Operations.

- In November 1999, senior officers from the Peruvian army participated in the planning process of the Cabañas 2000 multinational combined peacekeeping operations exercise in the United States. In addition, a contingent from the army participated in the Cabañas 2000, Cabañas 2001, and Cabañas 2002 exercises in Argentina.
- In November 1999, Peruvian armed forces officers participated in the international military observer course in Argentina's Joint Training Center for Peacekeeping Operations.
- In February 2000, officers from the Peruvian armed forces participated in the course on civilian-military cooperation in peacekeeping operations and the predeployment training course for military observers at the Lester B. Pearson Peacekeeping Operations Training Center in Halifax, Canada.
- From June 18–30, 2001, officers from the armed forces participated in the Equinox 2000 peacekeeping operations takeover exercise at the Eloy Alfaro Military Academy in Quito, Ecuador, organized by United States Southern Command and the Ecuadorian Armed Forces.

FACTORS INFLUENCING PERUVIAN PARTICIPATION IN MINUSTAH

After the end of the fight against internal subversion, the Peruvian armed forces again considered the possibility of participating in peacekeeping operations. Five factors were influential. The first of these, and possibly the most important, was the desire for reinsertion of the Peruvian armed forces in the Western military community. The war against internal subversion had brought about serious human rights violations by the armed forces and this had hurt their prestige at the international level, and obviously internally as well. Added to this was the high degree of corruption that involved not only the high-ranking officers, but even intermediate-ranking officers of the military during the government of Alberto Fujimori. As a result of this, the three top commanding generals, the chairman of the joint chiefs of staff, and the minister of defense ended up in prison. The post-Fujimori governments of Valentin Paniagua (2000–2001) and Alejandro Toledo (2001–present) presented themselves as reformers of the armed forces, and the latter, in turn, were anxious to be reinstated among their Western peers and to overcome the bad times of the 1990s. The drive for participation in Haiti therefore had an initial political objective: reinsertion in the Western military environment. This was clearly seen in 2001, when Roberto Danino, the first chairman of the council of ministers of President Alejandro Toledo, formed a commission to restructure the armed forces, which among other recommendations stated that the armed forces should actively participate in peacekeeping operations. Accordingly, on November 11, 2003, the foreign affairs minister signed a memorandum of understanding whereby a battalion and a frigate were made available to the United Nations to conduct peacekeeping operations.

Furthermore, in January 2004, the national defense council approved the National Security and Defense Policy, which included conducting peacekeeping operations with the United Nations. In addition, a multisector peacekeeping operations committee was formed with the purpose of increasing the participation of the Peruvian armed forces in peacekeeping operations within the UN context. This committee is charged with negotiations with the United Nations to define the type of peacekeeping mission in which the country is going to participate, how long the mission will last, how they will participate, and the equipment they will contribute. The final decision on sending Peruvian personnel to an operation of this nature, however, is vested in the president.

Along with the political consideration was the intent to attain prestige and a presence on the international stage that the armed forces could otherwise not achieve. For a military that during the Fujimori administration had strayed from the international environment and stopped attending military courses, conferences, and meetings outside its borders for fear of being accused of violating human rights and supporting an authoritarian regime, the way to regain a presence and reinstate itself in the international context was to participate in missions around the world with the military elements of other countries.

The third consideration that influenced the decision to go to Haiti was economic. The United Nations pays the armed forces of the various countries for their participation in this type of mission, and according to ministry of defense calculations, this payment not only covers the expense but also leaves a positive balance for the military branch and the participating personnel. For the Peruvian armed forces, which were suffering serious problems with financing from their own government, this was an especially important incentive. These funds would enable them to get certain military equipment in operating condition and to create a fund to finance operations, in addition to benefiting the income of officers, noncommissioned officers, and particularly troops, who in early 2004 were earning the equivalent of US$13.85 a month. By January 2005, that income had increased to US$29.76—a significant fact, considering that the salary of a female domestic in Lima fluctuates between US$100 and US$130 a month. In these circumstances, it is no wonder the Peruvians had trouble recruiting soldiers, especially considering that military service has been voluntary since 1999. In this context, United Nations peacekeeping missions can contribute to finding a partial solution to this problem.

It is important also to note the subject of training. A peacekeeping mission helps in the training of infantry forces in field situations close to what could be encountered in a military operation. Although this is not true for other heavy units such as armored units or helicopters, for infantry units this training is certainly useful. This view is prevalent and is defended in the Peruvian army.

Last, another factor, although the least considered one, was collaborating with the United States in an operation that appeared not to be within its scope of interest, taking into account that relations with Washington had become problematic for a number of reasons.

In the first place, it is important to note the U.S. pressure for Peru to sign a bilateral agreement that would guarantee not to make U.S. personnel available to the International Criminal Court. In the 1980s and 1990s, Washington was putting pressure on the Peruvian armed forces for human rights violations during the antisubversion war. At the same time, the military was complaining that these accusations were being made without contributing any type of support in the internal war against the subversives. Finally, the government of Peru gave in to the pressure from Washington and began to be concerned with the subject of human rights and take it seriously, resulting in the country's inclusion in the Protocol of Rome, in which the International Criminal Court was created to judge those who had committed serious human rights violations in wars. Faced with this, the U.S. position changed, and due to the risk of its personnel being accused of human rights violations in the invasion of Afghanistan and Iraq, it began to exert pressure in the opposite direction. Now the United States wanted Peru to guarantee that it would not send Americans to the court; if it did, the United States would cut off military aid. The Peruvian defense minister recommended yielding to the pressure from Washington in order to maintain military support at a time when the minister of economy had cut the funds allocated to the armed forces to a minimum. On the other hand, the Peruvian foreign affairs department opted for a position of principle and refused to yield. The result was that Washington did not halt current aid but did cut off aid that had been planned for the future.

In the second place, after the meeting of the World Trade Organization in Cancun in September 2003, where the elimination of agricultural subsidies from developed countries, generic drugs, and more equality in international trade were unsuccessfully discussed, a number of developing countries formed a group to support alternative trade policies. They were called the Group of 21, and Peru was among them. The United States therefore pressured Peru to withdraw from the group, threatening not to discuss the Free Trade Treaty with the Lima government if it insisted on remaining in the group. On that occasion, the U.S. pressure was successful, and Peru withdrew from the Group of 21 just 48 hours after joining it. This caused problems with Brazil, which was one of the leaders of the group, and with which Peru had recently signed a strategic alliance agreement.

Lastly, the biggest disagreement Peru had with the United States was associated with drug policy. Peru was introducing an alternative development policy. While Washington supported this solution, in practice it was allocating more funds to a military solution through the interdiction by the Peruvian air force of the planes used in drug trafficking. Peru ended up accepting this solution, and by 1998 had had great success. The price of coca leaf had dropped from US$4 to less than US$1 per kilo, a price at which it was not profitable for farmers to produce coca leaf. Coca farmers abandoned production at their own initiative, and the Peruvian state saved itself the trouble of initiating a confrontation with them. In 2001, a Baptist church plane was shot down accidentally, resulting in the death of a church member and her daughter. The church sued the U.S. Government for an initial amount of $50 million, eventually receiving a settlement for $8 million. As a result of this incident, U.S. support for interception was interrupted, but the requirement to eradicate coca producers was not. This meant that Washington was pressuring Lima to continue with forced eradication and directly confront well-organized and armed groups of coca producers that had twice marched on the capital. Peru, on the other hand, had opted for concerted eradication, which, to Washington, seemed slow. Peru, however, claims that the United States is pushing it toward a serious confrontation with the coca traffickers that could create renewed clashes in an area that had been free of problems and subversive influence for nearly a decade, at the same time it is preventing the use of airborne interception that would make it possible to eradicate coca crops without having to directly confront traffickers.

In the midst of this situation, U.S. Embassy officials and defense ministry officials met to explore the possibility of Peruvian participation in a peacekeeping mission in Iraq. At the time, Peru was trying to secure a position on the Security Council, with the precedent that the relations between the United States and the United Nations on the subject of Iraq had been in conflict. The Peruvian foreign affairs department was opposed to the U.S. approaches; in this situation, the worst thing Peru could do to consolidate its position as a candidate for the Security Council was to participate with the United States in a peacekeeping mission in Iraq not authorized by the United Nations. The initial response was negative. A second approach included a possible U.S. offer to put into operation four of the Peruvian air force's five C–130 transport planes that were rusting due to lack of funds to purchase spare parts. In exchange for having the aircraft operational, Peru would have to agree to send two of them to Iraq for 6 months. When the kidnappings and murders of non-U.S. personnel occurred in Iraq, Washington suggested Peruvian participation in Afghanistan instead. This offer was not successful in the end, but it was indicative of the U.S. desire for Peru to participate in some peacekeeping operations in which Washington was present. In these circumstances, Haiti appeared to be the perfect place to allay Washington's concerns and at the same time conduct a coordinated operation under the flag of the United Nations. This last factor was considered, although it was not the deciding factor when the decision was made to accept the mission. Peru's participation in Haiti, in these circumstances, appeared to be more viable than a previous effort to send men on a mission to Cyprus along with Argentina.

HOW THE DECISION WAS MADE

The decision to participate in the Haiti mission was complicated and difficult. After the Peruvian foreign affairs department offered in November 2003 to send a battalion and a frigate to conduct peacekeeping missions, in 2004 Peru received a request from the United Nations to send a force to Cyprus by March. The armed forces joint chiefs of staff were charged with putting together a force. That is when the problems began to become evident. Due to years of neglect in internal processes associated with military procurement and maintenance, the army did not have any new vehicles, and the ones it had were not in operable condition. The decision was therefore made not to send vehicles and to replace them with a group of only 24 men with light weaponry that would have to be part of an Argentine battalion. This substitution complicated things further. The United Nations only covers the deployment costs of autonomous units from their base of origin to the area of operations. Those that send groups that have to be incorporated in an autonomous unit have to finance the travel to the headquarters of that autonomous unit themselves. This meant that Peru would have to finance the round trip from Lima to Buenos Aires for 24 men and their equipment twice, since 6 months later, another group of 24 men had to relieve the first contingent. However, the ministry of economy and finance initially refused to issue the funds for the trips; by the time it relented, the time frame scheduled to send the force had ended. For that reason, it was agreed that Peru would send its small force in the second relief effort in September 2004. At the same time, the United Nations asked Peru to send a full battalion to Haiti. The armed forces joint chiefs, already aware of the difficulties in sending 24 men, replied to the foreign affairs department that the armed forces were not capable of sending any contingent.

The refusal was a concern not only to the foreign affairs department but also to the vice minister of logistics and the director general of policy and strategy of the defense ministry, who had participated both in the commission to restructure the armed forces and in the preparation of the National Defense Policy, documents in which participation in peacekeeping missions was considered an essential task. In addition, mid-level officers of the joint chiefs felt that an important opportunity to participate in this type of mission was being allowed to slip away and that the economic gains could be significant, so the opportunity should not be missed. The major stumbling block was again the ministry of economy and finance, which systematically refused to give funds to the defense ministry. In principle, Peru would be participating with an autonomous unit, so the cost of deployment of the unit would be borne entirely by the United Nations. But the problem now was that the battalion would have to take approximately 55 vehicles, and the entire army had only 9 that were operable and in good condition. It would have to repair the rest, which again meant asking the ministry of economy for funds, knowing their consistent negative replies in advance.

In addition, the joint chiefs had discovered that the funds given by the ministry of economy for the mission in Cyprus were not new funds, but were an advance on the budget allocated to the defense ministry that would be deducted from future items. The total defense ministry budget was approximately 2.8 billion soles (about US$800 million)—just about enough to pay wages, with little left for operations. Any deduction from the budget would affect the sector's ability to meet its payrolls. In these circumstances, a scenario was considered in which any new money released by the ministry of economy would be deducted at the end of the year. Although the United Nations would pay the money, it would probably not arrive until 2005, which would put a hole in the 2004 budget that would not permit the normal operation of the sector. The joint chiefs' response was therefore negative for the second time.

So the foreign affairs department pressured the defense ministry, and several alternatives were studied. The first was to ask the United States to donate the necessary vehicles. A delegation from defense and foreign affairs appealed to the U.S. Embassy to negotiate this, but the Americans were already involved in their own problems. The schedule for the mission in Haiti was very short, and Peru's request had arrived too late to process all the authorizations that would be asked for in Washington. It was even proposed that the Peruvian battalion would "inherit" the equipment of the U.S. battalion that would be relieved in Haiti, but even then the time for the formalities was extremely short. The second solution proposed was to purchase new equipment or second-hand equipment in good condition, ask that it be delivered to the island, and defer payment until the funds arrived from the United Nations. Unfortunately, the schedule was very tight in this case, too. Finally, the United Nations took it upon itself to solve the problem by proposing that Peru send not a battalion of 640 men but an airborne detachment of 205. Even this proposal entailed problems, because although the number of vehicles had been reduced, it was still more than Peru had in good condition. The joint chiefs were again inclined to avoid problems and say no, but the insistence of the foreign affairs department turned it around, and under the combined pressure of foreign affairs and the defense ministry, the ministry of economy yielded and issued the funds necessary to conduct the mission.

The ministry of economy and finance's constant refusal to issue funding for a mission that is apparently beneficial, even from an economic standpoint, may appear strange. The reason for this systematic refusal is that Peru has signed a letter of intent with the International Monetary Fund whereby it agrees not to have a fiscal deficit greater than 1.9 percent of its revenues. The deficit must in addition decrease and not exceed 1.5 percent by 2004 and 1 percent by 2005. This agreement ended up being a straitjacket that prevented Peru from freely investing and therefore obligated the entire state to have significantly low investment rates. Since the defense sector was not considered a priority, expenditures in that sector were always lower than in the rest of the public administration.

The last element that must be mentioned in this analysis is the congress, which did not play any role during the discussion within the executive branch concerning sending troops to Haiti. The subject was finally approved without any discussion, which has a positive aspect—depending on the angle from which it is considered; it means that the congress does not become a political obstacle when the time comes to discuss and decide on this type of mission and there seems to be no interest on the subjects of security and defense within the congress.

DESIGNING AND PLANNING THE MISSION

The mission was designed and planned by the operations division of the armed forces joint chiefs of staff.[6] The initial concept was that the mission be conducted by a joint unit made up of the army, navy, and air force, in which no troops would participate, only officers and NCOs. The reasons for not sending troops were that due to the small budget available, troop training would have been affected, and that because of the low level of pay for troops, those who came to apply for voluntary service would not be the best candidates. The armed forces themselves were not confident in the capabilities of their troops, especially conducting a mission in such a complex political and social environment as that of Haiti. This caused problems that were on the verge of aborting the mission. The initial thought was to send a battalion, but since no troops would go to propose a joint operation as an option, the numbers of officers and NCOs requested of the navy and air force were too high compared to the numbers the two branches had available. This could have affected the conduct of their traditional missions inside the country. In this scenario, the opinion of the two branches was not to participate. This opinion was supported by the chairman and the operations director of the joint chiefs, both air force generals. Finally, after pressure exerted by the foreign affairs department, those branches and the joint chiefs decided to change their mind. In September 2004, Peru sent a heavy infantry company of 205 men, made up of 113 men from the army, 49 from the navy, and 43 from the air force.

The mission, which would consist of guarding the Port-au-Prince airport, was planned by the United Nations. It is important to note the participation of the Committee for the Prevention of Human Immunovirus/Acquired Immune Deficiency Syndrome, which is part of the defense ministry, in the preparation of the men who would be sent to Haiti.

POLITICAL, ECONOMIC, AND MILITARY OBJECTIVES OF THE MISSION

The mission had four political objectives:

- reinsert the Peruvian armed forces in the international military environment
- honor the offer made to the United Nations in 2003 to participate in peacekeeping operations
- participate in a peacekeeping mission of interest to the United States
- collaborate in the pacification of Haiti.

The two economic objectives were to:

- get the armed forces their own source of revenue, however small
- improve the revenue of the armed forces military personnel.

The mission had three military objectives:

- gain prestige and a military presence
- train personnel in situations similar to those of a military operation
- protect the Port-au-Prince airport.

EFFECTIVENESS OF COMBINED MILITARY FORCES IN PEACEKEEPING MISSIONS

Peacekeeping missions differ substantially from the wartime operations for which conventional armies normally are prepared. The main difference is that in most cases, these operations do not require the use of arms. The political role in a peacekeeping operation is perhaps more important than the military role itself, so officers and NCOs must be appropriately trained to play this type of role. In the same vein, it is indispensable to have the skills for negotiations participants may be involved in with the population and with political groups that are often hostile. But this negotiating skill must not only be used for groups that are apparently in conflict; it is also useful in interacting with the many civilian agencies and nongovernmental organizations in the area that have agendas that are dissimilar and sometimes opposed and that in many cases have some degree of suspicion and mistrust of the military.

In order to have personnel who meet the necessary requirements for missions of this type, they must receive good training. Officers and NCOs with conventional training cannot be expected to be able to face the countless problems posed by a mission of this type. If the various components of a force have to be combined (made up of different countries), the situation can be even more complicated. The only way to overcome this problem is to offer the units prior training before they begin to work together in peacekeeping operations so that they adhere to and apply the same doctrine. Furthermore, the implementation of a single military operations doctrine is the ideal, since units of different origins are going to share the same command, so they must share the same language, in operations as well as logistics.

In addition, experience in this type of mission can be decisive with respect to performance variables. In a peacekeeping operations course conducted in Buenos Aires in 2003, the performance of the Peruvian officers was rated as good by the U.S. evaluation personnel. Their assigned mission was to guard an airport. During this drill, other contingents had casualties, while the Peruvians had none. The reason appeared obvious to the Peruvians themselves: The Peruvian army had experience in conducting this sort of mission for nearly 15 years in its fight against the subversion of *Sendero Luminoso* and the MRTA. So this type of task was nothing new to the Peruvian forces.

RECOMMENDATIONS FOR POLITICAL DECISIONMAKERS

Based on the Peruvian experience, a series of recommendations arise that could be considered useful for political decisionmakers. In the first place, a United Nations peacekeeping operation can in most cases be considered a good investment for many reasons. Some money can be earned from them, at the same time that the forces are gaining prestige. The United Nations pays the country that sends a contingent the expenses it incurs at a rate that greatly exceeds the actual expenditure. In addition, the wages of the personnel, at least in South American terms, are much higher than the wages that personnel earn in their respective countries. To all of the above are added the prestige, presence, and training that such a mission signifies.

In the second place, personnel who are not skilled or prepared should not be sent on a mission of this type. Just as an army prepares and trains for war, it must also prepare and train to conduct peacekeeping missions. Drills are one of the best tools for this, and there is already a series of international schools where personnel can be prepared.

In the third place, similar military and peacekeeping operations doctrines should be implemented when combined contingents are going to be used. Otherwise, the result could be massive confusion, which could jeopardize the principal objectives of the mission.

In the fourth place, it is obvious that sending forces that are not autonomous, thinking that it will save resources at the same time it affords a presence, is a serious error. When forces are not autonomous, they already know they will have to pay for their travel to the headquarters of the autonomous unit they are a part of. Furthermore, the presence will be that of the country under whose flag their unit is deployed, thereby losing the objective of presence and prestige. The only reason for sending forces that are incorporated in a unit belonging to another country is to familiarize a contingent with the experience of other units in peacekeeping operations. However, if the unit is not properly trained, equipped, and financed, it may end up becoming an additional problem for the unit that has an autonomous command.

In the fifth place, the location where a contingent is sent for a peacekeeping operation must be carefully selected, must meet the requirements of the country's foreign policy, and must have a reasonable possibility of success. There is always the possibility of sustaining casualties in peacekeeping operations, but there are places where these possibilities are higher, and the decisionmaking criteria must include considering whether the possible number of casualties that could occur during a peacekeeping operation is actually in the country's interest. This may be one of the most important recommendations.

Along with this recommendation, the force sent must be adequate to conduct the assigned mission to ensure that the mission will not be changed in midstream. Such changes of scenario can result from an operation that was initially a peacekeeping operation turning into a situation in which the troops may face a confrontational scenario for which they are not adequately prepared. The political objective and the force necessary to achieve it must always be consistent.

The selection of the force to be sent on a peacekeeping mission can be based on two criteria. The first is to try to send the largest possible number of personnel and rotate them so the largest possible number has the benefit of the experience and the extraordinary economic gains deriving from participation in the mission. The other possibility is to have some units that are experts in such operations and to send only those units, which ensures experience and the success of the missions. In this respect, we favor the second option since it goes to the country's prestige, and being able to have units with optimum training in this skill guarantees the success of the missions. The first option may be more democratic, but at the same time it is less efficient. Lastly, the primary objective of the mission must in fact be to achieve the pacification of the country to which the contingent is sent.

It is of great importance to maintain consistency between the country's policy and its actual capability of implementing it. In the case of Peru, the foreign affairs department asked the armed forces if it were feasible to make a battalion and a frigate available to the United Nations, and the answer was yes. When, as a result of the initial offer, the United Nations asked for the battalion, it was discovered that a basic element in the decisionmaking chain, the ministry of economy, had not been consulted, and that it did not have the least intention of outlaying the funds required, arguing that the needs of the defense sector were not among its priorities. It is imperative in a country for the priorities of all sectors to be similar and coordinated when an activity is involved in which several sectors must participate. This results in the creation of the Multisector Commission for Peacekeeping Operations, in which foreign affairs and the ministries of defense, the interior, and economy must be participants from the very beginning. If that commission had existed from the start, many of the setbacks discussed above would have been avoided.

Another point worth mentioning is the lack of coordination at the international level. Although peacekeeping missions are important to the United Nations, as they also are to the United States, it is indispensable for the countries that support these peacekeeping missions to have the appropriate logistical capability to provide the necessary troops, vehicles, aircraft, and boats. This would mean that they would have to invest in those capabilities. This is even more important when the participation of a given number of countries is required so that the international force is legitimate and representative, and not made up of a high percentage of troops from the United States or just a few countries. Analyzing the cases of countries like Peru and Argentina, which suffered serious difficulties in order to send a battalion to Haiti, it is possible to reach the conclusion that their armed forces have some structural limitations that prevent their being used for such purposes. This is due in part to the fact that their governments do not invest or allocate the necessary funds to sustain them at optimum levels of adequate readiness, added to the pressures exerted on them by multilateral organizations such as the International Monetary Fund. The economic mindset of the past decade has been to reduce military costs, which may be very laudable due to the high poverty rates registered in the region. However, these restrictions generate problems when at the international level the government wants to participate with armies poorly prepared for the conduct of peacekeeping operations. In these circumstances, a crisis in the region would not provide the means to be able to deploy a credible international force, obligating other more developed and better resourced countries to fill the void.

In such circumstances, it is indispensable to refine the political and military needs of the United Nations and the United States and harmonize them with those of international agencies such as the World Bank and the International Monetary Fund, which often pressure developing countries to reduce their military budgets, whereby the armed forces sacrifice their operational capabilities. A nonoperational military force may be the worst expenditure of all. It would be better to get rid of such a force than to continue a useless expenditure that does not produce what is expected of it: security.

Lastly, the lack of armed forces operability clearly can result in a lack of political decisions to participate in peacekeeping missions. Peru was on the verge of not participating in the Haiti mission due to lack of military operability. If that had happened, the country's credibility for participating in such missions would have been compromised, and turning down future United Nations requests could have become a bureaucratic habit. So it is necessary to maintain minimum operability in some armed forces if there is a desire for them to participate in future peacekeeping operations.

NOTES

[1] See <http://www.cinu.org.mx/temas/paz_seguridad/pk_despleg.htm>.

[2] See <http://www.un.org/Depts/dpko/missions/minustah/mandate.html>.

[3] Interview with Colonel Rodolfo Gaboa Obeso, Ministry of Defense, June 15, 2004.

[4] Ibid.

[5] See <http://www.ejercito.mil.pe/contribucion.htm>; <http://www.un.org/Depts/dpko/missions/minustah/background.htlm>.

[6] The information given here is first-hand since the author acted as director general of policy and strategy for the defense ministry during the course of these events.

Chapter Twelve

Lessons Learned from Haiti: Capacity Building for Peacekeeping

JOHN T. FISHEL AND ANDRÉS SÁENZ

T he ongoing United Nations (UN) mission in Haiti that began with the Multinational Interim Force–Haiti (MIFH) and continues with the UN Stabilization Mission in Haiti (MINUSTAH) raised questions about the capacity of the nations of the Americas to lead and conduct peacekeeping operations (PKO). To what degree were the individual states capable? Why would they choose to participate or not? What factors influenced the participants to do so? To what degree did the participants see the necessary capacity as an interagency effort? How well prepared were they to coordinate with other countries? What skill sets are required for effective strategic-level participation in PKO? What are the measures of effectiveness for a PKO? And, last, what can the United States do to help the nations of the hemisphere improve their capacity to participate effectively in peacekeeping operations?

In this concluding chapter, we seek to reflect on these questions in light of the research conducted on each of the participating countries. We draw conclusions based on that research which, while generally supporting our initial hypotheses, does suggest that certain modifications are in order. Finally, we offer a series of recommendations for the governments of the nations of the Americas if they desire to increase their PKO capacity. We emphasize here cooperative and collaborative actions that states can take together.

KEY FACTORS INFLUENCING THE DECISION TO PARTICIPATE

Our first hypothesis focuses on political capabilities, in particular, political will as the central determinant of participation. Our research questions highlighted a number of factors that contribute to political will. The first of these factors is *prestige*, a term we use in the same sense that Hans Morgenthau did. That is, prestige is "the third basic manifestation of the struggle for power on the international scene."[1] Nearly all the research papers cite prestige as a key determining factor, most in a very direct form. The major exception is the United States, where prestige plays an important but indirect role. For the United States, failure in Haiti results in a perceived loss of existing prestige, whereas success adds nothing.

For Brazil, prestige is a very direct and explicit factor. As Eugenio Diniz[2] argued, Brazil believed that, at best, its participation and leadership role would enhance its efforts to achieve a permanent seat on the UN Security Council. At minimum, it believed that this role would give Brazil an increased voice in world affairs. For Chile, according to Enzo Di Nocera and Ricardo Benavente, an important motive was "to send a message that Chile's participation, along with that of Brazil and Argentina, in MINUSTAH constituted a strong signal of cooperation and leadership in the region." Luciana Micha argued that for Argentina, rivalry with the other two major Southern Cone Common Market (MERCOSUR) states, Chile and Brazil, was influential, both positively and negatively, in the Argentine perception of prestige attached to the Haiti mission. Argentina's failure to commit its forces rapidly precluded it from one of the two key leadership positions in MINUSTAH. Chile's political leadership role in providing the Special Representative of the Secretary-General (SRSG) and its rapid deployment of forces to both the MIFH and MINUSTAH, along with Brazil's providing both the force commander and the largest troop contingent, made Argentina's participation imperative if it did not want to lose prestige. During the workshop, Paraguay, too, indicated that prestige was a factor in its participation.

In short, a peacekeeping mission in the region, led by Latin American states (with Brazil providing the force commander and Chile the SRSG) and Latin Americans providing the bulk of the forces, was perceived as enhancing the prestige of both leading and following states. The prestige attached to being a part of this PKO was a significant driver of political will.

A second, and very important, factor influencing the decision to participate is the sense of international obligation on the part of the force contributors. The research showed that these countries, far more than the United States, see an obligation to participate in PKO authorized and directed by the United Nations. The participants from all nine countries indicated in their respective research papers the importance they attach to their nation's obligations under the UN Charter. In the case of Paraguay, as is true of many Latin American states, an international treaty not only has the force of domestic law, but also is hierarchically superior to all conflicting domestic laws. For Paraguay and others, the Charter of the United Nations is just such a treaty.

Canada enters UN PKO as a longstanding matter of national policy. According to the most recent *Defence White Paper* (1994), a central part of the Canadian forces' mandate is "to contribute to global stability." Specifically, states Glen Milne, "Canada will maintain multi-purpose, combat-capable maritime, land and air forces able to defend Canada and Canadian interests while providing the Government with the flexibility to contribute to international peace and security initiatives."

A third, and related, factor is that of hemispheric solidarity. This factor was specifically mentioned in the papers of about six of the nine participating countries (exclusive of the United States). Two of these are particularly revealing. Micha notes that the Argentine minister of defense stated explicitly, "It is time that Latin America shows that it has put on long pants." Milne reviews Canada's increasing commitment to the hemisphere since about 1990.

While most of the countries engaged in MINUSTAH have some peacekeeping experience, several have either a long tradition or have established centers for PKO training. Uruguay is one of those countries with a tradition that dates back to the Chaco War between Bolivia and Paraguay in the late 1930s. As Jorge Rosales states, this gives Uruguay more than 70 years of PKO experience. In addition, he notes that, "Uruguay is the country with the greatest [PKO] presence in the world after China." It is "involved in 11 of the 16 current UN missions . . . and has more than 2,500 troops in [PKO] missions outside the country." Other countries with major PKO traditions, although they generally date from after the Cold War, include the guarantor powers of the 1942 Rio Protocol dealing with the Ecuador/Peru border—Argentina, Brazil, Chile, and Peru. The four guarantors, including the United States, as well as Peru and Uruguay, have had long involvement in the Multinational Force and Observers mission in the Sinai. Finally, Canada can lay claim to having invented modern UN peacekeeping with its leading role in the 1956 United Nations Emergency Forces mission following the Israeli/Egyptian disengagement after the first Sinai war.

The long-term commitment of Argentina, Brazil, Canada, and Chile has resulted in PKO training and education centers in each of these countries. The two oldest are the Pearson Peacekeeping Centre (PPC) in Canada and Argentina's Joint Peacekeeping Training Center (*Centro Argentino de Entrenamiento Conjunto Para Operaciones de Paz* [CAECOPAZ]). Although Chile's Joint Peacekeeping Training Center (*Centro Conjunto de Operaciones de Paz de Chile* [CECOPAC]) is relatively newer, it has already established a strong cooperative relationship with the PPC. The existence of these centers provides the potential for synergy in common PKO training for the countries of this hemisphere.

As the late Speaker of the U.S. House of Representatives, Tip O'Neill, is reputed to have said, "All politics is local." This statement is clearly true for all the countries participating in MINUSTAH, but for none so much as Canada. Milne points out that Montreal's Haitian community is estimated at 70,000 to 120,000. It goes without saying that Haitian Canadians living in the Province of Quebec are French speakers. What needs to be made explicit, however, is that Haitian Canadians see themselves as Canadians, not as *Quebecois*, and have provided the margin of victory for a united Canada in recent referenda. As a result, Canada has provided significant developmental aid to Haiti, and participated in the Multinational Force (MNF) of 1994, the United Nations Mission in Haiti (UNMIH) and its successors—providing the leadership as well as troops and police—MIFH, and MINUSTAH. In addition, Milne notes, "On November 26, 2004, Prime Minister Paul Martin announced the appointment of a Special Advisor for Haiti, Denis Coderre, Member of Parliament for Bourassa, in the province of Quebec where the majority of Haiti's immigrants to Canada reside."

For the United States, of course, a critical issue in 2004—as it had been in 1994—was illegal immigration, especially to south Florida. Joseph Napoli points out that the United States took great pains in the chaotic period prior to the deployment of the MIFH to preclude illegal Haitian migrants from reaching its shores. According to Guillermo Pacheco, Guatemala's national leadership took advantage of the request for UN forces to "position the political leadership in the armed forces decisionmaking process," something that had never been part of the Guatemalan political culture. In fact, Guatemala introduced the PKO participation concept as one objective of a more ambitious defense transformation program that envisions new roles and rules for the Guatemalan army in the post-internal conflict period.

Enrique Obando suggests that the decision to restructure Peru's armed forces for PKO—although hardly so overt as Guatemala's decision—had important civil-military relations goals. With regard to Argentina's participation, Luciana Micha notes the extensive debate in the Argentine congress over the law authorizing the sending of troops and the political charges that the delay incurred placed Argentina at a disadvantage with respect to Brazil and Chile. The fact that Argentina, like many other countries of the region, must seek specific legislation to participate in PKO is significant. Finally, it should be noted that in Chile there was some opposition to the deployment of the *Carabineros* (national militarized police).

For some countries, there were clear economic and military incentives to participate. In some cases, such as Peru, this amounted to "a significant increase in resources not only for the participating soldiers but also for the military institution itself." Obando also points out that for Peru, participation provided excellent training opportunities for its forces, especially infantry.

Pacheco suggests that Guatemala is attempting to use participation in UN peacekeeping operations as a method to fund its armed forces modernization program, through the UN monetary reimbursements allocated to participating countries. The wisdom of this approach is questionable, especially with respect to sustainability over the long term.

For a number of countries—perhaps the majority—the Haiti PKO provided an opportunity to support the United States on an issue of some importance while, at the same time, remaining true to their own strongly expressed preference for multinational operations within a UN context. Several researchers noted that their countries saw this operation as a chance to ease somewhat strained relations with the United States over their stances on the Iraq war.

All of these reasons support the notion that political will in all its forms is the critical factor in determining participation in the PKO mission. Nevertheless, the case of Paraguay strongly suggests that political will is a necessary but insufficient condition for participation to actually take place. Carlos Torales pointed out that first the Paraguayan military and then the Congress approved participation. Paraguay then identified 200 soldiers and began training them. At this point, the economics of participation took over. Paraguay simply did not have the resources to support a deployment. Its expectation that those resources would be provided by others did not materialize, and Paraguay's participation has been limited to six officers deployed to staff assignments. The deployment of the 200 remains in limbo due to a lack of resources.

THE INTERAGENCY CONTEXT OF PKO

All of the researchers pointed out the interagency nature of PKO. In every one of the countries, the defense ministry and the foreign ministry were involved in the decisionmaking process. The finance ministry was also involved in most of the countries. And in a number of countries the legislature had to approve and, in some cases, be convinced that it was in the national interest to participate in the Haiti PKO mission. Nevertheless, the capacity for interagency coordination in all of the countries, including the United States, leaves much to be desired.

National Interagency Capability

Although the United States has been addressing the problem of interagency coordination in a conscious way since the end of the Cold War, it is clear both from experience and recent press accounts that U.S. interagency coordination still has a long way to go. The effort that resulted in the plans for the 1994 Operation *Uphold Democracy* in Haiti included the first-ever interagency political-military plan that the U.S. Government produced. Yet when it came time to rehearse the plan, one key agency had simply done nothing and had failed to notify the others.[3]

Milne points out that Canada has a well-developed interagency process and applies it regularly to PKO. He states that "the decisions to participate in Haiti early in 2004 came primarily from the top, the Prime Minister, with assistance from bottom up scanning, analysis, options and recommendations from committees of officials and Cabinet ministers." The principal agencies involved were foreign affairs, defense, international aid, and federal police. "When the UN Security Council passed its resolution re Haiti on February 29th an options paper was prepared within a few hours by a special inter-agency task force of middle level officials and sent up to the Prime Minister." It was signed by all of the ministers involved. The decision was slightly differ-ent from the options "because it reflected some inputs from . . . [the Prime Minister's] senior advisors, a committee of deputy-ministers (heads of de-partments) discussion of the options by a Cabinet Committee, and consider-ation of costs by the Department of Finance." As an aside, it should be noted that the Canadian system reflects a parliamentary model that most resembles that of the countries of the Anglophone Caribbean.

A particularly revealing case is that of Peru, as relayed by Obando (who, at the time, was the director general of policy and strategy in the ministry of defense). When the United Nations requested that Peru send a battalion to Haiti, the joint command of the armed forces "took the easy way" and told the foreign ministry that it lacked the capability to meet the request. This response bothered the senior leadership of the defense and foreign ministries since it flew in the face of the new national defense policy. In addition, these officials, as well as some middle-level staff officers within the joint command, saw political, military, and economic advantages in participation. The two ministries ultimately prevailed over the joint command (or won it over); how-ever, the principal obstacle was the ministry of economy and finance, which refused to provide the necessary funding because of its agreements with the International Monetary Fund (IMF) for a stabilization program. The prob-lem was finally resolved by the UN suggestion of a smaller Peruvian contingent.

The Peruvian case points to two important conclusions. First, a lack of resources may well result in a significantly diminished capability, reflecting a lack of political will on the part of one or more of the agencies engaged in the decisionmaking process. Second, the impact of the stabilization agreement with the IMF on the finance ministry points to the criticality of the inter-agency process at both the national and international levels. Note that in this case there was also conflict between two parts of the UN family of organiza-tions: the IMF and Department of Peacekeeping Operations.

In contrast to Argentina, where the role of the legislative debate over participation greatly reduced its ability to respond rapidly to the UN call for MINUSTAH participants, the role of the Guatemalan legislature was mar-ginal. Instead, Pacheco points to a comprehensive assignment of roles and responsibilities to the institutions of the executive branch of government most directly responsible for PKO. The ministry of foreign affairs, the ministry of defense, and the joint defense staff have developed the capabilities for the design and planning of the various aspects of these missions. The highest level decisionmaking directly involved the president, the minister of foreign affairs, and the minister of defense, demonstrating a capability to link staff planning to political decisions.

International Capability for Integrated Operations

As Enzo DiNocera and Ricardo Benavente point out, the UN mandate for Haiti contemplated a mission undertaken in part under Chapter VI and in part under Chapter VII of the UN Charter. They note that some countries have legislation that restricts their participation in Chapter VII missions. In this same vein, Eugenio Diniz noted that Brazil does not like operating under Chapter VII and, for that reason, has reduced its participation in PKO in recent years. Yet Brazil accepted both the force command and a major role in providing forces under this mandate, although it nevertheless sought to confine its role to one under Chapter VI. This situation appears to have produced a degree of conflict between the Brazilian force command and the Brazilian contingent command—a problem of international interagency coordination played out between two components of the armed forces of the same nation.

DiNocera and Benavente also point to the lack of PKO experience of some countries that hampers their effectiveness. DiNocera, in his remarks, strongly argued for predeployment training of the international force engaged in a PKO mission. In a similar observation, Walter Kretchik, writing of the UNMIH mission, states, "In late February to early March 1995, the UNMIH headquarters staff underwent group training in planning and decisionmaking under the tutelage of a U.S.-led international team." This training took place at Fort Leavenworth under the auspices and using the methodology of the U.S. Army's Battle Command Training Program. Yet according to Kretchik, "For reasons that remain unknown, no UN mission since then has undergone similar pre-deployment training."

TRANSCULTURAL CAPABILITIES

An area of significant weakness among the participating countries that was identified by a majority of the researchers was what we are labeling here as *transcultural capabilities*. These include basic intelligence, language skills, and foreign area specialization. Of these, it should be noted that only basic intelligence is a collective capability; the other two are individual skills that in sufficient quantity can provide a force with a significantly greater capacity to operate in the PKO human environment. In fact, when required by special operations forces, these individual skills can produce collective capabilities.

Basic intelligence refers to a body of knowledge about the area of the operation that is needed to conduct effective PKO, as well as other operations. Most MINUSTAH participants knew little about Haitian history, economics, politics, or culture. They were largely unaware of the factional conflicts at play, the relations of Roman Catholicism to *Vodun*, the history of internal Haitian violence dating back to its war for independence, or the class conflicts between mulattos and blacks. They generally did not know that nearly all Haitians speak Creole but that only the upper class speaks French. Not only were most of the contingents woefully ignorant about Haiti, they also lacked the basic intelligence documents with the needed information.

Of the hemispheric countries participating in MINUSTAH, only Canada is French-speaking, and it alone has a significant population of Creole speakers. Thus, the lack of the right language skills makes the Latin American participants dependent on interpreters who may, or may not, be trustworthy.

In dealing with Haiti, there is no country that specifically trains its officers or diplomats to specialize in that culture. Even the United States generally assigns Africa specialists to attaché duty in Haiti rather than Latin American specialists. But Haiti is not Africa; neither is it like its Latin American fellows. If Haiti is a special case, it nonetheless illustrates the more general situation that few nations have comprehensive education and training programs to prepare their diplomats and military officers for assignment to a particular cultural area of the world. Thus, cultural skills tend to be haphazard at best. Only the United States has a foreign area officer program—and then only for its military (and only really effective for the Army)—but not for its diplomats. And only the United States has special operations forces Special Forces, Psychological Operations, and Civil Affairs that have area specialization. The result is that in the area of transcultural capabilities, Latin American PKO partners will be dependent on either ad hoc adaptations or U.S. support.

MEASURES OF EFFECTIVENESS

The issue of how to measure the effectiveness of the MINUSTAH operation has given the least clear results of any of the research questions. Part of the reason is that there were multiple interpretations regarding what was being asked. Another partial explanation is because we don't really know how to measure the effectiveness of peacekeeping capacity. The researchers generally divided into two groups. The first group defined the question in terms of the UN mandate. They asked whether the political-military mission was accomplished. The second group looked more at the capabilities to conduct PKO, but these tended toward the tactical. A few researchers attempted to bridge the two, with limited success.

As far as MINUSTAH is concerned, the UN mandate has been met only if it is defined in the narrowest possible way. As with all previous multinational missions in Haiti dating to MNF in 1994, MINUSTAH has had little impact on the Haitian future. While it has generally kept Haitians from killing each other, it has yet to institutionalize democratic and responsive government; perhaps it has not even been successful in the basic establishment of such a government. In any case, for the purposes of this research, evaluating success in terms of the mandate is of little use. Our concern was to address the relative capacity for PKO evidenced by the hemispheric countries participating in MINUSTAH.

Obando argues that what is essential for PKO is adequate training at all levels, and Rosales suggests that the way to achieve this objective is through staff and field training exercises. He cites U.S. Southern Command (USSOUTHCOM) staff exercises as particularly useful for the standardization of planning and operational procedures. He also cites field training exercises like the Cabañas series to standardize field operating procedures. The common element of these exercises is the after-action review, where senior observers give a "no holds barred" critique of the decisions made.

Pacheco suggests that the critical measure of effectiveness is that of integration—both internal to the force and external with the other organizations engaged as well as the host country authorities and population. Milne identifies how this integration might be done:

- conduct interviews and workshops with representatives of all PKO forces on "lessons learned, sharing best practices, and ideas for future operations"
- conduct interviews and workshops with local leaders, aid organizations, and citizens on "lessons learned, sharing best practices, and ideas for future operations."

The essence of using training exercises is to establish standards and procedures that can be evaluated in preparation for a PKO. The essence of the operational evaluation is to make use of the standards and procedures developed in the exercises to focus the evaluation of the lessons of real operations as well as to modify those standards and procedures based on experience in the real world.

RECOMMENDATIONS TO INCREASE CAPACITY FOR PKO AND OTHER INTEGRATED OPERATIONS

The collective results of this research project suggest that there are a number of areas in which hemispheric governments can improve their capacity to conduct peacekeeping operations and, by extension, other integrated operations. The areas of recommendations are those in which the research was conducted:

- motivation for PKO participation
- interagency capacity
- transcultural capacity
- measures of effectiveness.

Motivation for PKO Participation

First among the motivations to participate in PKO is international prestige. Merely to participate offers prestige, especially for the smaller countries. Taking a leadership role—either political (as did Chile) or military (Brazil)—or being able to provide a PKO contingent on short notice (Chile) greatly enhances the prestige of the nation playing that part. As the Argentine defense minister stated, participation in PKO is evidence that the American states wear "long pants." This same recognition resulted in the demonstration of Argentine maturity in accepting a follower role in MINUSTAH. By extension, then, states need to be realistic about what they can and cannot contribute. A commitment that cannot be supported is one that is better not made, since it results in a loss of prestige rather than the desired increase.

As shown above, the Latin American states view their obligations under the UN Charter as both more important and more positive than does the United States. Therefore, to the extent possible, requests for participation should be made in terms of UN (and/or Organization of American States) obligations. Indeed, it is best if the United States is perceived as acting on behalf of, or in a supporting role to, the United Nations in seeking force contributions from the region.

There is significant residual support for the United States throughout the hemisphere. At the same time, countries are seeking to act independently of the United States and, at times, contrary to U.S. policy. Countries seeking better relations with the United States, even when demonstrating their independence, may well find it in their interest to offer to contribute forces to a PKO that is clearly a U.S. policy objective.

Finally, when it is in the interest of the American states to gain the widest possible participation in a PKO, it will be in the collective interest to help countries where resources are in short supply, but the political will to participate exists. Therefore, mechanisms need to be found to rapidly transfer the required resources. This will require significant multinational coordination and may require legislation (to include the appropriation of funds for this purpose) by several of the individual states.

Interagency Capacity

Building interagency capacity is an important goal inside the United States as well as for the region. Although we know what is needed, we have been less than totally successful in institutionalizing this capacity in our own country. Thus, we need a concerted effort to build the required capabilities at both the national and international levels. Several approaches commend themselves for consideration.

First, there is an educational (as opposed to training) dimension. Here we recommend that the established components of the Center for Hemispheric

Defense Studies (CHDS) basic course that deals with interagency coordination be expanded, as well as the current Interagency Coordination and Counterterrorism course. The latter might be expanded to two courses with the second, conceivably, having its secondary focus on PKO rather than counterterrorism. Another possibility is to expand the CHDS Advanced Policymaking Seminars to include interagency coordination. Finally, crossing over into the training area, we recommend increased emphasis on the interagency coordination dimension of the CHDS National Security Policymaking Workshops.[4] In a similar vein, we suggest that Strategic Leadership for Defense and Crisis Management (*Curso de Dirección Estratégica para la Defensa y Administración de Crisis* [CEDEYAC]) course in Peru, the various national and service war colleges, and civilian universities expand their courses to include a greater emphasis on interagency coordination both at the national and international levels.

This leads us into consideration of training for interagency coordination and PKO. Several venues can be utilized and expanded. We should point out that the principal training facilities or programs that can be used for this purpose include several peacekeeping institutes and centers in the hemisphere—the PPC in Canada, CAECOPAZ in Argentina, CECOPAC in Chile, and the new Brazilian center—that all provide a training capability. The United States should support and encourage efforts by these institutions to provide PKO training that emphasizes interagency coordination. In addition, the United States should participate both by providing exchange instructors and students. Moreover, we should support collaborative training efforts among these institutions and with USSOUTHCOM and U.S. Northern Command (USNORTHCOM). As Rosales suggests, the USSOUTHCOM exercise program of both staff and field training exercises should be expanded to include a significant interagency component.

Based on the successful training for the UNMIH staff conducted at Fort Leavenworth in 1995, the United States should work with the peacekeeping centers to develop a staff training program for deploying multinational PKO staffs. These should include the civilian as well as the military staff of the mission. A critical component of all training is the after-action review. This can be conducted in the formal manner that the U.S. military uses or in the mode described by Milne, but it should take place in both training events and as part of ongoing operations.

Transcultural Capacity

If the United States is serious about building the capacity of international partners to participate in PKO and other integrated operations, then transcultural capabilities are essential. The first step is to build up the basic intelligence database beyond what already exists in both unclassified and classified form.

A good beginning would be to get the Area Handbook series (published by the Federal Research Division of the Library of Congress) up to date. This action should be followed by their translation into Spanish and Portuguese. The books could then be made available to all our hemispheric partners at no cost, perhaps by offering electronic versions. There is no reason that the United States exclusively should support this effort. Rather, all the countries of the Americas have the kind of expertise required to produce this kind of open source basic intelligence. The United States should also seek the reinvigoration of classified basic intelligence documents, making every effort to identify as much documented information as possible that can be released to our allies in the Americas and elsewhere. In both cases, the development of these electronic documents should be prioritized based on best estimates of countries where PKO missions are likely.

With regard to language skills, the executive branch of the U.S. Government should seek Congressional authorization for the language training of members of the armed forces of the Americas at the Defense Language Institute and the Foreign Service Institute outside the parameters of international military education and training (IMET) funding. The argument can be made that such training is in the mutual national interests of all the American states since it will give needed skills to allied armed forces in ways that will relieve demands on U.S. military personnel and enhance the effectiveness of those armed forces in the conduct of PKO.

Increasing the foreign area specialization skills of our regional partners suggests the need for a different kind of program. The three components of the U.S. Army Foreign Area Officer program are a language skill, an academic master's degree in the relevant area studies program, and an in-country training phase. The United States should develop a fellowship program for military officers and diplomats that would lead to area studies master's degrees at U.S. universities that are of interest in terms of potential future PKO. This program should also be funded outside the current IMET system.

As far as special operations forces are concerned, the armed forces of the hemisphere should undertake the development or expansion of psychological operations and civil affairs capabilities.[5] Both unit skills are particularly useful in PKO, and especially so when the units have access to good basic intelligence on the area to which they will be deployed and are leavened by a few officers with foreign area specialization.

Measures of Effectiveness

The problem of identifying measures of the capacity of hemispheric states and their armed forces to conduct PKO is complex and reasonably difficult to define. The temptation is to seek measures to evaluate mission success or failure. That process, however, represents an exercise in frustration because it is dependent not only on the capabilities that the forces and civilian officials bring, but also on the will of their governments and the relevant international organization to see the mission through to the end.

Rather than evaluating mission accomplishment, this research suggests that what is needed is a method to evaluate the capabilities that each state and its institutions bring to a PKO mission, as well as the degree to which those capabilities can be institutionalized as capacity. Following this line of reasoning, it appears that the most promising approach would be the development of standards and procedures against which interagency capabilities and other PKO skills can be measured. As recommended above, USSOUTHCOM and USNORTHCOM should sponsor and support both staff and field training exercises using PKO scenarios. The regional peacekeeping centers, in collaboration with U.S. military organizations, should establish standards and procedures for PKO and other integrated operations that will be exercised. Exercise participants would be critiqued during the after-action review and the lessons captured for inclusion in the Joint Unified Lessons Learned system and the curriculum of the peacekeeping centers. The review process would also be used to evaluate performance during ongoing peacekeeping operations and the captured lessons would be used to modify both doctrine and curriculum. The Joint Center for Lessons Learned, with the support of the Service institutions such as the Center for Army Lessons Learned and the Army Institute for Peacekeeping and Stability Operations, should be given the responsibility to address this recommendation for the United States. In addition, there needs to be a memorandum of understanding among all the U.S. institutions and the peacekeeping centers in the hemisphere to share data, doctrine, and curricula.

A FINAL COMMENT

This project has shown that scholars and practitioners from around the region can bring together real expertise that both enhances our collective knowledge and provides practical suggestions for the successful building of the capacity to conduct peacekeeping operations. This capacity can be extended to many other kinds of integrated operations. If a professional research team can be put together and produce a quality product of this nature in a relatively short time and cost-effective manner, then there is no reason why the Americas cannot become the world leader in all aspects of peacekeeping and integrated operations.

All this requires is the recognition that Latin American states now wear the "long pants" in the hemisphere. With that recognition, a full partnership is well on its way to development.

NOTES

[1] Hans Morgenthau, *Politics Among Nations* (New York: McGraw-Hill, 1993, 84. See also, all of Chapter 6, 84 - 98).

[2] The persons and papers cited in the text are the contributors to the workshop. Some of the comments appeared in the prepared papers; others were made in the context of the workshop.

[3] See Walter E. Kretchik, Robert F. Baumann, and John T. Fishel, *Invasion, Intervention, "Intervasion": A Concise History of the U.S. Army in Operation Uphold Democracy* (Fort Leavenworth, KS: U.S. Army Command and General Staff College Press, 1998), chapter 2.

[4] It should be noted that these recommendations can apply equally to the other four regional centers.

[5] Both Peru and Guatemala have demonstrated significant expertise in psychological operations, while the latter has a well-developed civil affairs capability.

Abbreviations

ADN	Alianza Democrática Nacionalista (Nationalist Democratic Alliance–Bolivia)
AI	Americas Initiative
AIDS	Acquired Immune Deficiency Syndrome
C⁴ISR	command, control, communications, computers, intelligence, surveillance, and reconnaissance
Cabañas 2000	Multinational Combined Peacekeeping Operations Exercise in the United States
CAECOPAZ	Argentine Joint Training Center for Peacekeeping Operations
CALL	Center for Army Lessons Learned
CARICOM	Caribbean Community (and Common Market)
CECOMAPA	Army Peacekeeping Coordination Center (Uruguay)
CECOPAC	Joint Peacekeeping Operations Center of Chile
CEDEYAC	Strategic Leadership and Defense Management Course/Peru
CEP	Provisional Electoral Committee (Haiti)
CF	Canadian Forces
CFAC	Central American Armed Forces Conference
CHDS	Center for Hemispheric Defense Studies
CIDA	Canadian International Development Aid Agency
CIMO	companies d'intervention et de maintien de l'ordre
CJTF–Haiti	Combined Joint Task Force–Haiti
CPLP	Community of Portuguese Language Countries
CSIS	Canada Security and Intelligence Service
DDR	Disarmament, Demobilization, and Reinsertion
DFAIT	Department of Foreign Affairs and International Trade
DND	Department of National Defence (Canada)
DOD	Department of Defense

DOMREP	Mission in the Dominican Republic
DPKO	Department of Peacekeeping Operations (UN)
EIPC	Enhance International Peacekeeping Capabilities
EMC	*Estado Mayor Conjuncto*
EMCFFAA	Armed Forces Joint Chiefs of Staff
EMDN	National Defense Staff (Guatemala)
FAC	Foreign Affairs Canada
FAd'H	Forces Armées d'Haïti
FAO	Foreign Area Officer
FAST	Fleet Antiterrorism Security Team
FC	Force Commander
FNCD	Front National pour le Changement et la Democratie
FRAPH	Revolutionary Front for Haitian Advancement and Progress
FTAA	Free Trade Area of the Americas
GIP	Group in India and Pakistan
GONUL	United Nations Observer Group in Lebanon
HNP	Haitian National Police
IADB	Inter American Defense Board
ICITAP	International Criminal Investigative Training Assistance Program
IGO	International Governmental Organizations
IMET	international military education and training
IMF	International Monetary Fund
INTERFET	International Force for East Timor
IPM	International Police Monitors
IPMM	International Police Monitoring Mission
IPSF	Interim Public Security Force
JCS	Joint Chiefs of Staff
JIAPG	Joint Interagency Planning Group
LOA	Letters of Assistance
MAGTF	U.S. Air Contingency Marine Air Ground Task Force
MAS	Movement Toward Socialism
MBL	Antonio Aranibar's Free Bolivia Movement
MERCOSUR	Mercado Comun del Cono Sur (Southern Cone Common Market)
MFO	multinational force and observers
MICAH	International Civilian Support Mission in Haiti
MICIVIH	International Civilian Mission in Haiti
MIF	Multinational Interim Force
MIFH	Multinational Interim Force–Haiti
MIH	Mission in Haiti

MILOBS	military observers
MINUGUA	UN Inspection in Guatemala
MINURSO	UN Mission for the Referendum in Western Sahara
MINUSTAH	United Nations Stabilization Mission in Haiti
MIPONUH	United Nations Civilian Police Mission in Haiti
MIR	Movimiento de la Izquierda Revolucionaria (Movement of Revolutionary Left, Bolivia)
MNF	multinational peacekeeping force
MNR	Gonzalo Sanchez de Lozada's National Revolutionary Movement
MONUC	UN Mission in the Democratic Republic of the Congo
MOU	memorandum of understanding
MRTA	Tupac Amaru Revolutionary Movement
NAFTA	North American Free Trade Agreement
NATO	North Atlantic Treaty Organization
NCO	noncommissioned officer
NGO	nongovernmental organization
NORDCAPS	Regional Peacekeeping Training Cooperation
NORTHCOM	United States Northern Command
OAS	Organization of American States
OCHA	Officer for the Coordination of Humanitarian Assistance
ONUC	United Nations Operation in the Congo
ONUCA	UN Observer Group in Central America
ONUSAL	UN Observers in El Salvador
OPL	Lavalas Political Organization (Organisation Politique Lavalas)
OSD	Office of the Secretary of Defense
PAC	Civilian Defense Patrols
PCC	United Nations Civilian Police Corps
PDT	Democratic Labor Party
PFL	Liberal Front Party
PKO	peacekeeping operations
PPC	Pearson Peacekeeping Centre
PPS	Socialist Popular Party
PSDB	Brazilian Social Democracy Party
PSEPC	Public Safety and Emergency Preparedness Canada
RCMP	Royal Canadian Mounted Police
ROE	Rules of Engagement
SFOR	Stabilization Force
SHIRBRIG	Multinational Standby High Readiness Brigade for United Nations Operations

SINOMAPA	National Peacekeeping Operations Support System (Uruguay)
SJFHQ	U.S. Southern Command Standing Joint Force Headquarters
SOFA	Status of Forces Agreement
SOUTHCOM	United States Southern Command
SRSG	Special Representative of the Secretary-General
TCC	Troop Contributing Country
TES	Training and Evaluation Service
TFH	Task Force Haiti
UCS	Max Fernandez's Civilian Solidarity Unit
UDP	Union des Patriotes Democrates
UN	United Nations
UNATAET	United Nations Temporary Administration Force
UNDOF	United Nations Disengagement Observer Force
UNDP	United Nations Development Programme
UNDPKO	United Nations Department for Peacekeeping Operations
UNEF	United Nations Emergency Forces
UNFICYP	United Nations Peacekeeping Force in Cyprus
UNIIMOG	United Nations mission for the observation, oversight, and control of the cease-fire between Iran and Iraq
UNMIH	United Nations Mission in Haiti
UNMIK	United Nations Mission in Kosovo
UNMOGIP	United Nations Military Observation Group in India and Pakistan
UNOCI	United Nations Operation in Cote d'Ivoire
UNSAS	United Nations Stand By Arrangement
UNSCR	United Nations Security Council Resolution
UNSCR 940	(September 1994) authorized all means necessary to restore democracy in Haiti under Chapter VII of the UN charter
UNSCR 944	(September 29, 1994) set the stage for eventual mission handover from the multinational peacekeeping force to the United Nations Mission in Haiti
UNSCR 1063	(June 28, 1996) United Nations Support Mission in Haiti was established to operate under Chapter VI
UNSCR 1086	(December 5, 1996) established a mandate extension with a new mission termination date of May 31, 1997
UNSCR 1123	(July 30, 1997) established the United Nations Transition Mission in Haiti

UNSCR 1141	(November 28, 1997) created the UN Civilian Police Mission in Haiti
UNSCR 1277	(November 30, 1999) extended UNSCR 1141 until March 15, 2000, to ensure a phased transition to another organization, the International Civilian Support Mission in Haiti
UNSCR 1529	(February 29, 2004) UN authorized the deployment of a Chapter VII Multinational Interim Force
UNSCR 1542	(June 1, 2004) Multinational Interim Force transitioned to United Nations Stabilization Mission in Haiti
UNSMIH	United Nations Support Mission in Haiti
UNTMIH	United Nations Transition Mission in Haiti
UNTSO	United Nations Truce Supervision Organization
USAID	U.S. Agency for International Development
USCG	United States Coast Guard
USSR	Union of Soviet Socialist Republics
WTO	World Trade Organization

About the Editors and Contributors

John T. Fishel is Professor Emeritus of National Security Policy and former Research Director at the Center for Hemispheric Defense Studies of the National Defense University from 1997 to 2006. He is also a Professor Emeritus from the School of International Service of the American University. Dr. Fishel currently is a member of the faculty of the School of International and Area Studies of the University of Oklahoma. He focused on national development and security and defense policy in Latin America, specifically researched in Peru, Mexico, El Salvador, and Panama, and served as President of the Midwest Association for Latin American Studies and North Central Council of Latin Americanists. Dr. Fishel served on active duty in the U.S. Army at the United States Southern Command where he was Chief of Policy and Strategy, Executive Officer of the Combined Assessment Team for the evaluation of the Armed Forces of El Salvador, and Deputy Chief of the U.S. Forces Liaison Group with the Panama Public Force. Dr. Fishel holds a Bachelor of Arts degree from Dartmouth University, and received his Master of Arts degree and PhD in Political Science from Indiana University.

Andrés Sáenz is Deputy Director of Departamento Administrativo de Seguridad (Colombia's national intelligence agency). Between 2001 and 2005 he worked as an Assistant Research Professor at the Center for Hemispheric Defense Studies. He was a researcher of terrorism, political violence, and proliferation of weapons of mass destruction in the Washington, DC, office of the Center for Non-Proliferation Studies within the Monterey Institute of International Studies. He has worked in issues related to hemispheric security, strengthening mutual trust measures, demining in Central America, and international terrorism. Mr. Sáenz holds a degree in Political Science from the Universidad de los Andes, Bogota, Colombia, and Master of Arts degree in strategic studies and military history from the War Studies Department of King's College, University of London.

Ricardo Benavente Cresta, retired Navy Captain, Staff Officer, specialist in weapon systems, is currently working as a professor at the Specialization and Graduate Programs of the Chilean Academy of Political and Strategic Studies. He holds a degree in International Defense Management from the Naval Postgraduate School in Monterey, CA, and a Master's degree in Naval and Maritime Sciences, specialized in Peacekeeping Operations. He served in the Peacekeeping Operations in Bosnia and Herzegovina and after that he was the Head of the Department of Peacekeeping Operations, Staff of National Defense.

Eugenio Diniz is a Professor of International Relations at the Pontifícia Universidade Católica (Catholic University) of Minas Gerais, Brazil and is a member of the International Institute for Strategic Studies. He holds a PhD in Strategic Studies, a Master's degree in Political Science, and Bachelor's degree in Philosophy.

Guillermo A. Pacheco Gaitan is an Assistant Professor of National Security Affairs at the Center for Hemispheric Defense Studies. Mr. Pacheco worked as a Political Advisor to the Guatemalan Ministry of Defense, Coordinator of the Demining and Explosive Devices Program of the Organization of American States, Legislative and Presidential Advisor in the Guatemalan Congress, and has been a diplomatic officer. He is a member of the Guatemalan Network for Democratic Security, the Security and Defense Network for Latin America and the Institute for International Relations and Studies for Peace, part of the Guatemalan Institute for Development and Peace. He is a consultant to the Latin American School for Social Sciences and to the UNDP for issues related with security, defense, and preparation of White Books and Defense Policies.

Enzo Di Nocera García, retired Aviation Colonel, Staff Officer qualified in Chile and Brazil, is the Director of the Department of International Studies at the Academia Nacional de Estudios Políticos y Estratégicos; is a member of the International Society of Air Safety Investigators, the Instituto Geopolítico de Chile, and is an Associate Researcher at the Centro de Estudios Aeronáuticos y del Espacio. He is an engineer in implementation of aeronautical systems, has a Master's degree in Military Administration Sciences, and was an Academy Professor specialized in Personnel and Staff, Strategy and National Security.

Walter E. Kretchik, PhD, is an Assistant Professor of History at Western Illinois University, Macomb, Illinois. He has taught at Bilkent Univerisity, Ankara, Turkey, and at the Combat Studies Institute, United States Army Command and General Staff College, Fort Leavenworth, Kansas.

Luciana Micha is the head of Logistics and Finance for the Armed Forces Joint Staff, within the Department of Peacekeeping Operations, in Argentina.

She was a professor at the University of Buenos Aires School of Social Sciences and worked for the United Nations in 2000. She holds a Master's degree in International Relations and a University degree in Political Science.

Glen Milne is an adjunct professor at Carleton University in Ottawa, Canada, and a strategic facilitation, design, and training consultant to the Canadian federal government. He is the author of *Making Policy: A Guide to the Federal Government's Policy Process* and several papers.

Colonel Joseph Napoli, USA, is currently Commander, U.S. Military Group, Argentina, in Buenos Aires. He is a graduate of the U.S. Army War College. Previously, he served as a Special Assistant to the Commander and Chief of the Commander's Action Group at U.S. Southern Command, the 101st Airborne Division, 2^d Infantry Division, 82^d Airborne Division, and the Joint Readiness Training Center at Fort Polk, and was assigned to the UN and Military Group in Venezuela.

Enrique Obando is the President of the Institute for Political and Strategy Studies. He was a member of the Commission for Restructuring of the Armed Forces and Commission for the Restructuring of the Peruvian Intelligence Counsel. He is the former Director General for Policy and Strategy of the Ministry of Defense and representative of the civil society before the Peruvian Commission to Combat Corruption and to Promote Ethics and Transparency in Public Administration. He was a professor of Political Science and Social Doctrine at the Pacific University and holds a Master's degree in Security Policies from George Washington University.

Rolando Sánchez Serrano, PhD, is a professor in the Sociology Department of the Universidad Mayor de San Andrés, in La Paz, and serves as an external consultant for the UNDP, Bolivia. He is the author of several books. He received his PhD in Social Science with experience in Sociology from the Colegio de Mexico, in Mexico, holds a Master's degree in Political Science, and a University degree in Sociology.

Lieutenant General Jorge Washington Rosales Sosa is the Commander in Chief of the Uruguayan Army. In 1974 he graduated as a Second Lieutenant of Infantry Weapons, was promoted to Major in 1987, served as Chief of the Uruguayan II Battalion in Mozambique in 1994, served as an Aide to the Senior Commander in Chief of the Army in 1995, was promoted to Colonel in 1996, and subsequently served on the General Staff of the Army as Deputy Chief of Staff and Chief of the Planning and Doctrine Department. In 2001 he served as Commander of the 4th Infantry Brigade, in 2002 and 2003 he held the position of Deputy Commander of the Western Hemisphere Institute for Security Cooperation, and in 2006 he was promoted to General and became Army Chief of Staff and then Lieutenant General and appointed as Commander in Chief of the Army.